NATIONALISM AND NON-MUSLIM MINORITIES IN TURKEY, 1915 – 1950

NATIONALISM AND NON-MUSLIM MINORITIES IN TURKEY, 1915 – 1950

Ayhan Aktar

TRANSNATIONAL PRESS LONDON

2021

SOCIETY AND POLITICS SERIES: 7

Nationalism and Non-Muslim Minorities in Turkey, 1915 – 1950

By Ayhan Aktar

Copyright © 2021 Transnational Press London

First Published in 2021 by TRANSNATIONAL PRESS LONDON in the United Kingdom, 12 Ridgeway Gardens, London, N6 5XR, UK.
www.tplondon.com

Transnational Press London® and the logo and its affiliated brands are registered trademarks.

Requests for permission to reproduce material from this work should be sent to: sales@tplondon.com

Paperback
ISBN: 978-1-80135-042-6
Digital
ISBN: 978-1-80135-043-3

Cover Design: Nihal Yazgan
Cover Photo: Ali Öz

Transnational Press London Ltd. is a company registered in England and Wales No. 8771684.

In memory of Şerif Mardin who left his mark in my life by inspiring critical thinking.

CONTENTS

ABOUT THE AUTHOR

Ayhan Aktar studied sociology at Bosphorus University and worked at the Department of Political Sciences, Marmara University until 2006. He later worked at the Department of Turkish and Middle Eastern Studies, University of Cyprus, Nicosia before joining to Istanbul Bilgi University in 2010.

Prof. Aktar is one of the first social scientists addressing the problems of discrimination, assimilation and forced migration of Turkish minorities during the late Ottoman and Republican period in Turkey. His research on notorious anti-minority tax of 1942-43 (Wealth Tax) is based upon field research and the British and US diplomatic correspondence of the period.

His books include *Varlık Vergisi ve Türkleştirme Politikaları* [Wealth Tax and Turkification Policies] (2000) and *Türk Milliyetçiliği, Gayrimüslimler ve Ekonomik Dönüşüm* [Turkish Nationalism, Non - Muslims and Economic Transformation] (2006), *Yorgo Hacıdimitriadis'in Aşkale – Erzurum Günlüğü (1943)* [The Diary of Yorgos Hacidimitriadis in Askale/Erzurum Labour Camp, 1943] (2011), and *Nationalism in Troubled Triangle: Cyprus, Greece and Turkey*, (Edited volume with Niyazi Kızılyürek and Umut Özkırımlı) London, 2010.

Finally, Prof. Aktar edited and introduced the memoirs of Captain Sarkis Torossian, *Çanakkale'den Filistin Cephesine* [From Dardanelles to Palestine] in 2012. Memoirs of the Armenian artillery officer had initiated heated debate in Turkey and abroad. An edited volume on this debate published by Bilgi University Press: *Tarih, Otobiyografi ve Hakikat: Yüzbaşı Torosyan Tartışması ve Türkiye'de Tarihyazımı* [History, Autobiography and Truth: Captain Torossian Debate and Historiography in Turkey] in 2015. *Journal of Genocide Research* (Vol. 19, No. 2, 2017) allocated an issue for this debate.

Prof. Aktar was selected as a fellow of National Library of Australia for 2017. He is conducting research on Gallipoli war memory, remembrance and Islamization of war narratives in Turkey. Ayhan Aktar is a Professor of Sociology at the Institute of Graduate Programs, Istanbul Bilgi University.

ACKNOWLEDGEMENTS

Chapters in this collection have been previously published in various journals. We are grateful to the editors and publishers for kindly allowing republishing of these works. Full bibliographical details of the original publications are as follows:

Debating the Armenian Massacres in the Last Ottoman Parliament, November – December 1918. (Published in *History Workshop Journal*, No. 64, Autumn 2007, pp. 240–270).

Homogenizing the Nation, Turkifying the Economy: Turkish Experience of Populations Exchange Reconsidered. (Published in *Crossing the Aegean: An Appraisal of the 1923 Compulsory Exchange between Greece and Turkey*. Edited by Renée Hirschon. Oxford: Berghahn Books, 2003, pp. 79–95).

Conversion of a 'Country' into a 'Fatherland': The Case of Turkification Examined, 1923 – 1934. (Published in *Nationalism in Troubled Triangle: Cyprus, Greece and Turkey*. Edited by Ayhan Aktar, Niyazi Kızılyürek and Umut Özkırımlı. London: Palgrave Macmillan, 2010, pp. 21–35).

'Turkification' Policies in the Early Republican Era. (Published in *Turkish Literature and Cultural Memory*. Edited by Catharina Duft. Wiesbaden: Harrassowitz Verlag, 2009, pp. 29–62).

Tax Me to the End of My Life: Anatomy of an Anti-Minority Tax Legislation, 1942 – 1943. (Published in *State-Nationalisms in the Ottoman Empire, Greece and Turkey: Orthodox and Muslims, 1830–1945*. Edited by Benjamin C. Fortna, Stefanos Katsikas, Dimitris Kamouzis and Paraskevas Konortas. London: Routledge, 2013, pp. 188–220).

Turkish Attitudes vis à vis the Zionist Project (with Soli Özel). (Published in *CEMOTI (Cahiers d'études sur la Méditerranée orientale et le monde turco-iranien)*, No. 28, 1999/2000, pp. 129–147.

Economic Nationalism in Turkey: The Formative Years, 1912 – 1925. (Published in *Boğaziçi Journal, Review of Social and Administrative Studies*, Vol. 10, No. 1–2, 1996, pp. 263–290).

FOREWORD

It was the summer of 1991... I clearly remember the moment when I was enjoying the breeze by the sea in a holiday resort somewhere around the Northern Aegean. Having published my doctoral dissertation as a book a year earlier, I was a bit bored and certainly detached from my doctoral research topic. It was a research based upon extensive sociological field-work on the silk producers of Bursa, Turkey. As a sociologist who had his foundation shaped in the early 1970s, I was aware that the topics that we deemed crucial (and probably fashionable!) in those days were fading away and becoming outdated soon. Research questions related to national identity, nationalism and minorities were becoming the center of attraction for social scientists in the post-1990 period.

After getting my degree, my professor had advised me to engage in a liberal reading and research program for two years. In the good old days, we were granted such liberty to browse and reflect for a while. Fortunately, the notorious 'publish or perish' approach was still not prevalent in those years. Starting from the summer of 1989, I used my two years of tranquility in reading books and memoirs related to late Ottoman and early republican period in Turkey (1875-1950).

On that particular day by the seaside, I was reading the memoirs of Faik Ökte (1901-1982) who was the Director of State Finances at Istanbul in 1942. Ökte's book was titled as *The Tragedy of the Turkish Capital Tax*. It was a quite a rare-book to find.[1] He was in charge of administering the Wealth Tax Law in 1942-43 which was a perfect example of the "anti-minority" policies implemented during the single-party period in Turkey. Approved by the Turkish parliament in November 1942, the Wealth Tax was used to expropriate especially non-Muslim minorities i.e., local Greeks, Armenians and the Jews. Exhausted at the end of this process some of them had to leave the country just after the World War II.

Ökte's memoirs contained the details of the Wealth Tax Law, such as drafting the law, the procedures whereby the special commissions would determine who was to pay how much tax. Tax payers who failed to pay their tax in time were dispatched to labor camps. At the labor camps in Aşkale in Eastern Turkey, twenty-one taxpayers, all of them non-Muslims, died due to several chronic illnesses and harsh working conditions mostly in temperatures below zero. I must admit Faik Ökte's memoirs gave a full description of the injustices done to non-Muslim tax payers. His account

---

[1] The original Turkish edition published in 1951. It was later translated into English, see Faik Ökte, *The Tragedy of the Turkish Capital Tax.* Translated by Geoffrey Cox (London: Croom Helm, 1987).

seems to be an exception within the genre of Turkish bureaucrats' memoirs. Unlike the other state officials, Ökte was sharp, conscientious, candid and to the point at all times. I must admit, these were rare qualities to be found among Turkish state officials.

On that day by the sea, I decided to visit Atatürk Library on my return to Istanbul and read the daily newspapers of 1942-43. My initial plan was to write a monograph on the media coverage of the period and observe how this anti-minority tax legislation fitted into the general framework of Turkish nationalism. In hindsight, I admit that this original resolution was an extremely naive one. I was innocent enough to dream about summarizing a whole gamut of unexplored material within a few months. I was undoubtedly seeing only the tip of iceberg.

A week later, I paid my first visit to the periodicals section of the Atatürk Library. How could I have known that these were the first steps of a journey that lasted for more than two decades. At the end of my first day at the library, I was devastated with the hate-speech against non-Muslims that was utilized in the press. Soon, I decided to conduct interviews with the persons who were involved in tax collection as finance officers and ordinary tax payers or their close relatives. I was lucky enough to find some of them who were still around in those days. My close friends among the Greek, Armenian and Jewish communities helped me to convince some of their old relatives and acquaintances to accept to be interviewed. Some of the older folks were still under the heavy burden of these terrible times after fifty years. Sometimes, my interviews were interrupted with tears. Few retired tax officers were extremely helpful. There were moments during the interviews when I felt like a Catholic priest administering a confession session. Still, there were others who were as cold as a marble headstone at a Turkish cemetery.

With the help of Marmara University's rector, late Professor Ömer Faruk Batırel, I obtained permission to work at the Istanbul Public Deeds Office Archives where all the records of property sales and transactions related to private property were kept. By recording all the property sales between December 1942 to June 1943 in the central business district of Istanbul and some other boroughs, I was able to quantify the amount of wealth in the form ownership of shops, offices, factories, storage units, homes, summer residences etc. transferred from one section of the population (non-Muslims) to another (Turkish/Muslims). In the summer of 1992, I was fortunate enough to meet late Professors Bernard Lewis and Stanford J. Shaw at an international conference in Istanbul. I mentioned them about my research and also complained that Turkish Foreign Ministry's archives are closed to researchers. Professor Lewis looked at me with a big smile and said "Never mind, Dr. Aktar. Let them keep it closed. British Public Records are open to researchers at Kew, London. Read the diplomatic correspondence between Ankara and London. You'll find everything you need in the dispatches of the British diplomats." Professor Shaw also advised me to read the microfilms of the "Records of the Department of State relating to the Internal Affairs of Turkey, 1930 - 44" prepared by the US National Archives Administration. He also added, "You don't need to go to Washington, go to Ankara. They are kept in the US Library over there. You can even save your travel money!" I kept their advices I am grateful to both of them.

My research was getting expanded. I really needed time to read other cases of anti-minority legislations during the interwar period in Europe and study the Holocaust experience. I applied for a sabbatical and decided to go the US. My dear friend, Professor Cemal Kafadar knew about my research and invited me to Harvard University. I spend two semesters at Harvard enjoying blissful academic environment and using the legendary Widener Library. It was a real paradise and I am grateful to Cemal for his invitation. The academic year of 1992-93 had really contributed to the essence and value of my research. During my stay at Harvard, late Professor Halil İnalcık was there as a visiting professor. He was an old-school Turkish scholar with high sensitivities on national matters. He did not like my revisionist terminology like "Turkification of the economy", "anti-minority legislations" and "elimination of non-Muslim minorities" etc. However, he was gracious enough not to quarrel. We were able to keep a distant but respectful relationship.

The British and American Archives enabled me to accumulate archive documents on 1920s and 1930s as well. My project turned out to be something more spread-out covering the early Republican and late Ottoman periods. I started to publish my articles, with the first one in Turkish, in 1996. In those days, Professor Renee Hirschon asked me to write a piece concentrating on the Turkish experience regarding the Greek-Turkish Population Exchange of 1923-24. A special 75th anniversary conference on the Great Exchange was to be held at Oxford University in the Summer of 1998. In those days, I had run into Professor İnalcık in an academic bookshop in Istanbul. He asked, "Dr. Aktar, are you still working on the years of World War II?" I answered back, "No Sir, I am going backwards a bit. Nowadays, I am writing on the Great Exchange of 1923-24. It is a bit weird, actually." He looked at me in a smiling manner and said "My dear son, this is normal. Historians always go backwards. I did the same." Going backwards in terms of research topics finally brought me to the Armenian genocide of 1915. In this collection, you will find two articles about it.

As you notice, I have been working on anti-minority policies in Turkey since 1991. Through such policies, Armenians were subjected to deportations and massacres (1915), Greeks were 'exchanged' (1922–1924) and Jews were forced to migrate abroad (after 1945). In the Ottoman Empire's final decade (in 1906), non-Muslims constituted 20% of the population; by 1927, they were reduced to 2.5% and, nowadays, they make up less than 0.02% of the population.

Like many other nation states in the Near East, Turkey has been able to homogenize its population on religious grounds within five decades. All non-Muslim minorities were discriminated against and their stories cannot be understood unless the Turkish state and its policies were placed at the center stage. Utilizing diplomatic correspondence in the British and US National Archives has enabled me to understand the anti-minority policies of the Turkish state as a whole and to comprehend the many dimensions of the subject. I believe, this is the distinguishing characteristic of my research. This collection of articles tells the story of this sad and painful transformation.

Finally, I would like to express my gratitude to Professor Şerif Mardin (1927-2017). While I was a Freshman studying Business Administration at Bosphorus University, he and his colleagues arrived from Ankara and initiated the Department of Sociology at Bosphorus University. I transferred to this newly formed department at once and became one of its first graduates in 1977. He was my dear professor and I learned a lot from him. Without him, I reckon, I would have been a frustrated business manager. Therefore, this book is dedicated to Şerif Mardin.

Ayhan Aktar,

April, 2021.

Ayaspaşa, Istanbul.

CHAPTER 1

DEBATING THE ARMENIAN MASSACRES IN THE LAST OTTOMAN PARLIAMENT, NOVEMBER – DECEMBER 1918

> No serious historian of the nations and nationalism can be a committed political nationalist, except in the sense of believers in the literal truth of the Scriptures, while unable to make contributions to evolutionary theory, are not precluded from making contributions to archaeology and Semitic philology. Nationalism requires too much belief in what is patently not so.

> *Eric Hobsbawm*[1]

Introduction

Perhaps the question "what happened to the Ottoman Armenians in 1915?" is deceptively simple. Certainly, the answer is far from straightforward; it is becoming progressively more politically encumbered and is now polarized into two distinct and uncompromising discourses. The first of these set up by a group of Turkish nationalist historians and their foreign colleagues in the early 1980s. They argued that during World War One the Ottoman Armenians staged an armed uprising in Eastern Anatolia and collaborated with the invading Russian army. Hence the Young Turks in power known as İttihat ve Terakki Cemiyeti (the Committee of Union and Progress, hereafter the CUP) in Istanbul decided to "relocate" the Armenian population to deserts in Syria and Iraq. According to this narrative, the decision for relocation should be interpreted simply as a strategic measure to secure the rear of the Ottoman Army fighting against the Russians on the Caucasus front. One of the major proponents of this "official thesis", was the late Ambassador Kamuran Gürün. According to him:

> Various deaths occurred for various reasons during the relocation. Some of the deaths were due to epidemics, some were due to climatic factors, some were due to the hardships suffered during the journey, some were due to attacks, because officials did not protect them or because officials engaged in illegal acts... Many others died while fighting against the Turks in the Russian Army which they joined as volunteers.[2]

---

[1] Eric J. Hobsbawm, *Nations and Nationalism since 1870: Programme, Myth, Reality* (Cambridge: Cambridge University Press, 1995), 12.
[2] Kâmuran Gürün, *The Armenian File: The Myth of Innocence Exposed* (London: Published jointly by K. Rustem

Naturally this mode of reasoning tried to minimize the death toll of Armenians, and justify as "collateral" the nature of the subsequent deaths during these massive deportations. Gürün also estimated conservatively that "the number of casualties of the Armenians of Turkey, for all reasons, did not exceed 300,000."[3] However, alternative opinions suggest a figure not less than 900,000.

Taking these "facts" as the main premise of analysis, a corpus of "semi- official" literature proliferated in Turkey from the early 1980s, which shared a common narrative structure.[4] Central to this structure was the unquestioned belief that Muslims and Christians had lived peacefully together within the Ottoman millet system until it dissolved in the second half of nineteenth century. This collapse was, to a large extent, the fault of the Great Powers who intervened in the domestic affairs of the Ottoman Empire and exploited the position of the non-Muslim minorities living there. Later, the Armenian revolutionary elites, captivated by the false promises of self-determination and independence, took up arms and organized rebellions against the Sultan. Finally, during the First World War the Armenians sided with the invading Russian army and consequently had to be deported to Syria and Iraq.

Next, this defensive line of argument against the "allegations of the so-called Armenian genocide" was replaced with a new and intensified counter-offensive. In the last decade, a group of state-sponsored Turkish historians have argued that it was actually the Muslim population of Anatolia which was massacred by Armenians and subjected to genocide. In order to prove this point, they exhumed "newly discovered mass-graves" in Eastern Anatolia and could thus wave bones and skulls to the cameras, of the Turkish TV. This was taken as proof of what was called the "innocent Muslim people" that were massacred by the armed Armenian rebels during the First World War.

But the debate has not belonged solely to local historians with different views on one chapter of late Ottoman history never discussed until the early 1970s. Instead, following the resolutions of several European parliaments in the last decade to recognize the deportation and massacre of the Ottoman Armenians as "genocide", and the approval of Turkey's candidacy for membership to the EU in 2004, the debate on the fate of Ottoman Armenians has reached the international stage, and as consequence, has become more and more contaminated with political considerations. A considerable proportion of the Turkish public has

and Weidenfeld & Nicolson, 1985), 214.
[3] *Ibid*, 219
[4] The most recent example of this literature is a compilation by Aysel Ekşi, *Belgeler ve tanıklarla Türk-Ermeni ilişkilerinde tarihî gerçekler* (İstanbul: Alfa Basım Yayım Dağıtım, 2006).

become convinced since the late 1990s that the pressures exerted on the nation by the Armenian diaspora and European parliaments to recognize the "so-called Armenian genocide" are another imperialist plot to divide the Turkish fatherland. So this debate not only triggered already deeply ingrained fears within the Turkish collective conscience, it has also begun to haunt the Turkish political agenda. Such fears find fertile ground in Turkey. For instance, American historian Justin McCarthy – who is one of the staunch supporters of the official Turkish line – concluded his lecture at a special session of the Turkish parliament in Ankara in 2005 with the following words:

> How can it be right to become a member of an organization [EU] that demands you lie as the price of admission? Would any honest man join an organization that said, 'you can only join us if you first falsely say that your father was a murderer?' ... History teaches that the Armenian nationalists will not stop their claims if the Turks forget the truth and say there was an Armenian Genocide ... I hope and trust that the EU will reject the demands of the Armenian nationalists ... But whatever the EU demands, I have faith in the honor of the Turks ... I know that the Turks will never say their fathers were murderers. I have faith in the Turks.[5]

Unsurprisingly, Professor McCarthy received a standing ovation from the deputies. But this type of political rhetoric could also create fear, and even paranoia, in a society where the individuals had been educated in such a way that the historical threat of dismemberment, xenophobia and self-victimization had been an indispensable part of their political socialization.

It must be clear by now that we are not dealing with a simple academic disagreement between historians. In fact Gerard Libaridian rightly argues, "the entrenched position of each side is now part of their [Armenians' and Turks'] respective identities, identities that not only define the boundaries of the ethno-cultural self-definitions but also the socio-political context within which they see their present and project the future."[6] Over the last two years conservative and nationalist political circles in Turkey have also exploited the Turkish-Armenian debate as a means of opposing reform processes and to hinder further negotiations with the EU.

The second discourse, the historiography produced by Armenian nationalists is very different, and rightly underlines the basic fact that the

---

[5] Justin McCharty, "The Truth about the Armenian Problem in the Ottoman Empire," Speech delivered at the special session of Turkish Parliament, Ankara, 24 March 2005. Translation is mine A.A.
[6] Gerard J. Libaridian, "The Past as a Prison, the Past as a Different Future," in *Turkish Policy Quarterly* 4, no. 4, (Winter 2005): 1.

deportations and massacres of 1915 brought to an end the collective existence of the Armenian people in Anatolia. For the sake of simplification, we can say that such nationalist Armenian historians believe that what happened to Ottoman Armenians in 1915 was the first coherent, well-organized and premeditated genocide of the twentieth century. But such historiography is problematic too, not least when early events like the inter-communal clashes between Muslims and Armenians are read in retrospect, and employing hindsight. Any kind of armed conflict between the Ottoman army, Kurdish regiments and Armenian revolutionaries in the 1890s therefore is interpreted within this teleological model as "dress rehearsal" or the preliminary events which led to an organized genocide in 1915.

A further, more theoretical, problem originates from the discipline of "genocide studies" itself. Many Armenian and pro-Armenian scholars start their analyses with the UN "Convention on the Prevention and Punishment of the Crime of Genocide" which became a document for international law from the day of its adoption in 1948. As a result, genocide studies stands at the junction where international law and history/social sciences intersect. Use of the legal concepts and categories embedded in this convention in order to interpret the historical data available for 1915 creates further complications. As Jacques Sémelin rightly argues, "there is an inherent difficulty in using a legal concept as a category in social science analysis."[7] In social sciences and history the data is used to try to reach "truth" through interpretation. The legal expert or a jurist on the other hand is searching for "legal evidence." Historical truth and "legal truth" therefore might differ considerably. Besides, it is unbecoming for historians to play amateur jurists, or public prosecutors transforming their historical writings into legal treatises. For instance, Vahakn N. Dadrian – one of the very few Armenian historians who can read sources in Turkish – tries to illustrate the "genocidal intent" of the CUP by underlining certain common denominators between the CUP and Nazis:

> Perpetration of genocide requires the presence of genocidal intent. The preceding discussion indicates, if not demonstrates, a certain interconnection at such a mental level between incidence of the Armenian genocide and of the Jewish Holocaust. An additional detail, to be discussed now, is the extent to which the murderous legacy of the Mongol warlord Genghis Khan emerges as a nexus, as a functional link between Ittihadists [the CUP] and the Nazis ... there can be no doubt that the example of Genghis

[7] Jacques Semelin, "From Massacre to the Genocidal Process," *Int Social Science J International Social Science Journal* 54, no. 174 (2002): 435.

Khan impacted the organization and implementation of both the Armenian and Jewish genocides.[8]

Vahakn Dadrian goes on to explain how Hitler admired the "merciless murderousness" of Genghis Khan and to highlight similar attitude among the Young Turks, citing the example of Enver Pasha's uncle, Halil Pasha, who was a commander on Iraqi front and ordered the massacre of thousands of Armenians. Drawing on the testimony of allied German Colonel Ernst Paraquin, who worked under the command of Halil Pasha, Dadrian informs us that Halil Pasha named his youngest son Genghis and daydreamed of conquering Turkistan in the near future!

Here, a third problem emerges. This line of argument was clearly rooted in Orientalist images of the "terrible Turk", prevalent in Europe. Many Armenian scholars base their explanations on such crude nationalist analyses and bitterly essentialist premises. Again Dadrian, in his major work, argues that the militaristic *weltanschauung* of the Turks, combined with the limited tolerance associated with Islam, created a cultural setting conducive to genocide against Christians.[9] What is inconsistent here is that neither the Islamic faith nor the military were the main instruments of massacre. Besides, is it not un-academic for a scholar to categorize any people or culture as inherently murderous? Michael Mann presents a more balanced argument in his excellent work: "[Armenian genocide] was not primarily an Islamic but a secular nationalist genocide, though the long European struggle between Christian and Muslim had left deep marks on community enmities."[10]

Some common ground might yet be found in the simple observation that since the mid 1990s Turkish society has entered the introspective process of "soul searching", regardless of opinion or affiliation. Many taboos are now openly discussed as the result of democratization and the requirements of candidacy to the EU. The opening of private TV channels has provided discussion programs with ratings comparable to soap operas or football matches. Many national myths have been brought under scrutiny and many long-silenced issues, previously swept under the carpet, have been discussed in public quite openly. The critique of Turkish nationalism and the question of the Armenian genocide is no exception, although such debates have proved divisive.

---

[8] V.N Dadrian, "The Historical and Legal Interconnection between the Armenian Genocide and the Jewish Holocaust: From Impunity to Retributive Justice," *The Yale Journal of International Law* 23, no. 2 (1998): 543.
[9] Vahakn Dadrian, *The History of the Armenian Genocide Ethnic Conflict from the Balkans to Anatolia to the Caucasus* (New York; Oxford: Berghahn Books, 2004), 157-163.
[10] Michael Mann, *The Dark Side of Democracy: Explaining Ethnic Cleansing* (Cambridge: Cambridge University Press, 2005), 172.

But to contest and challenge such entrenched nationalist historical paradigms, supported by the establishment, is no easy task. When a group of social scientists and historians teaching in Turkish universities and abroad started to discuss "what really happened to the Ottoman Armenians in 1915?" their discussions were conducted in private first and later found their way into the Turkish press in the form of interviews. Of course, the works of the Armenian or pro-Armenian scholars were translated into Turkish and read extensively, despite being tagged with "politically incorrect" labels, negative stereotypes and many essentialist statements about Turks and Islam in general. Eric Hobsbawm's words concerning believers who have absolute devotion to Scriptures were certainly applicable to Armenian nationalist historiography, which had "too much belief in what is patently not so." Revengeful assertions and generalizations based upon nationalist sentiment reduced the credibility of this literature, although it contributed a lot to our understanding of the processes of mass murder. Furthermore, the narrative structure and style of these works was similar to legal indictments in a criminal tribunal. The quest for the "politics of genocide recognition", and the goal of trying to prove "genocide" and especially "premeditation and genocidal intent" at all costs, regrettably transformed some Armenian scholars of the diaspora into amateur jurists.

In May 2005 a group of critical and anti-nationalist Turkish scholars, myself included, organized a conference in Istanbul entitled "The Ottoman Armenians during the Demise of the Empire: Issues of Democracy and Scientific Responsibility." This triggered much public debate and was immediately branded a "genocide conference" in the Turkish media. The aim had been to present the multiplicity of perspectives that existed within Turkish academia and the public sphere, hitherto not included in the official accounts. Hence, the three-day program was designed so as to include more than fifty Turkish scholars and public intellectuals analyzing various dimensions of the Armenian question. A day before the conference opened the president of Bosphorus University decided to postpone it because of mounting pressure from the Turkish government and the state, as well as increasing concerns about the threat from protesters to the security of participants. The *coup de grace* that confirmed the postponement came from a discussion in the Turkish Parliament on the same day, when an opposition-party deputy, retired Ambassador Şükrü Elekdağ, brought the issue to the floor and accused both Bosphorus University and the conference participants of "committing treason against the Turkish nation." The government spokesman, Cemil Çiçek, Minister of Justice, responded not only by concurring, but by accusing the conference of "stabbing the Turkish nation in the back", borrowing an expression from Adolph Hitler and his friends.

The conference was finally held four months later at a different university (23–25 September 2005). The nationalist militants were again mobilized, and threw tomatoes and eggs at the participants. A day before, the "Association of Retired Army Officers" threatened to parade in front of the university's gates. Regardless, and with the assistance of the AKP government, the conference was successfully held under the strictest security measures. This article is the English version of the paper I presented at this conference.

***

> In this book, great effort has been put forth to describe the pure reality by taking into account nothing but humanity. All the greedy actions: killing people, scrambling for land and overwhelming mankind by blood and fire, must be in our conviction, condemned absolutely ... My soul equally suffers for all the Turks and the Armenians who have painfully perished during this terrible period.[11]
>
> *Ahmet Refik (1876–1937)*

The quotation above is taken from the foreword to *İki Komite, İki Kıtâl* (Two Committees, Two Massacres) a memoir by the prominent historian Ahmet Refik (later Altınay) who had first published his recollections in *İkdam* daily newspaper between December 1918 and January 1919. One of the committees referred to in the title of this book is the *İttihat ve Terakki Cemiyeti* (the Committee of Union and Progress), effectively in power from 1913 to 1918, which carried out the Armenian deportations and massacres. The second committee is the *Dashnakzutiun* (Armenian Revolutionary Federation, hereafter ARF) the Armenian nationalist political party. It is of particular significance that the author chose the term *kıtâl*, meaning 'massacre'.

The first chapter of this book covers the impressions of Ahmet Refik Bey relating to the year 1915 when he was in charge of "The Military Transportation Commission" in Eskişehir, in Central Anatolia. Ahmet Refik does not hesitate to confront the Armenian Question, describing the oppression and misery the Armenians suffered, seized from homes in various parts of Anatolia and forced to join the grim and arduous deportation marches. He harshly criticized the CUP administration responsible for the deportation policy and its implementation. In the second chapter he recounts his observations as a journalist reporting from Erzurum at the Caucasus front after the withdrawal of the Russian army

---

[11] Ahmet Refik Altınay, *İki komite iki kıtâl* transcribed by Hamide Koyukan (Ankara, 1994), 8.

in 1918. In great detail he also narrates the massacres carried out by the members of the ARF in that region.

Ahmet Refik was one of the few intellectuals who succeeded in keeping a critical distance from the bloody nationalistic confrontation that took place in the Ottoman lands from 1912 to 1922. He ends his foreword: "For a historian coming a hundred years later, this little book will be a document revealing the reality in all its tragedy."[12] Indeed, eighty-eight years after its publication, Ahmet Refik's book has gained in significance because it provides the first-hand impressions of an Ottoman intellectual related to the Armenian massacres.

The aim of this article is to draw on the debates about the Armenian Question in the Ottoman Parliament during the last two months of 1918 and to analyze certain issues in detail. I shall observe that some of the views repeatedly put forward nowadays by official circles in Turkey were originally expressed first in the Ottoman Parliament in 1918. Further, I shall try to analyze how conditions resulting from the Armistice period and the occupation of Istanbul affected these discussions.[13]

The Allied Occupation of Istanbul and Political Turmoil

The resignation of the Talat Pasha cabinet and the signing of the Mudros Armistice with Britain on 30 October 1918 by the Ahmet İzzet Pasha cabinet created political turmoil in the Ottoman capital. With the Armistice, it was understood that the country would be occupied, so to evade prosecution the CUP leadership left the country on the night of 1 November 1918 on board a German submarine. The political atmosphere in the Ottoman capital was highly charged.[14]

First of all, the political opposition, suppressed since 1912, argued vehemently both in the press and in Parliament that the CUP was responsible for all disasters caused by the First World War. Secondly, the agenda of the Ottoman parliament was dominated by the attempt to hold the CUP accountable for the Armenian massacres, and thereby absolve the rest of the political establishment in Turkey from responsibility. In this way, the Ottoman elite tried to prepare its defence against the accusations which could be expected at the imminent Paris Peace Conference of 1919, and to secure the rights of Ottoman citizens

---

[12] Ibid.

[13] Taner Akçam, A Shameful Act: The Armenian Genocide and the Question of Turkish Responsibility (New York: Metropolitan Books, 2007).

[14] Members of the Union and Progress who fled on the German submarine were the following: Enver Pasha; Talat Pasha; Cemal Pasha; former Police Director Bedri; Dr. Nazım; Chief of Teşkilat-ı Mahsusa (the Special Organization), Dr. Bahaeddin Şakir; Cemal Azmi. These people were afterwards found to be responsible for the Armenian deportations and massacres. See, Sina Akşin, 100 soruda Jön Türkler ve Ittihat ve Terakki. (Istanbul: Gerçek Yayınevi, 1980), 311.

vis-à-vis the victors of the war.

During the war the CUP government had censored all publication pertaining to the negative course of the war. Though it did indeed lift political censorship by June 1918, it had decided to continue military censorship in order to conceal from the public the fact that the situation at the fronts had turned to the disadvantage of the Ottoman army. From summer of 1918 on, numerous newspapers and magazines commenced publication: a result of first the relaxation and later the total removal of censorship. After the flight of the CUP leadership in the first week of November, political pressure on the press ceased. At this point the destruction, defeat and misery suffered between 1912 and 1918 began to be questioned in the press. In short, the Ottoman capital rediscovered political opposition and self-criticism in a relatively free political environment.

At the final party congress, held a week after the Mudros Armistice was signed, the CUP legally dissolved itself. At the same party congress, *Teceddüt Partisi* (Renewal Party) was founded instead, under the leadership of Fethi Bey [later Okyar]. The members of Parliament previously affiliated with the CUP became deputies of the new party. In the following two months there was a burst of political participation and nearly twenty new political parties and associations were established. Besides newspapers and magazines which functioned as mouthpieces of the newly-founded political parties and associations, there were also publications that tried to cultivate a more independent position. In this period an important source of tension was the fact that according to Clause 7 of the Mudros Armistice, Istanbul was under occupation. The occupation forces of the Entente Powers did not directly seize the administration of the city, preferring that the Ottoman public bureaucracy continue to operate. The decision to keep the Ottoman Parliament functioning at that time was in accordance with the intention of the occupation forces not to intervene in local politics. Yet on

21 December 1918 Parliament was dissolved by the order of Sultan Mehmet Vahdettin under the pretext of holding new elections. However, the elections were postponed for a long period. When Parliament finally reconvened with the newly-elected deputies on 12 January 1920, it was dominated by supporters of the resistance movement which had developed in Anatolia, under the leadership of Mustafa Kemal Pasha (later Atatürk). This alarmed the occupation forces, which raided the Parliament on 16 March 1920, terminated its juridical existence and sent many of the deputies into exile in Malta. Remaining deputies fled to Ankara and later formed the legislative body of the new parliament that assumed administrative functions during the Turkish War of

Independence, 1920–22. From March 1920, the occupation of Istanbul was official and the Ottoman cabinets, severed from the Parliament, worked under the command of occupation forces that had the last word in the administration of Istanbul.[15]

In February 1919, when allied forces under the command of French General Franchet d'Esperay held formal occupation ceremonies, the Muslim/ Turkish population of Istanbul realized that the war was completely lost. Moreover, the enthusiasm of non-Muslim minorities for the occupation forces had aroused anger and resistance. Four months earlier, on 13 November 1918, sixty-one allied warships anchored in the harbor and brought maritime transport between the two shores of Istanbul to a temporary halt. Just a week before, Mustafa Kemal Pasha, who had been in charge of Ottoman forces in Syria, left his mission after the collapse on the Palestinian Front and the occupation of Mosul by British forces. Interestingly, on the day the allied ships took control of the Bosphorus, Mustafa Kemal Pasha arrived at the train station on the Asian shore and was subjected to a long wait before he could cross to the European side of the city. It is reported that the view of the foreign battleships in the harbor inspired him to comment: "They will go back the way they have come!"[16]

It is hardly surprising that all these rapid changes caused great frustration and disappointment among the Muslim/Turkish population of Istanbul. The people of Istanbul, unable to obtain accurate information from the front between 1914 and November 1918, continuously misinformed by the government and comforted by false promises of "final victory", now experienced "total surrender" in the course of only a month. This began on 8 October 1918, with the resignation of the last CUP cabinet, was followed by the signing of the Armistice on 30 October, and ended on 13 November, when enemy battleships anchored at the entrance of the Bosphorus. October and November of 1918 can thus be summed up as "a period of social trauma" for the Ottoman elite and the Muslim/ Turkish people of Istanbul.

During this period the renowned calligrapher Tuğrakeş İsmail Hakkı (1873–1946) wrote *'Bu da geçer Yâhû'* (O God, this too shall pass!) and put it up in his shop window (Fig. 1). This sentence, originating from the Sufi perception of the transitory nature of everything, good or bad, was rapidly transformed into a slogan of national resistance and began to decorate all shop windows belonging to Muslim/Turkish tradesmen.[17]

[15] Bilge Criss, *İşgal altında İstanbul* (Cağaloğlu, İstanbul: İletişim Yayınları, 1993), 14.
[16] Orhan Koloğlu, *1918 aydınlarımızın bunalım yılı: Zaferi Nihai'den tam teslimiyete* (İstanbul: Boyut Kitapları, 2000), 325.
[17] After nationalist forces under the command of Refet Pasha entered Istanbul and the occupation was

Fig. 1. 'Bu da geçer Yâhû' (O God, this too shall pass!), by the famous calligrapher Tuğ rakes, _Ismail Hakk| (1873-1946), from the Sufi perception of the transitory nature of everything, good or bad. This was displayed in his shop window during the occupation years, 1918-22. It rapidly became a slogan of national resistance and began to decorate all shop windows belonging to Muslim/Turkish tradesmen

Yahya Kemal's poem titled 1918 conveys the emotional climate of that period - the combination of feeling ill - treated and repressed, of *ressentiment* and pain:

The dead ones had already passed away,
We're suffering with the living ones.
In our own country, we're no more than a despised community
The dead ones, at last, were liberated from this chaos

At the back of their eyelids, the vision of the good old fatherland,
Remained as 'our place' until Doomsday.
Those who are left behind: young, old, women and men
They're all in, wrecked, living with the suffering of such a destiny,
With the pain of seeing the enemy in the fatherland.

In our country we are in the middle of a nightmare, it's true
But this cannot last long,
The dawn will certainly break.
One day, our army will wipe the stain away with fire and blood,
That is this [Mudros] Armistice, a black smudge on humanity.[18]

---

ended in 1922, Calligrapher İsmail Hakkı wrote, 'Gel keyfim gel!' [How pleasant it is!], and put it up on his shop window, this time as an expression of his happiness.

[18] Yahya Kemal Beyatlı, *Kendi gök kubbemiz* (İstanbul: İstanbul Fetih Cemiyeti, 1974), 79.

15

After the CUP leadership fled abroad and city's occupation by the
Entente Powers, it was assumed that the victorious countries would start
to determine who was responsible for the Armenian massacres and take
legal action against them. It is possible to trace through the press of that
time, the attempts of the Ottoman elite or representatives of certain
institutions to argue that they had not been involved in the massacres. In
the atmosphere of Armistice and occupation, everybody seemed too
eager to emphasize their innocence.

In his memoirs Refik Halid [later Karay], a prominent Turkish
novelist, mentions a reception hosted by Grand Vizier Damat Ferit Pasha
in 1919 at the Lycée Impérial de Galata-Serai. The Grand Vizier, imitating
European statesmen of the period by holding a reception in an elite
school, invited not only the commanders of the occupation forces, but
also foreign journalists. Before the dinner, the Grand Vizier and Ali
Kemal Bey, the Minister of Education, made speeches. Refik Halid
recounts the speech of Ragıp Bey, a graduate of the Lycée:

> One of the directors of the Board of Public Debts Office and a
> graduate of the school, Ragıp Bey made a beautiful speech in
> French; there was one sentence within it that was both true and
> very precious for the school. 'Gentlemen,' he said, 'Not a single
> person educated in the Lycée Impérial de Galata-Serai is among
> those responsible for the war, deportations and mass-killings, this
> place is the home of free and virtuous people.[19]

Ottoman intellectuals tried to avoid any accusation of being embroiled
in the Armenian massacres, and also to stress that oppression and
atrocities committed against Armenians were the work of a small minority
in power, and that it was thus wrong to blame all.

Debate in the Parliament: Why did we enter this war?

Discussion of the Armenian massacres in the Ottoman Parliament
began with motions calling the Union and Progress governments to
account. When on 4 November 1918 the Ottoman Parliament convened
in Istanbul the political attempts to find the perpetrators started with the
first motion, tabled by Baghdat-Divaniye deputy Fuat Bey a few days
earlier. This demanded that the members of the Sait Halim Pasha and
Talat Pasha cabinets be tried by the High Court.[20] The motion's ten

---

[19] Refik Halit Karay, *Anılar: Minelbab ilelmihrab : 1918 Mütarekesi devrinde olan biten işlere ve gelip geçen insanlara dair bildiklerim* (İstanbul: İnkilâp Kitabevi, 1992), 137.
[20] During the same session, the motion of Fuat Bey was accepted and the 'Fifth Branch Office' that was to work as a commission of investigation and inquiry was assigned. For minutes of this investigation and the following trial, see Osman S. Kocahanoğlu, *İttihat-Terakki'nin sorgulanması ve yargılanması: Meclis-i Mebusan tahkikatı, Teşkilat-ı Mahsusa, Ermeni tehcirinin içyüzü, Divan-ı Harb-i Örfi muhakemesi* (İstanbul: Temel

clauses enumerated the actions of the two cabinets which had led the country towards destruction: entering World War One without valid reason; making false declarations in Parliament about the motivation for entering the war; rejecting proposals from the Entente Powers before war was declared; dragging the country into the war without obtaining certain guarantees from Germany; wasting lives during the war through individual misdeeds and frenzied actions without justification in military science; turning the country into a scene of catastrophe through "provisional laws" that contradicted the spirit of general law and the Constitution; concealing the course of the war from the public; rejecting every single peace proposal made by Entente Powers during the war and thus bringing about this ominous end; enabling certain sections of the population to be enriched by speculation and profiteering and thus ruining the economic life of the country and limiting the freedom of press by applying censorship without relying on any specific law. Clause 10 made direct reference to the Armenian deportations and to the *Teşkilat-ı Mahsusa* (the Special Organization), an irregular military force organized by the CUP leadership that had carried out deportations and massacres. In this final clause the offences of the CUP- backed governments were summarized as follows:

> Creating administrative chaos within the country and facilitating attacks of certain gangs against security of life, property and chastity [of the people] and thus contributing to the atrocities these gangs brought about.[21]

In the same session, Aydın Deputy Emanuel Emanuelidis, İzmir Deputy Vangel and Çatalca Deputy Tokinidis put forward a motion with more detailed claims, asking the new government about their attitude to the offences of CUP-backed governments, and their plans to deal with them. The crimes were listed in eight 'acts of government':

1. A population of one million people guilty of nothing except belonging to the Armenian nation were massacred and exterminated, including even women and children.

2. Two hundred and fifty thousand people of the Greek minority, which has been a true agent of civilization in this country for at least forty centuries, were thrown out of the Ottoman territory and their properties were confiscated.

Yayınları, 1998). See also, Vahakn N Dadrian, "The Documentation of the World War I Armenian Massacres in the Proceedings of the Turkish Military Tribunal," *Int. J. Middle East Stud. International Journal of Middle East Studies* 23, no. 04 (1991): 552-554.

[21] *Meclisi Mebusan Zabıt Ceridesi* [Parliamentary Minutes], 3rd Period, 5th Year of the Assembly, vol. 1, Ankara, 1992, 103.

3. Before the war five hundred and fifty thousand Greek people were also massacred and exterminated along the coasts and inland districts of the Black Sea, Dardanelles, Marmara and the Prince's Islands, and their properties too were confiscated and usurped.

4. By prohibiting non-Muslims from engaging in any commercial activity and by leaving trade to the monopoly of certain influential people, nearly the entire nation was robbed.

5. [Armenian] deputies Zohrab Efendi and Varteks Efendi were murdered.

6. The treatment deemed proper for noble Arab people has constituted the main reason for recent disasters.

7. The lives of the two hundred and fifty thousand people [who were mainly non-Muslims] of the Labor Battalions constituted by way of mobilization were wasted as a result of starvation and deprivation.

8. Entering the World War without any reason and leaving a section of the country to the Bulgarians in order to attain this ominous honor.

The motion ended with three succinct questions:

What does the new government in power know about the perpetrators, how does it view the true nature of these acts and when will it start to take measures against all this? [22]

With this motion, the Armenian deportations and general anti-minority policies of the Unionists (the CUP and its successors) were clearly set out in Parliament for the first time. The main objective of the three deputies (all non-Muslim) was to force the Ahmet İzzet Pasha cabinet, which was perceived as the "rearguard cabinet" of the CUP, to take a stand on this issue.[23] Moreover, they hoped with this motion to cause trouble for the new government by also exploiting the flight abroad of the CUP leadership, and thus ensuring that immediate action could be taken to punish those involved in the Armenian deportations and massacres.

Yet it could not be expected that a government which included Unionists and which had signed the Mudros Armistice right after its foundation, would act in a tough and decisive manner regarding the Armenian question.[24] Aydın Deputy Emmanuel Emanuelidis insisted that

[22] *Meclisi Mebusan Zabıt Ceridesi* [Parliamentary Minutes], 109.
[23] For the foundation of Ahmet İzzet Pasha's cabinet and the approach of Sultan Mehmet Vahdettin towards this cabinet, see Sina Akşin, *İstanbul hükümetleri ve millî mücadele: 1918-1919* (İstanbul: Cem Yayınevi, 1976) 27-34.
[24] There were many Ministers in Ahmet İzzet Pasha's cabinet originally from the core staff of the CUP: Cavit Bey (Minister of Finance), former Sheikh-ul Islam Hayri [later Ürgüplü] (Minister of Justice), Fethi [later Okyar] (Minister of Interior), Rauf [later Orbay] (Minister of Navy), etc.

his main aim was to understand what the new government's vision regarding this issue:

> My intention is to know what the program of the new government on this issue is. All the existing laws were unable to prevent this disaster. All the measures concerning this issue have failed. Does the new government have any internal policies in this regard? [25]

Naturally the answer to this question was neither short nor simple. The members of the Ottoman Parliament had held their seats since the last election in 1914. There were Unionist deputies who could not raise their voices against the acts of the old governments during the war; indeed, some of them had been directly involved in the Armenian deportations and massacres. Moreover, there were deputies from regions like Yemen, Jerusalem, Medina, Baghdad, Aleppo, Mousul, Basra, Beirut and Damascus which had been under Ottoman rule for the 1914 election, but by the time of these debates were under British occupation. Thus it was politically impossible for the new government, obliged to make use of its executive power by relying on such a shaky base, to provide satisfying answers to the above-mentioned questions and to punish those involved in the Armenian massacres.

But Turks have suffered too!

Fethi Bey, the Minister of the Interior and leader of the *Teceddüt* Party, which was founded to replace the CUP, replied to the motion of Aydın Deputy Emanuel Emanuelidis. He began by stating that the disasters experienced by the non-Muslim minorities had also happened to the Turkish people.

> As you gentlemen know, within the last four years very bad and hazardous currents have passed through the atmosphere of the country and turned the country upside down. Because of this I assure you, Turkish people have suffered equal or even greater harm than the Greek, Armenian and Arab minorities. I wish that Emmanuel Efendi had also mentioned that Turkish people suffered the same, or maybe even more than all these minorities. [26]

Minister of Interior Fethi Bey then summarized the aim of the government as follows:

> The approach of the government will be to grant freedom and perfect equality to all segments of society without making any distinction as to race or religion. Apart from this, it is the intention

---

[25] *Meclisi Mebusan Zabıt Ceridesi* [Parliamentary Minutes], 110.
[26] Ibid.

of the government to cure every single injustice done up until now, as far as the means allow, to make possible the return to their homes of those sent into exile, and to compensate for their material loss as far as possible. And activities have started to be carried out in this regard. But it is also our common duty to make sure that such an event does not recur, that nobody dares to commit such deeds and that officers or any other person who attempted to perpetuate such actions are prosecuted.[27]

Emmanuelidi Efendi reclaimed the floor after these remarks, and noting that as a member of the Ottoman Parliament he had the right to comment on various non-Muslim minority groups, he responded:

They have expressed that the Turkish segment of the society too has very much suffered and that they wish me to make a reference to this. I am just as affected by the suffering of Turkish people as I am by that of the Greek minority. The reason I did not mention the Turkish people is the fact that at present sovereignty is exercised in the name of the Turkish majority. (Cries from the benches: 'God willing, always').[28]

When we read the minutes of Parliament in that period, we notice something else: while deputies of minority origin brought the actions of old governments on to the agenda and proposed motions aimed at pushing the new government to take a political stand against the cruelties and crimes committed, the Unionist deputies either tried to hinder the discussion by making use of the advantages granted them by internal statute, or took the position that "in the past, bad things happened; let's not stir up these issues."

The motion put forward by deputies of Armenian origin Deputy of Kozan, Matyos Nalbantyan; Deputy of Aleppo, Artin Boşgezenyan; Deputy of Erzurum, Medetyan; Deputy of Sıvas, Dikran Barsamyan; Deputy of İzmir, Onnik and Deputy of Maraş, Agop Efendi during the session on 4 November 1918 was intended to force the government to take a clear position. It placed on the agenda demands that the deportation decision of 27 May 1915 and the decree of 27 September 1915 concerning expropriation of abandoned properties and real estate should be revoked, and that those deported from their native land be permitted to return. It further asserted that the administrative measures facilitating the sharing out among local notables of properties that had belonged to deported Armenians went absolutely against the spirit of the Ottoman Constitution of 1876. The last part of the motion demanded:

---

[27] Ibid.
[28] *Meclisi Mebusan Zabıt Ceridesi* [Parliamentary Minutes], 111.

What does our Government think of doing to restore justice to destroyed families … [restore justice] for the crushed dignity and honor [of those individuals] and for all Ottoman citizens who perished, their orphans and widows who died unnecessarily and for the confiscated wealth and sacred things which all was the result of the laws and decrees put into force?[29]

The government was asked to declare all the measures to be taken regarding this issue. Deputy of Kozan, Matyos Nalbantyan Efendi, who had signed this motion, declared that he supported it not only as a representative of the Armenians but in the name of the "whole Ottoman nation." Stating that all deputies already knew the issue, he underlined how widespread its effects had been.

I find it superfluous to say here how people were treated on the basis of these laws and to what conditions people were exposed. I saw many friends expressing their grief by shedding tears. I know those who could only speak with tears in their eyes. Therefore sensitivity on this issue should not be attributed to things like 'fanaticism'. In the name of humanity, I appeal to your conscience; these matters have made us all weep. In my opinion, many family hearths were put out without any distinction of race and religious conviction. Yet their smoke is still rising. Today many women live in misery here and there.[30]

The chairman of the session, Hüseyin Cahit (later Yalçın), then proposed to proceed to the next clauses and his proposal was accepted. In response to Nalbantyan's remarks, Minister of Interior Fethi Bey said that the government would try to provide "the return of the deported [Armenians] to their districts", but added that it was uncertain whether those who returned would find any place to live or a hot meal to eat; thus, things should be taken care of slowly. Moreover, he reminded the parliament that complaints against officers committing atrocities and injustices had to be filed on an individual basis.

Still at the 4 November session, Minister of Interior, Fethi Bey placed on the agenda the repeal of the decree dated 27 September 1915 concerning the sale of abandoned properties and Armenian deportations. Deputy of Aleppo, Artin Boşgezenyan Efendi made a speech about this temporary law:

This is a knife. This is an axe that has caused great cruelty. By blunting this knife, this axe we cannot do away with that cruelty … There is still the blood of those who suffered on it … The

[29] Ibid, 112.
[30] Ibid, 113.

houses it demolished are countless ... We should not only repeal it but also request that those who relied on this law to ruin the country should be punished; those who passed and used this law for the purpose of murder should be punished too.[31]

Up to that point the discussion had been conducted between deputies of minority origin and members of the government. Then Deputy of Trabzon, Mehmet Emin Bey took the floor, saying that during the discussion of the parliamentary inquiry he had not been able to voice his opinion. He challenged the figures given in the earlier eight-clause motion from Deputy of Aydın Emmanuel Emanuelidi ('besides 550,000 people of Greek minority, 1,000,000 children and women were exterminated solely because they were Armenian while 250,000 people of Greek minority were deported'). This was the first mention in the Ottoman Parliament of the "debate on the casualty figures" which is still an inevitable part of all discussion about the Armenian question. Mehmet Emin Bey announced that as long as those involved in Armenian deportations were not punished, he would give no vote of confidence to the government:

> It is not right to undo one injustice by means of another injustice. I believe Emmanuelidi Efendi has exaggerated on this point and understood that he departed from the issue a little bit. Yes, Gentlemen, I also say that our officials butchered many Armenians, including women and children and that their properties were plundered. But there was a beginning to all of this.[32]

Mehmet Emin Bey then started to relate his impressions of 1907 in Muş, where he was public prosecutor. He said that a document belonging to an Armenian nationalist had made clear that Armenians were always trying to prove that their population in the region was higher than it actually was, and suggested that Emmanuelidi Efendi had obviously been influenced by such figures. He asked too why Emmanuelidi Efendi did not mention the Turks who had also suffered atrocities in this context. At this point, the discussion began to get heated. Mehmet Emin Bey was interrupted by cries such as "Let us not open up this issue again!" Later on Mehmet Emin said that claims about the deportations of the Greek minority were correct, but explained that Greeks had taken guns and ammunition from Russian enemy ships coming to the shores of the Black Sea and had engaged in brigandage, and for this reason were forced into involuntary migration "as it was deemed necessary." At the end of Mehmet Emin's speech, he stressed that nothing had happened "without

---

[31] *Ibid*, 114.
[32] *Ibid*, 115.

cause!" Artin Efendi responded "May God curse the tyrants", to cries of "Amen" from other deputies.

Mutual Killings or Massacres?

On 8 November 1918, four days after these discussions, the cabinet of Ahmet İzzet Pasha resigned and Tevfik Pasha formed another cabinet, which received the full support of Sultan Mehmet Vahdettin. The formation of this new cabinet, which contained no Unionist deputies, was a source of tension for the Unionists and for journalists close to *Hürriyet ve İtilaf Partisi* (Freedom and Harmony Party), who accordingly intensified their criticism.

At the session on 18 November the program of the new Tevfik Pasha cabinet was read out by Minister of Foreign Affairs Mustafa Reşit Pasha and discussed. It consisted of very general wishes for peace, and made no mention of any measures directed at those involved in the Armenian deportations and massacres. Deputy of Aleppo, Artin Boşgezenyan during this session expressed his views pertaining to the efforts for peace. He brought up the issue of the Armenian deportations, which he felt would probably come up at the Paris Peace Conference that was soon to convene:

> Soon every nation, be it victorious or defeated, will sit around the conference table. I say that we should not go to that table with empty hands. We should go there prepared to defend ourselves and protect our rights. Let us speak frankly: Gentlemen, you know that in the eyes of the world of civilization and of politics, Turkey is today in the dock. (Cries of 'God forbid!') ... There has been a great murder that constitutes the most mournful, the bloodiest phase of Ottoman history. This great murder that has shaken both earth and heaven is known as the Armenian massacre, the Armenian tragedy. The Turkish nation is being accused of this crime. But in fact those who should be blamed are not the Turkish people but the former Turkish government and/or administration. (Cries of 'Bravo')...I say that this great murder, of which they are accusing the Turkish nation, was committed by the former administration, to be more exact, by a gangster administration. The most dreadful link in the chain of suspicion thrown around the neck of the Turks, namely the Armenian tragedy, was committed by a small but noisy minority in the center, and their officers in the provinces, such as governors, local governors, commanders of the gendarmerie, police chiefs, soldiers of the gendarmerie, the Special Organization, etc. To me, blaming a whole nation for the crimes of a few murderers, and some lunatics, is an act worthy of a gang. There can be a murderer or five murderers following such a policy but it is not

appropriate to condemn a whole nation because of this. This [accusation] would be [a kind of legal] banditry – I cannot find any other expression.[33]

The efforts of Deputy of Aleppo, Artin Boşgezenyan to explain all that had happened by comparing the CUP leadership to a gang and his proposal to punish everybody involved in these affairs before the Paris Conference so that the Turks would not go there with "empty hands", caused a heated debate, during which Deputy of Sivas, Dikran Barsamyan demanded that the new government immediately take action in favor of Armenians whom he referred to 'remnants of the sword'. Deputy of Muş, İlyas Sami Bey next took the floor, trying to explain it all:

> Gentlemen, was this a massacre or mutual killing? I will determine this in your presence. [Artin Boşgezenyan Efendi] absolved the Turks. I am now asking officially for the re-evaluation of this great murder, of which they absolved every member of the nation. Was it murder or mutual killing? I am addressing all humanity with the voice of my conscience and saying that although the secondary matters, the consequences, the particulars were painful, deplorable and tragic, I believe that no one has considered how all this began. At its inception, this situation was a mutual killing. Gentlemen, if it is a necessity for the present Parliament and Government and humanity to understand all this, then please allow me here to present the realities in all clarity. That is, please do not lose your temper.[34]

After summarizing the development of the Armenian nationalist movement, İlyas Sami Bey turned to the rebellion in Van that took place at the beginning of the First World War, saying that seventy per cent of the Muslim population in Van was killed. That rebellion, according to him, "the weapon thrust into the heart and soul of the Ottoman government by Armenians", had "brought about the tragic consequences which I myself hate and am disgusted by", when the Turkish side had responded with massacres. Mutual massacre followed, according to İlyas Sami Bey, but it was Armenians who started it all. He demanded punishment of everyone involved, on both sides, saying that "Muslim or Armenian, whoever they are, they are to be beheaded like a dragon; they are to be squashed. This should be recorded exactly in these words."

In this speech İlyas Sami Bey justified the things done by arguing that "if in Britain such a rebellion had taken place and a part of the society had betrayed [the British government], it would discipline and destroy them

---

[33] *Ibid*, 141.
[34] *Ibid*, 157.

by pouring cannon balls of stone and iron on to them." The fact that Britain was cited as an example is very meaningful because during the Easter days of 1916, as a result of the rebellion started by the IRA, the administration of Dublin had been taken over by the rebels for a period. That rising was brutally repressed by British forces. In fact during this section of İlyas Sami's speech, those on the benches of the Parliament cried: "As in Ireland!"[35]

After some further debate it was Deputy of Kozan, Matyos Nalbantyan's turn to speak. Pointing out that İlyas Sami Bey claimed that the Armenian question was limited to certain events and mutual massacres in Eastern Anatolia. He posed a challenge.

> Then I ask İlyas Sami Bey: if a band [of Armenians] comes out and causes some incidents, and inhabitants of that region [Eastern Anatolia] participate in those events and perform some illegal acts, would this situation necessitate the removal and extermination of all Armenians including for instance those Armenians in the West like in Edirne, İzmit and Armenians living along the [Western Anatolian] coast, the complete destruction of their honor and the confiscation and plunder of their properties? ... To what extent was it right for the government to observe all this happen and find all Armenians guilty and then take such a decision about them? Did the government get out of control? Individuals and tribes might get angry and out of control but the principle of government action is the treatment of all matters with justice and equality.[36]

This speech by Nalbantyan Efendi was an important intervention, pointing out the individual responsibility for crime from the juridical point of view. He wound up with these words:

> The government cannot execute me because of the crimes committed by my son. Neither can it behead me nor destroy me in any way. This is unacceptable. To say that Armenians caused all this to happen is by no means reasonable and cannot be accepted... We will punish those responsible and will return the damaged properties to the owners. We have to make clear that we will give back their legitimate wives, their girls and the little children who are still in the hands of the savages. We have to demonstrate our sensitivity towards the world of civilization, our humaneness and our veneration of all things sacred.

He thus made clear that he was expecting the government to take a

---

[35] *Ibid*, 158.
[36] *Ibid*, 161.

political and moral stand.[37] After this a motion to end the debate was submitted in order to proceed to a vote of confidence concerning the program of the government.

At the session on 11 December a debate was started by deputies of the Greek community about the forced migration of the Ottoman Greeks in Anatolia and Eastern Thrace during the war and the plunder of their properties. The quarrel between Deputy of Trabzon Yorgo Yuvanidis Efendi and the Deputy of Edirne Mehmet Faik Bey is indicative of the CUP policies pertaining to forced migration of the Greek population and the Turkification of Anatolia during the First World War.[38]

At the same session, the Deputy of Edirne Mehmet Faik Bey argued that the Ottomans had not invented forced migrations and deportations. They had learned such tactics from neighboring countries like Greece and Bulgaria. (This was a reference to the ethnic cleansing of 450,000 Rumelian Muslims during the Balkan Wars, 1912–1913.) He stressed that a total of 28,800 Ottoman Greeks had left the country to join the Greek army during the Balkan Wars and the First World War and had fought against the Ottomans. He did accept that 82,000 Ottoman Greeks from the settlements around the Sea of Marmara had been deported to the inner parts of Anatolia, saying that the deportation recommended by the Ottoman Chief of Staff. During the Gallipoli Campaign in 1915, he said, allied submarines passed the Dardanelles and conducted "hit and run" operations against the Ottoman Navy in the Marmara Sea

According to Ottoman military intelligence reports the local Greeks were instrumental in provision of food and other necessities to these submarines.[39]

In next day's session, on 12 December, Deputy of Kozan, Matyos Nalbantyan Efendi responded forcefully to renewed claims about the sufferings of Turks:

> [Deputy of Mosul Mehmet Emin Bey] says we have suffered, Turks have suffered, too. But the suffering of Turks is the suffering of a majority in power ... Some people [namely] Armenians were killed like animal herds. Of course, I accept the

---

[37] Ibid.

[38] *Ibid,* 295-302. Homogenization of Anatolia was completed after signing the convention on the compulsory exchange of populations between Greece and Turkey in 30 January 1923. As the result of this treaty 1,200,000 Anatolian Greeks were exchanged with 400,000 Rumelian Muslims. On the social and political repercussions of this first "ethnic cleansing" in history, achieved through diplomatic negotiations in Lausanne, see Ayhan Aktar, "Homogenizing the Nation,Turkifying the Economy: Turkish Experience of Population Exchange Reconsidered," in *Crossing the Aegean: An Appraisal of the 1923 Compulsory Exchange between Greece and Turkey,* ed. by Renee Hirschon, Oxford, 2003: 79–95.

[39] Rıza Bey, *A.E. 2 denizaltı gemisini Marmara'da nasıl batırdım?* (İstanbul: Akca Basımevi, 1947).

suffering of the Turks. But as a matter of principle, there are two types of death: one is noble, the other is ignominious. In any case, we have to acknowledge this. Turks died heroically at the frontiers, Armenians were killed ignominiously.

The point Matyos Nalbantyan Efendi wanted to stress here was that the battlefield deaths of the Turks in defense of their country at Gallipoli, the Russian front and Palestine, should not be compared to the deaths of those who were massacred by the roads.

Debates in the Ottoman Senate: Who is responsible?

At the Ottoman Senate (*Meclis-i Ayan*), which convened on 21 November 1918, the motion of Ahmet Rıza Bey was read out.[40] Ahmet Rıza had been a senior member of the Young Turk movement and had opposed the despotic regime of Abdulhamid II (1876 – 1909) for many years from Paris. His motion called for those responsible for the decision to enter the war to be immediately identified by a proposed Parliamentary Investigation Committee and those culpable to be brought before the High Court. Furthermore, he demanded that "the atrocities committed under the name of deportation' be investigated; that its adverse impact throughout the country be determined; and that those involved in these affairs be prosecuted. The final section of the motion declared that "many acts and even crimes were perpetrated against all Ottomans; in particular, unprecedented injustices in Ottoman history were committed against my Arab, Armenian and Greek fellow-citizens." Ahmet Rıza Bey demanded that the government investigate these atrocities at the High Court, that the perpetrators be put on trial; and that these atrocities be accepted as individual crimes. In short, they had to be prosecuted by the Public Prosecutor's Office and ultimately those found responsible "delivered to the grip of justice."[41]

As in the Parliament, Major General Rıza Pasha replied that among those who suffered atrocities and maltreatment there were also Turks, but that in the motion of Ahmet Rıza Bey there was no mention of Turkish people. Turks, he said, 'suffered no less than the other minorities. Therefore

I insist on my proposal. The term "Turks" should be added to the motion.'[42] Ahmet Rıza Bey, who opposed efforts to generalize the issue,

---

[40] According to Clause 60 of the 1876 Constitution, the Senate (*Meclis-i Ayan*) consists of members directly appointed by the Sultan, whose number does not exceed one third of the total number at the Parliament. The Senate functions as an upper chamber.

[41] *Meclis-i Ayan Zabıt Ceridesi* (Minutes Book of the Senate), 3rd Period, 5th Year of the Assembly, Volume 1, 1990, 117.

[42] *Ibid*, 118.

began to speak again and summarized his motion with great clarity within the framework of constitutional law:

> Briefly I repeat that I do not acknowledge the CUP or any other organ as the perpetrator of the crime. I acknowledge only the executive power. There is no Union and Progress within the executive power. It is the executive power that is responsible for the war, for the crimes. Even if a secret association or others encourage such criminal acts, the blame falls again on the government for having allowed that. It is the government that did not perform its duty. As the government is unfortunately the Turkish government, I did not refer to what the Turks have suffered. Yes, they suffered, too. That government had no pity on the Turks either.[43]

At the same session, former governor and Minister of Interior, Reşit Akif Pasha made a very important speech. He had been a member of Ahmet İzzet Pasha's cabinet as the head of Şurâ-yı Devlet, the Ottoman Council of State. This short-lived cabinet, known as the "rearguard cabinet" of the CUP, ruled the country less than a month and signed the Mudros Armistice with Britain on 30 October 1918. During his short term Reşit Akif Pasha conducted an administrative inquiry into the organization of Armenian deportations and massacres in 1915. Although the scope of his research was limited, his findings were crucial to an understanding of the mechanisms behind this extensive mobilization and the massacre of the Ottoman Armenians. Reşit Akif Pasha summarized his findings:

> There are certain confidential things that I learned during my public service, which did not last more than 25 to 30 days, in the Ahmet İzzet Pasha cabinet. In that respect, I encountered something quite strange. These orders of deportation had been given by the well-known Minister of Interior [Talat Pasha] and officially communicated to [governors in] the provinces. Following these official communique's, the Central Committee [of the CUP] sent orders everywhere in order to secure the gangs to complete their devilish duty. Therefore, the gangs went further and cruel mutual killings took place. Here, [the activities of] this assembly known as the Central Committee [of the CUP] – that cruel and ruthless group which was solely responsible for these massacres and the countless troubles which we inflicted on the [Ottoman] State and innocent nation – was more effectual than the official orders. In my opinion, it is crucial to be able to

---

[43] *Ibid*, 119.

decipher the soul of the matter when sufficient research and investigation be conducted. For ten years – not four! – there has been a treacherous group of people destroying not only the Islamic world but all of humanity. This [group] must be identified and made known to the public. If this is done properly the whole truth will be revealed in its clarity and it will later serve as a terrible lesson to our children and to the next generations.[44]

From this speech of Reşit Akif Pasha, we can deduce the following. First of all, we note the central position of the Minister of Interior, Talat Pasha, in the deportation and massacre of Armenians. He is strategically placed as Minister of Interior and Head of the Central Committee of the CUP. Secondly, Talat Pasha had first sent the official deportation orders to governors and local officials in the provinces from his office in the Ministry of the Interior. At the same time, as the head of party organization he cabled another set of orders to local representatives of the CUP "to complete their devilish duty." Talat Pasha had been a post-office clerk before 1908 and he had a telegraph apparatus installed in his Istanbul home from where these "special orders" were sent.[45] Thirdly, while Talat Pasha organized the deportation of Armenians by using the Ottoman public bureaucracy in the provinces centrally attached to the Ministry of the Interior, he also mobilized the gangs of *Teşkilat-ı Mahsusa* (the Special Organization) so as to initiate the massacres and the plundering of Armenian property. From the speech of Reşit Akif Pasha we can conclude, therefore, that the system worked efficiently, while most of the higher- ranking CUP members in Istanbul knew nothing about all these massacres unless they travelled to Anatolia which was difficult due to the war conditions. There is no doubt then that the communications system developed by the Minister of Interior Talat Pasha enabled the whole operation to be conducted discreetly.

On 9 December 1918, Minister of Justice, Haydar Molla, came to the Senate in order to respond to Ahmet Rıza Bey's motion. First of all, the Minister made a general presentation of the crimes and their perpetrators as indicated by this motion. He particularly enumerated the types of crimes committed within the framework of the Armenian deportations. First, were the crimes committed by state officials, which had to be brought before the High Court. Second, were the crimes committed by politicians. Third were the crimes that may have been committed by the ordinary people other than politicians or state officials.

---

[44] *Ibid,* 123.
[45] US Ambassador Morgenthau mentions that Talat Pasha had installed a telegraphic system in his mansion. See, Henry Morgenthau, *Ambassador Morgenthau's Story* (Ann Arbor (Mich.): Gomidas Institute, 2000), 93–6.

The Minister of Justice said that in order for public prosecutors to be able to start an investigation of "ordinary citizens" who committed the above- mentioned crimes, they required either information about the committed crime or a formal written complaint by the victims. He also pointed out that state officers and politicians could not be put on trial without a preliminary investigation. According to the fifth clause of the "Provisional Law Concerning the Trial of State Officials", issued while the CUP government was in power and still valid, the crimes committed by state officials while in office must first be investigated by their superiors, who would function as the "investigative magistrate." According to this provisional law, investigations of state officials involved in the Armenian deportations and massacres would be excluded from the jurisdiction of investigative magistrates and public prosecutors who worked under the Ministry of Justice.[46]

The legal obstacle presented by Minister of Justice Haydar Molla as an excuse for not being able to proceed rapidly with the investigations was in fact a rule binding the government. In addition to all this, when a commission of their superiors made a decision such as "no prosecution is necessary" of state officers against whom there were various claims, there was no mechanism by which public prosecutors could overrule this decision.

Which authority, then, was competent to investigate these crimes and put on trial the state officers suspected of collaborating with the inhabitants of the cities where Armenian deportations and massacres took place? According to Minister of Justice Haydar Molla, there was a never-ending conflict of authority between the Ottoman High Court of Appeals (*Mahkeme-i Temyiz*) and Council of State (*Şurâ-yı Devlet*). The Ministry of Justice worked to bridge this legal gap, overcome the obstacles emerging during the investigations and complete the investigations as soon as possible by appointing inspectors.

Another point stressed by the Minister of Justice was that if superiors decided that a Lieutenant Governor or a Governor should be tried for crimes he committed while in office, then he should be put on trial by the Criminal Section of the Ottoman High Court of Appeals in Istanbul. For instance, if a Governor had practiced oppression, and a group of 100 or 200 people filed a complaint against him, then they would have to travel together to the Ottoman capital and present their cases personally. This was a very long process that made trial impossible in practice. Minister of Justice Haydar Molla said that a draft law had been submitted to the

---

[46] It is interesting to note that this law is still implemented in Turkey. Most of the human- rights violations, such as maltreatment and torture, cannot be prosecuted easily due to the legal obstructions created by superior officials trying to protect their subordinates.

Parliament concerning this issue, which proposed trying state officers not in the capital city, Istanbul, but in local courts of first instance, as was the prior practice.

Thus it is understood from Ahmet Rıza Bey's motion and from the explanations of the Minister of Justice that the amendments made by the CUP leadership had rendered the Ottoman legal system incapable of putting perpetrators of Armenian massacres on trial and punishing those responsible. The legal process that could bring to light those responsible for the deportations and massacres, a matter of interest to hundreds of thousands was blocked by some minor alterations made in the legal system and the guarantee of immunity for state officials.

Ottoman Bureaucrats resisting the Armenian deportations and massacres

One of the speeches made in the Ottoman Parliament at this time concerned an issue which has remained off the agenda even today in discussions concerning the Armenian massacres: the individuals who resisted the deportation decision taken by the CUP leadership and the Armenian massacres that followed it. Recent studies of the Armenian genocide make little or no mention of the Ottoman bureaucrats who resisted the deportation orders sent from Istanbul. These governors and local administrators opposed the deportation orders both directly and by delaying them. Other individuals and groups refused to implement the orders for religious, humanitarian, ideological, or cultural reasons. In the literature on the Armenian genocide there is a tacit assumption that all Ottoman subjects wholeheartedly agreed with the Armenian deportations, and that nobody resisted the decisions of the CUP government. However, the speech of Aleppo Deputy Artin Boşgezenyan Efendi at the parliament 18 November 1918 is of great significance, both for acknowledgement of people resisting the deportations and for an understanding of the feelings and thoughts that motivated such resistance:

> I know of gentle, good-tempered, humanist, pious Turks who shed tears of blood along with me during the time of this tragedy. And they cursed the ones who undertook it. (Cries of 'Bravo'.) Was this all done only by individuals? There are cities whose inhabitants are true Muslim Turks; in order to rescue the helpless Armenian subjects from this cruel deportation, the Muslim people in these cities collectively opposed Government orders. But they could not in this way defeat the cruel order. They submitted when they saw that anyone who opposed the order or the acts of the Government was hanged in front of his own door. There are, for

instance, the people of Erzurum. There are such cities [like Erzurum] that apart from protecting the Armenians who were their fellow countrymen, also provided refuge to those who happened to be 'the remnants of the sword' dispatched from other locations to their city. There are [for instance] the people of Konya. These are the true, honest, unspoiled, pious, helpful Muslim Turks! [47]

The final words of the deputy of Aleppo were interrupted by the deputy of Konya, Ali Haydar Bey saying, "Thank you, Artin Efendi." Besides making general reference to the protective and humanist residents of a city, Artin Efendi went on to mention high-ranking Ottoman bureaucrats who resisted the Armenian deportations:

I know of such a Governor who after protecting the population of his own city also protected helpless Armenians who had taken refuge in this city. A mature and glorious Governor! ... I personally know such a Governor who was distinguished with the highest virtue granted to human beings by God, namely mercy, who rather than commit such a murder, gave up his office for good. A provincial governor (*mutasarrıf*) surpassed his colleagues in competing with all other officers in providing comfort to the needy. There is no need to prolong the speech by enumerating their names. But their number is limited and known. As opposed to them, there were very cruel governors and administrators. [48]

During the debates in Parliament, the Governor of Trabzon, Cemal Azmi, along with the local administrators working with him, was mentioned as an example of cruel governors. For instance, Deputy of Trabzon, Mehmet Emin Bey, in his speech on 11 December 1918, told how:

There was a Lieutenant Governor in Ordu district. He filled a boat with Armenians on the pretext of sending them to Samsun and tipped them into the sea. I heard that Governor Cemal Azmi treated them in the same way. I could not go that far. I had to return from Ordu district. As soon as I arrived here, I told all that I witnessed to the Minister of the Interior [Talat Pasha]. Thereupon they sent an inspector and dismissed the Lieutenant Governor. They put him on trial. But I could not make them do anything more against the Governor. I struggled for three years, but I could not succeed. [49]

[47] Meclisi Mebusan Zabıt Ceridesi, 141.
[48] Ibid.
[49] *Meclis-i Ayan Zabıt Ceridesi* (Minutes Book of the Senate), 300.

Another Governor infamous for his cruelty during the Armenian deportations was the Governor of Diyarbakır, Dr. Reşid Bey. He was tried in Istanbul in 1919 for being involved in the Armenian deportations and massacres and was sentenced to capital punishment, but he broke out of prison. On the point of being recaptured he committed suicide. A prominent Turkish journalist, Abidin Nesimî, who was a child in those days, later wrote in his memoirs how the Governor of Diyarbakır had first invited his father, the Lieutenant Governor of Lice, Hüseyin Nesimî Bey, to his office and then had him killed by an ambush laid by the gang of Harun the Circassian, who was also a member of the Special Organization:

> During the governorship of Dr. Reşid many crimes were committed whose agents could not be found. The most important of these are the murders of Governor of Basra Ferit, Governor of the Province Müntefek Bedii Nuri, Lieutenant Governor of Lice, my father Hüseyin Nesimî, Representative Lieutenant Governor of Beşiri, Sabit and journalist İsmail Mestan. All these people killed were either socialists or philanthropists. It was impossible to carry out the Armenian deportations with the Circassian gendarme team and members of Bedirhâni, Millî, Karakeçili tribes who were actually Kurdish militia, because these groups were interested in plunder and pillage. Unable to realize deportations they transformed them into massacres. Hence the elimination of the administrative staff that would oppose to this plunder and pillage was also inevitable. Therefore this cadre deemed the elimination of the above- mentioned persons necessary, too.[50]

So according to the memoirs of his son, Hüseyin Nesimî Bey and some other public administrators were killed by the gangs loyal to Governor of Diyarbakır Dr. Reşid because they did not allow members of the Special Organization (Teşkilat-ı Mahsusa) to plunder and pillage.[51] The most important feature of the discussions in the Ottoman Parliament is the revelation of the existence of loyal and dignified Ottoman bureaucrats who opposed the Armenian deportations and massacres.

Conclusion: Thinking about the 'reality of fear'

In this article I have brought to light some key moments of the debates concerning the Armenian genocide that took place in the Ottoman Parliament in the fall of 1918 and described their political and emotional

---

[50] Abidin Nesimi, *Yılların içinden.* (İstanbul: Gözlem yayınları, 1977), 39-40.

[51] Dr. Reşid defended himself against the accusations concerning the murder of the above-mentioned local administrators in his memoirs, which he wrote while under arrest. See, Mehmet Reşit Bey, *Dr. Reşid Bey'in hatıraları: Sürgünden intihara* ed. by Ahmet Mehmetefendioğlu (İstanbul: Arba, 1993).

context. Considering that those who took part in the debates consisted of witnesses who actually experienced the Armenian deportations and massacres, I would like to make the following points.

First, none of the deputies, Muslim or non-Muslim, took the position of complete denial of the atrocities and massacres. Nor were the press and Parliament legally hindered in discussing the subject at first. However, the motions of Armenian and Greek Deputies demanding a more detailed debate of the subject and the punishment of those responsible were inhibited by limits set by the internal statute of the Parliament. In a Parliament where the former CUP deputies constituted the majority, this was not surprising.

Second, we see that many positions articulated by Turkish official circles today concerning the Armenian massacres were first developed at the Ottoman Parliament. It is interesting to note that complaints made by the Unionist deputies such as "Turks died, too", on the one hand, and the references to those responsible for massacres as "gang members" and demands for their punishment, by Deputies of minority origin, on the other, could all be expressed under the same roof. This demonstrates that the deputies of the Ottoman Parliament were able to remain calm even while discussing such an important issue.

Third, nowadays there are two poles in discussions of the Armenian deportations and massacres: at one end there are those who argue that it was a 'genocide *par excellence*' meticulously planned beforehand; at the other are those who attempt to explain the deportation of hundreds of thousands of people as "a simple administrative measure necessitated by the state of war." It is very difficult to carry on an academic discussion in an environment where the voices of social scientists have become restrained and they sometimes feel they are being accused of "treason to fatherland."

At this point the questions we have to ask ourselves are these. What are the political, academic and psychological reasons that keep the Turkish political elite from discussing this issue calmly in the way their grandfathers did in 1918? What is hindering the Turkish political establishment today from questioning the CUP's acts relating to the Armenian deportations when even the deputies elected from the lists of the CUP at the Parliament in 1918 could demand that the people who had dragged the country to war be held responsible? How can we explain the persistence of the need to unconditionally defend the leadership of Union and Progress Party after ninety years? Why does it seem so hard for some people today to repeat the words written by historian Ahmet Refik Bey in 1918, "my soul equally suffers for all the Turks and the

Armenians who have painfully perished"?

It might also be appropriate to consider the sentiments of Amin Maalouf, who lived through the civil war in Lebanon and later became a world - famous novelist. In *On Identity* (1998) Maalouf considers the ethnic conflicts in the Balkans and the Middle East:

> After each ethnic massacre we ask ourselves, quite rightly, how human beings can perpetrate such atrocities. Certain excesses seem incomprehensible; the logic behind them indecipherable. So we talk of murderous folly, of bloodthirsty ancestral and hereditary madness. When an otherwise normal man is transformed overnight into a killer, that is indeed insanity. But when there are thousands, millions of killers; when this phenomenon occurs in one country after another, in different cultures, among the faithful of all religions and among unbelievers alike, it is no longer enough to talk of madness. What we conveniently call 'murderous folly' is the propensity of our fellow-creatures to turn into butchers when they suspect that their 'tribe' is being threatened. The emotions of fear or insecurity don't always obey rational considerations. They may be exaggerated or even paranoid; but once a whole population is afraid, we are dealing with the reality of fear rather than reality of threat.[52]

It is obvious that the Turkish political elite has always dealt with the conflicts it was involved in or observed, from the 'reality of threat' perspective. In appreciating the words of Maalouf might we consider for a moment that certain things we perceive as a threat today are merely the consequences of our own fear? When we begin to think in this way, perhaps we may discover what actually frightened us in the first place. And thus, we may realize how that legacy of fear has penetrated deep into our souls and how it has evolved into a system that works subconsciously today. We should not forget that Turkey is the only country whose national anthem starts with the statement, "Do not fear!" (*Korkma!*) We should however courageously face the fears that have "made us the way we are." It seems apparent that there is no other way to demolish "the kingdom of fear" that is deeply ingrained in the Turkish psyche. Only by transcending our fears may we reach a maturity that in the end will allow us to discuss everything calmly – even the Armenian "genocide."

---

[52] Amin Maalouf, *On Identity* (London: Harvill Press, 2000), 24.

Bibliography

Official Publications

Meclisi Mebusan Zabıt Ceridesi [Parliamentary Minutes], 3rd Period, 5th Year of the Assembly, vol. 1, Ankara, 1992.

Meclis-i Ayan Zabıt Ceridesi (Minutes Book of the Senate), 3rd Period, 5th Year of the Assembly, Volume 1, Ankara, 1990.

Academic Works and Memoirs

Akçam, Taner, A Shameful Act: The Armenian Genocide and the Question of Turkish Responsibility. New York: Metropolitan Books, 2007.

Aktar, Ayhan "Homogenizing the Nation, Turkifying the Economy: Turkish Experience of Population Exchange Reconsidered," in *Crossing the Agean: An Appraisal of the 1923 Compulsory Exchange between Greece and Turkey*, ed. by Renee Hirschon, Oxford: Berghahn Books, 2003: 79–95.

Akşin, Sina. İstanbul hükümetleri ve millî mücadele: 1918-1919. İstanbul: Cem Yayınevi, 1992.

————. Yüz 100 soruda Jön Türkler ve Ittihat ve Terakki. Istanbul: Gerçek Yayınevi, 1980.

Altınay, Ahmet Refik, *İki komite iki kıtâl*. Ed. by Hamide Koyukan. Ankara, 1994.

Beyatlı, Yahya Kemal. *Kendi gök kubbemiz*. İstanbul: İstanbul Fetih Cemiyeti, 1974.

Criss, Bilge. *İşgal altında İstanbul*. Cağaloğlu, İstanbul: İletişim Yayınları, 1993.

Dadrian, Vahakn. The History of the Armenian Genocide Ethnic Conflict from the Balkans to Anatolia to the Caucasus. Oxford: Berghahn Books, 2004.

Dadrian, Vahakn N. "The Documentation of the World War I Armenian Massacres in the Proceedings of the Turkish Military Tribunal." *Int. J. Middle East Stud. International Journal of Middle East Studies* 23, no. 04 (1991): 549–76.

Dadrian, V.N. "The Historical and Legal Interconnection between the Armenian Genocide and the Jewish Holocaust: From Impunity to Retributive Justice." *The Yale Journal of International Law* 23, no. 2 (1998): 503–59.

Ekşi, Aysel. Belgeler ve tanıklarla Türk-Ermeni ilişkilerinde tarihî gerçekler. İstanbul: Alfa, 2006.

Gürün, Kâmuran. *The Armenian File: The Myth of Innocence Exposed*. London: Published jointly by K. Rustem and Weidenfeld & Nicolson, 1985.

Hobsbawm, Eric J. Nations and Nationalism since 1870: Programme, Myth, Reality. Cambridge: CUP, 1995.

Karay, Refik Halit. Anılar: Minelbab ilelmihrab. 1918 Mütarekesi devrinde olan biten işlere ve gelip geçen insanlara dair bildiklerim. İstanbul: İnkilâp Kitabevi, 1992.

Kocahanoğlu, Osman S. İttihat-Terakki'nin sorgulanması ve yargılanması: Meclis-i Mebusan tahkikatı, Teşkilat-i Mahsusa, Ermeni tehcirinin içyüzü, Divan-ı Harb-i Örfi muhakemesi. Istanbul: Temel Yayınları, 1998.

Koloğlu, Orhan. 1918 Aydınlarımızın bunalım yılı: Zaferi Nihai'den tam teslimiyete. İstanbul: Boyut Kitapları, 2000.

Libaridian, Gerard J. 'The Past as a Prison, the Past as a Different Future', in *Turkish Policy Quarterly* 4: no. 4, (Winter 2005).

Maalouf, Amin. *On Identity*. London: Harvill Press, 2000.

Mann, Michael. The Dark Side of Democracy: Explaining Ethnic Cleansing. Cambridge: CUP, 2009.

Mehmet Reşit Bey, and Ahmet Mehmetefendioğlu. *Dr. Reşid Bey'in hatıraları: Sürgünden intihara*. İstanbul: Arba, 1993.

Morgenthau, Henry. *Ambassador Morgenthau's Story*. Ann Arbor (Mich.): Gomidas

Institute, 2000.

Nesimî, Abidin. *Yıların içinden.* İstanbul: Gözlem yayınları, 1977.

Rıza Bey, A.E. 2 Denizaltı gemisini Marmara'da nasıl batırdım? İstanbul: Akca Basımevi, 1947.

Semelin, Jacques. "From Massacre to the Genocidal Process." *International Social Science Journal* 54, no. 174 (2002): 433–42

CHAPTER 2

ORGANIZING THE DEPORTATIONS AND MASSACRES: OTTOMAN BUREAUCRACY AND THE CUP, 1915 – 1918[1]

Around May 1917, Yervant Odian, the editor of Armenian daily *Jamanag* in Istanbul, had finally reached El Bousera, a small town further east of Der Zor in today's Syria. El Bousera, those days an Arab village of a few hundred households was located at the point where the Euphrates and Khabur rivers joined. Next day, the local government official, *Nahiye Müdürü,* wanted to see the Armenians deported there. Odian's impressions of the government official are worth quoting:

> He was a 55 year-old bearded man with an honest face. It was the first time that we'd faced an older official. Until that time the officials we'd met - *vali, mutesarrif, kaimakam* and so on had all been 30-35 years old, dyed-in-the-wool Ittihadists and Armenophobes. We had already heard that the *mudir* was a good man and had done as much as he could to protect the Armenians.[2]

Odian's description of the late Ottoman bureaucracy under the Young Turks was very accurate one. Between 1909 and 1915 the administrative elite of the empire had been transformed into a young, energetic group of officials who had adopted the Turkish nationalist ideology preached by the Committee of Union and Progress (CUP hereafter). Indeed, the local governor of El Bousera, who had treated deported the Armenians kindly must have been one of the remnants of the old regime.

Starting from April 1909, the CUP leadership did everything possible to re-shape and transform the Ottoman public bureaucracy and the army. The political and military developments, i.e., the armed uprising of certain army units in Istanbul in April 1909 and the catastrophic defeat of the Ottoman Army in the Balkan Wars of 1912-13, granted the opportunity to the CUP leadership to dismiss and eliminate the old guard inherited

---

[1] First version of this article was presented at 'The State of the Art of Armenian Genocide Research: Historiography, Sources, and Future Directions,' Strassler Center for Holocaust and Genocide Studies at Clark University, 8 - 10 April 2010. This article is a by-product of an ongoing joint research conducted with Professor Abdulhamit Kırmızı on the 'Righteous Turkish Bureaucrats' who resisted deportation orders sent from Istanbul in 1915. The author wants to express his gratitude to Taner Akçam, Abdulhamit Kırmızı and my dear student Daniel Ohanian who had read the paper very carefully and made valuable suggestions. I would like to thank Professor Abdulhamit Kırmızı for transcribing the archive documents from the Ottoman Archives. Of course I am responsible for all possible mistakes.

[2] Yervant Odian, *Accursed Years: My Exile and Return from Der Zor, 1914-1919.* Translated by Ara S. Melkonian, (London: Gomidas Institute, 2009), 154.

from Sultan Abdülhamid's neo-patrimonial regime.

In their political vocabulary, the act of 'transforming' meant the appointment of younger, more able and better-educated personnel. However, apart from newly appointed officials' age, audacity, talent and education, their most important characteristic must have been their loyalty to the unionist ideology. I argue that the unconditional support of the newly appointed officials and party cadres in the provinces enabled the CUP leadership to implement genocidal polices towards Anatolian Armenians in 1915. I shall also contend that although the CUP secured the loyalty of the Ottoman bureaucracy, but the "bureaucratic culture" based upon corruption, bribery and nepotism remained intact. This, in turn, enabled some of the wealthy Armenians to buy their way and survive the deportations. Finally, I shall try to analyze the organizational structure of the Ottoman public bureaucracy under the CUP dictatorship in relation to the execution of the deportation and massacres of the Ottoman Armenians. In doing so I will focus on the archive material recently made available in the Ottoman Archives in Istanbul.

Stages of Bureaucratic Purges and Cleansing

During the reign of Sultan Abdülhamid II (1876 – 1909) the role of the *Sublime Porte* was reduced into "a subservient administrative arm of the state."[3] The high-level bureaucrats who were once acting autonomously during *Tanzimat* period (1839-1876) lost their autonomy and control over governing practices. They became simply the extension of the Yıldız Palace, where Sultan Abdülhamid II exerted his unbearable weight on decision-making. Reducing *Tanzimat* bureaucrats into a group of technocrats, the Sultan demanded a kind of personal loyalty of high-level Ottoman officials. The shift of power towards Yıldız Palace required unconditional allegiance of the Ottoman bureaucratic elite to the Sultan, an allegiance strictly monitored by an army of informers all around the empire. In return for loyalty, some of them received higher salaries, expensive gifts, shiny decorations, or donations in cash or in the form of lavishly decorated mansions on the Bosphorus. The Sultan's generous rewards naturally increased competition for service and facilitated obedience among the elite. By the last decade of the 19th century, the once powerful and reformist Pashas of the *Tanzimat* period who were negotiating and sometimes balancing the power and authority of earlier Sultans were all gone. The ones still holding their tenures were aging and becoming obsolete and old-fashioned in the rules of conduct.

Establishing his autocratic rule and securing the individual loyalty of

[3] M. Şükrü Hanioğlu, *A Brief History of the Late Ottoman Empire* (Princeton: Princeton University Press, 2010), 123-125.

40

his bureaucratic elite, Abdülhamid II also tried to institute bureaucratic reform. Şükrü Hanioğlu summarizes the process as follows:

> At the Sultan's behest, a host of new bureaucratic schools were established, including the Royal Academy of Administration [*Mekteb-i Mülkiyye*], which became a college. These schools turned out bureaucrats and technocrats of different sorts, ranging from provincial governors to customs officials and veterinaries ... Furthermore, in support of the vision of an efficient bureaucracy in control of the periphery. Abdülhamid II linked the provinces to the center by means of a new invention, the telegraph.[4]

Although Abdülhamid II was an enlightened despot whose authority, power and decisions were not restricted by any means. But the administrative power of his bureaucrats limited by the laws and regulations. The speed and tempo of social and economic modernization under Abdülhamid II's rule was impressive indeed. During his reign, he was able to transform the infrastructure of a traditional empire into an emerging European state. His reliance on such traditional institutions like the Caliphate as a source of legitimacy and power did not necessarily held his administration back as a traditional one in that the regime did not close its doors to the technical innovations of his time.[5] While Abdülhamid II was utilizing every occasion to celebrate the grandeur of the Ottoman Empire in a pompous manner - for instance, on the 600th anniversary of the formation of Ottoman state - he did not hesitate to permit the crossing of the Orient Express in 1878 through the imperial gardens of his ancestors' "well-protected house", the Topkapı Palace.[6]

Middle class youth born between 1870 and 1890 had the opportunity to receive a proper education in the schools initiated by Abdülhamid II. Some of them even had obtained state scholarships to study abroad, learned foreign languages and internalized European ways of thinking. The Young Turks, who later organized themselves under the broad umbrella of the CUP to overthrow the regime of Abdülhamid II, shared some of these common sociological characteristics. First of all, nearly all of them came from middle-class families; in other words, they had modest backgrounds. Therefore, they lacked the means to connect themselves to the palace in order to get promoted in the bureaucratic service or in the

---

[4] Ibid.

[5] For technological developments in the late Ottoman Empire, see Ekmeleddin İhsanoğlu and Mustafa Kaçar, *Çağını yakalayan Osmanlı!: Osmanlı devletinde modern haberleşme ve ulaştırma teknikleri* (İstanbul: IRCICA, 1995).

[6] It is interesting to note that Abdülhamid II had also exploited all possible instruments in order to legitimize his power, like charitable donations, rebuilding the tombs of earlier Ottoman Sultans etc. See, Selim Deringil, *The Well-Protected Domains: Ideology and the Legitimation of Power in the Ottoman Empire, 1876-1909* (London; I.B. Tauris, 2009).

army. In short, they were not as privileged as the sons of Abdülhamid's loyal Pashas or high-level bureaucrats. Second, in the beginning they enrolled into public service as medical doctors, engineers, bureaucrats, local governors, judges or simple army officers. They had the education and the ability and they expected to be employed according to merit. However, the bureaucratic structures in which they were embedded did not permit them upward mobility; the system was corrupt, open to nepotism and full of dead-ends. These young and aspiring individuals soon developed resentment towards their superiors who managed to stay in power by personal alignment to the Sultan. Nepotism and clientelism originating from the upper echelons of the state apparatus, corruption in the daily matters of bureaucratic rule of conduct, encountering ignorant/poor masses in provinces and the permanent threat of disintegration of the empire soon infuriated these youngsters. Finally, they realized that the only way out was to resort to revolutionary activities and overthrow the Sultan.

First Wave of Cleansing: July – August 1908

On the 24th of July 1908 when the CUP succeeded in forcing Abdülhamid II to end his autocratic rule and to reinstitute the Constitution of 1876, the CUP was still a very weak political entity in terms of cadres and organization. Its political center was in Salonica. However, we know that this political change triggered a wave of celebrations among the Ottoman subjects coming from different ethnic and religious backgrounds. Sensations of celebration and joy prevailed until the first week of August 1908.

The first wave of bureaucratic cleansing started just after the revolution in 1908. In the summer months, some members of Abdülhamid's cabinet ministers and pashas, notorious in their corruption and oppressive rule of conduct, asked for political asylum in various European countries. Those who remained in their posts were arrested immediately and their property was confiscated. Many of them were sacked immediately or their salaries reduced. At the end of July 1908, the Sultan was forced to pass an Imperial decree mandating that nearly 30,000 informers operating throughout the empire be dismissed at once. In Bursa, an angry mob had lynched notorious Fehim Pasha, who was the head of the informers.[7]

While the masses were celebrating the restoration of constitutional monarchy in the streets, one of the demands pronounced was that the Sultan apologise for the oppressive policies conducted during his long

---

[7] Nuri Akbayar (ed), *II. Meşrutiyet'in ilk yılı: 23 Temmuz 1908-23 Temmuz 1909* (İstanbul: YKY, 2008), 67.

rule. In addition to that, all political prisoners were released at the end of July 1908. Later, this wave of amnesty was extended to ordinary convicts. One of the first actions of the CUP was to invite all army officers to take an oath, promising that they were going to be loyal and obedient to the Constitution and its protector, the CUP. This was the first instance where the CUP had asked individual loyalty of army officers. Very strong language was used in the wording, especially in the last section of the oath:

> I shall support the CUP; and whomever ventures to conspire against the CUP I shall kill with my own hands; and to our beloved *Padişah*, who has granted us this favor; to my religion, nation and motherland I shall give service with complete loyalty and servitude; I ensure upon my virtue and honor, placing my hand on the most glorious *Kur'an*; by *Allah*, I so swear.[8]

In the provinces, there was already chaos. Angry mobs occupied government offices and demanded resignations of governors, oppressive police officers, judges and many other corrupt bureaucrats. A flood of telegrams was reaching to the Interior Ministry and other central organizations in Istanbul, forcing the ministers to act according to the wishes of local forces. All progressive individuals came together and formed local branches of the CUP in the provinces without getting permission from its headquarters in Salonica and tried to administer justice. These so-called local branches of the CUP mostly headed by army officers and it was difficult to resist their demands.

For instance, in Izmir, some bureaucrats were arrested and shipped to Salonica to be put on trial. In Bursa and Diyarbakır, governors' offices were occupied by angry mobs that produced a list of bureaucrats to be dismissed immediately. In Kayseri, the office of the local *Mutasarrıf* was raided and he dropped dead of a heart attack. *Kaymakam* of Antep was taken out his office and beaten up by the shop-owners in the market place, and later kicked out of the town.[9]

On the 6th of August 1908, the governors of Trabzon, Erzurum, Hejaz, Kastamonu, Beirut and Adana were dismissed by the orders of the Ministry of Interior.[10] Within a month all local governors including the *mutasarrıf*s were discharged.[11] Sultan Abdülhamid II had lost nearly all of his faithful local governors in the provinces.

---

[8] For complete text of the oath, see M. Naim Turfan, *Rise of the Young Turks: Politics, the Military and Ottoman Collapse* (London: I.B. Tauris, 2002), 146.
[9] Kudret Emiroğlu, *Anadolu'da devrim günleri: İkinci Meşrutiyet'in ilanı, Temmuz - Ağustos 1908* (Kızılay, Ankara: İmge Kitabevi, 1999), 125-226.
[10] II. Meşrutiyet'in İlk Yılı: 23 Temmuz 1908 – 23 Temmuz 1909. Istanbul: YKY, 2008, p. 72.
[11] Erkan Tural, *Son dönem Osmanlı bürokrasisi: II. Meşrutiyet dönemi'nde bürokratlar, İttihatçılar ve parlamenterler* (Ankara: İmge, 2016), 280.

In the appointment of new ones, the most important criterion was loyalty to the spirit of constitution and revolution. Having no prior plan and preparation on how to rule the empire, the CUP was trying to influence and control new cabinet ministers in order to secure the appointment of new cadres loyal to revolution. Soon personal loyalty of bureaucrats to the Sultan was replaced by loyalty to the CUP. Members of the CUP who were elected to the parliament were acting as the sole authority to measure loyalty to the new regime.

Second Wave of Cleansing: Special Law on Reorganization, 1909

It is no wonder that the first wave of cleansing had created a massive discontent among the former officials who developed hatred and resentment towards the CUP. Soon they started to fill the ranks of the Liberal Party (*Ahrar Fırkası*) in opposition. Army officers who were once loyal to the Sultan had also developed a feeling of distrust towards the Unionist officers. As one can imagine, the dominant theme of opposition had a religious cloak. The ones who were sacked by the new regime characterized the Young Turks as a group of heretics and freemasons planted by the Great Powers in the Ottoman lands in order to disseminate chaos and instability.

Some army units in Istanbul revolted on the 13th of April 1909. Suddenly the city was in chaos. There was fighting in the streets, and the rebellious hot heads raided the parliament and searched the members of the CUP who were seeking refuge in their friends' houses. Soon, regiments controlled by the members of CUP in Salonica - later named the "Liberators' Army" - marched towards Istanbul and restored law and order. Martial law was declared, and night curfew was established in the city. Military courts were formed and leaders of the rebellion were hanged. However, the CUP and its supporters sensed the danger. On the 27th of April 1909, the Ottoman parliament proclaimed its decision to depose Sultan Abdülhamid II; only then could members the CUP take a sigh of relief.

Now there was a good excuse for another wave of cleansing or, more aptly, "purges" in the bureaucracy and the army. In the spring of 1909, a set of committees was formed in Istanbul in order to prepare a draft of a "Special Law on Reorganization in Bureaucracy." While the committees were active in the parliament, the press was putting a lot of pressure on them. Finally, on the 29th of May 1909 the draft law came to floor of the parliament. After fierce discussions in the parliament it was approved on the 9th of July 1909. Carter Findlay explains the process of cleansing and its consequences as follows:

There was to be in each ministry or department a special commission consisting of three members of that department under the chairmanship of a member of the senate and the vice-chairmanship of a member of the Chamber of Deputies. These commissions were to examine the service records and abilities of each official, determine the number officials actually needed in the department, and fill all vacancies, giving preference to the best qualified of those who either were serving or had served in the department. Those who were excluded from cadres and judged fit for employment (*caiz-ül istihdam*) were eligible to receive an unemployment stipend on condition that they accepted, unless they had a legitimate excuse, any position subsequently offered to them... For many officials the purges marked the end of their careers and thus in a personal sense, the fundamental meaning of the revolution. ... The British Ambassador's annual report for 1909 indicates that by then some 27,000 officials had already been removed from the payrolls of the various branches of service, with or without unemployment stipends.[12]

Anticipated dismissals and the subsequent reorganization were the most important topic covered in Istanbul press and fiercely debated in government circles. Even in the official correspondence between Istanbul and the provinces, there were references to expected dismissals. For instance, a telegram received from the Deputy-Governor, Major General Naim Bey from Diyarbekir, states that "the local gendarme regiment cannot be expected to act according to the principles of constitutional monarchy and revolution. A deep and complete cleansing is required in Diyarbekir. In that respect, a group of young and vigorous officers need to be appointed."[13] Special emphasis on being "young and vigorous" (*genç ve dinç*) is worth underlining here. The committee that drafted the law on reorganization and submitted it to the Ottoman parliament had also utilized these two adjectives "young and vigorous" for future bureaucrats in the draft text.

During the summer months of 1909, the Istanbul press supported the CUP extensively. For instance, in the editorial of daily *Tanin* on August 11, 1909, Hüseyin Cahit Bey enthusiastically approved the appointment of "able individuals without rank [he means young and vigorous bureaucrats!] as ministers, governors and local governors." Being a

---

[12] Carter V Findley, *Bureaucratic Reform in the Ottoman Empire: The Sublime Porte, 1789-1922* (Princeton: Princeton University Press, 1980), 296-297.

[13] Telegram from Diyarbakır to Ministry of the Interior dated 6 June 1909, BOA [Ottoman Archives / Istanbul], DH.MKT 2840/27 cited in Abdulhamit Kırmızı, 'Meşrutiyette İstibdat Kadroları: 1908 İhtilalinin Bürokraside Tasfiye ve İkame Kabiliyeti,' in *100. yılında Jön Türk devrimi*, Sina Akşin et al., eds., (Beyoğlu, İstanbul: Türkiye İş Bankası Kültür Yayınları, 2010), 340.

prominent member of the CUP, Hüseyin Cahit argued that this was the only way to improve organization of the state. In the same editorial, he expressed his happiness about "the recent appointment of Talat Bey, a former post-office clerk as the Minister of the Interior."[14]

One of the first organizational developments that took place under Talat Pasha was the enactment of the new 'General Law on Provincial Administration' dated 26 March 1913. This law not only provided the basic framework for provincial administration, but also permitted a considerably high degree of decentralization. Provinces could have their own budgets and assume responsibilities in the management of certain financial affairs such as paying salaries, raising some taxes, etc.

Perhaps one of the most important innovations that this law introduced was the appointment process of governors. On the one hand, the new law granted authority to provincial governors (*vali*) to appoint staff to echelons below them (*mutasarrıf* and *kaymakam*), on the other it prevented all possible interventions by the palace and the Sultan in the appointment process of governors. In this sense, the new law of 1913 was a kind of anti-thesis of the Hamidian regime during which the Sultan used to intervene in nearly all high-level appointments. Under the new law, the confirmation of the Sultan with an imperial decree was necessary only for certain appointments. Even this privilege was reduced to a level of formality.[15] In other words, under Talat Bey, the Ministry of Interior was transformed into a semi-autonomous domain in terms of its administration.

Enjoying a high level of autonomy in the management of his ministry, Talat Pasha had also succeeded in incorporating the Ministry of Interior to the Sublime Porte. The enclosed depiction of the organizational chart of the Ottoman central administration in 1914 by Carter Findley is quite revealing. With the "Foreign Ministry" and the "Council of State" - which was only an advisory body with limited personnel - the Ministry of the Interior was positioned into the core of late Ottoman civilian bureaucracy. As we shall demonstrate later, being at the heart of the government and enjoying a relative autonomy must have given a free hand to Talat Pasha to initiate the Armenian genocide later.

Executing Deportations: Formation of 'General Directorate for Settlement of Tribes and Refugees'

In the midst of the Balkan Wars, the CUP organized a *coup* and came

---

[14] Ali Birinci, *Hürriyet ve İtilâf Fırkası: II. Meşrutiyet Devrinde İttihat ve Terraki'ye Karşı çıkanlar* (İstanbul: Dergâh Yayınları, 1990), 32.
[15] Findley, *ibid*, 312.

to power in 23 January 1913. The Ottoman army had just been defeated in the first Balkan War and the Ottoman state had lost 83 per cent of its European territory and 69 per cent of its population living in Europe. Simultaneously, Eastern Thrace was under the occupation of the Bulgarian Army. The first group to suffer from this catastrophe was the Rumelian Moslems living right at the heart of this theatre of war. [16] When the advancing Bulgarian army was halted on the outskirts of Istanbul, nearly 250,000 Turkish/Moslem refugees flooded the imperial capital.[17]

Deportation of the Armenian men from Mamuret-ul-Aziz, May 1915
(Source: Armeniangenocide100.org)

It was the first time Istanbul had ever received such a large number of refugees in its history. In order to solve refugee problem, a special regulation called "Regulation for the Settlement of Immigrants" adopted on 13 May 1913. This regulation mandated the formation of an organization called the "General Directorate for the Settlement of the Tribes and Refugees" (*İskân-ı Aşairin ve Muhacirîn Müdiriyeti, hereafter IAMM*) directly answerable to Minister of the Interior. Recent research in the Ottoman Archives shows us that within the IAMM, a "scientific committee" (*Encümen-i İlmiye Heyeti*) had been formed to study the distribution of ethnic, linguistic and religious minorities in Anatolia from May 1913.[18] This committee had prepared a set of statistical tables and

---

[16] Arnold J. Toynbee, The Western Question in Greece and Turkey: A Study in the Contact of Civilizations (Boston: Houghton Mifflin Company, 1922), 138

[17] Ayhan Aktar, 'Homogenizing the Nation,Turkifying the Economy: Turkish Experience of Populations Exchange Reconsidered' in Renée Hirshon ed., Crossing the Aegean: An Appraisal of the 1923 Compulsory Population Exchange between Greece and Turkey (New York: Berghahn Books, 2004), 79-95.

[18] Fuat Dündar, 'The Settlement policy of the Committee Union and Progress: 1913-18' (Paper presented

ethnographic maps of Anatolia by instructing local authorities to collect information all the way down to the village level. The findings were collated in Istanbul and updated meticulously every three months, and changes in the ethnic and religious composition of the local population were recorded fastidiously.

From the outbreak of war in November 1914 until October 1918, Ottoman subjects were banned from travelling within the country for business or pleasure, and the railway transportation system fell under the complete control of the military authorities. Total censorship of the press accompanied these moves with only the official communiqués, prepared by the officers in the Ottoman Military HQs, published in the newspapers. Therefore, war conditions actually gave a free hand to the CUP to implement policies of long-term demographic engineering of Anatolia on a massive scale.

For the CUP the basic principle of demographic engineering was quite simple:

1. It was decided that the ratio of non – Muslims (Greeks, Armenians, Jews) or non – Turkish minorities (Kurds, Bosnians, Arabs, Georgian Muslims, Albanians, Gypsies etc.) within any of the provinces would not be more than 10 per cent. For example, if in one province the percentage of any kind of minority in the total population was 15 per cent, then one third of this community had to go elsewhere.

2. If deportation or forced migration was not implemented due to certain technical difficulties, then the incoming Balkan or Caucasian refugees were settled in that particular region. Consequently, the population had to be increased until the percentage of minority groups within the total population went below the critical threshold of 10 per cent.[19]

Therefore, the basis of such demographic engineering in this period could be summarized as "mixing of the populations" in order to transform Anatolian territory into a "melting-pot" where preferably Muslim population of Anatolia united to form a single national community. As in the case of Anatolian Armenians, whenever the policies of "mixing and melting" did not work out, the deportations and massacres had to be initiated by Ministry of the Interior. For instance, the data accumulated in the IAMM shows that the CUP leadership carefully

---

at the workshop titled as "Ideologies of Revolution, Nation and Empire: Political Ideas, Parties, and Practices at the End of the Ottoman Empire, 1878-1918, Salzburg, Austria, April 15-17, 2005), 3.
[19] For a detailed analysis of demographic engineering policies, see Taner Akçam, *Young Turks Crime against Humanity: The Armenian Genocide and Ethnic Cleansing in the Ottoman Empire*, (Princeton: Princeton University Press, 2012), 239-280.

monitored population movements in Anatolia.[20] Whenever necessary, Minister of the Interior Talat Pasha issued orders from Istanbul to local governors on the settlement, forced migration and deportation of different communities throughout Anatolia. The underlying principle behind these orders was to create a fatherland where the Turkish/Muslim majority would feel secure, and where the minorities' claims for "national self-determination" could be defeated militarily at once. In essence, cultural and ideological loyalty to the political regime was to be secured by the strategic mixing and significant reshuffling of the entire Anatolian population.

Organizational Structure of the 'General Directorate for Settlement of Tribes and Refugees'

Just after the formation of the IAMM, Şükrü Bey[21] was appointed as the first General Director of the department. In his telegrams to provinces, Talat Pasha mentions the name of Şükrü Bey frequently. For instance, in his telegram to the governors in Anatolia, Talat Pasha informs that the 'General Director of IAMM, Şükrü Bey was on his way to visit provinces in order to inspect the groundwork done to deport Armenians to their determined destinations, please act within the limits of his instructions.'[22]

However, we do not have much information about the organizational structure of the IAMM in its early days. Only in the State Annual (*Sâlname*) of 1917-18 can we find detailed information about the departments under the IAMM and the names of the individuals running these divisions in the center. After the resignation of Şükrü Bey in 1918, Hamdi Bey was appointed as the Director of the IAMM. Here is the organizational chart and personnel of the IAMM at the center in Istanbul:[23]

---

[20] Fuat Dündar, *İttihat ve Terakki'nin Müslümanları İskan Politikası (1913 – 1918)*. Istanbul: İletişim yayınları, 2001. Summarized from the conclusion, pp. 245-252.

[21] Born in 1883 at Istanköy island [Kos on the Aegean], Şükrü Bey studied at the Galatasaray Lycee and the Faculty of Law at the Istanbul University. He later enrolled into public service; first in the Foreign Ministry and later in the Ministry of the Interior. In 1918, he resigned from his position and moved to Izmir. Later he was arrested by British occupation forces and exiled to Malta in relation to Armenian massacres. He escaped from Malta and spent some time in Europe. He joined the National Resistance later and moved to Ankara. Şükrü Bey was in Ankara as an MP between 1923-1938. He took the surname Kaya in 1934. He was the Minister of Interior of all of the İsmet İnönü cabinets throughout 1930s. Şükrü Kaya died in 1959. In relation to his files in Malta, see Vartkes Yaghiayan, *Malta Belgeleri*. Istanbul: Belge yayınları, 2007, 123-125.

[22] BOA.DH.ŞFR, 55-A/16, Telegram sent from the Minister of the Interior, Talat Pasha to Governors of Konya, Ankara, Hüdâvendigâr [Bursa], Adana, Aleppo and Mutasarrıfs of İzmit, Eskişehir, Kütahya, Karahisâr-ı Sâhib, Maraş dated August 31, 1915.

[23] *Salnâme-i Devlet-i Aliye-i Osmaniye, 1333-1334* [Ottoman State Annual of 1917-1918], (Istanbul, 1918), 209-211. Cited in Nedim İpek, *İmparatorluktan Ulus devlete: göçler* (Trabzon: Serander, 2006), 146-147.

General Directorate for Settlement of Tribes and Refugees – Organization Chart of 1917/18

Deputy General Director   **Hamdi Bey**

Department of Settlement

Director	İbrahim Bey
Assistant-Directors	Münir Bey and Muzafferiddin Bey
Asst. Director - Naturalization and Immunities	(?)

Department of Scientific Committees

Director of Agricultural Affairs	(?)
Director of Medical Affairs	Asım Bey
Director of Construction Works	Ömer Kâni Bey
Officer in Charge of Cartography,	(?)

Department of Deportations

Director	Süleyman Hikmet Bey
Deputy-Director	Alaaddin Bey
Officers in Charge of External Deportations	Ali Fehmi, Hilmi, Mehmet Mithat Bey

Department of Nomadic Tribes

Director	Zekeriya [Sertel] Bey
Assistant Director in Charge of Anatolia	Veli Necdet Bey
Assistant Director in Charge of Arabia & Hejaz	Mustafa İhsan Bey
Assistant Director in Charge of Iraq and Syria	Hasan İhsan Bey

Department of Documentation and Communications

Director	Sabri Bey
Officer in Charge of Files	Cemil Bey

Department of Statistics and Personnel

Director	Maruf Bey
Assistant Director, Personnel affairs	Said Seyfi Bey
Assistant Director in Charge of Statistics	Talat Bey

Committee of Inspection

Chief Inspector	Midhat Bey
Inspectors	Bahaeddin Bey, Kerameddin Bey

Department of Accounting

Director	Muzaffer Bey
Clerk	(?)
Officer in charge of Administration and Logistics	Hasan Bey

Apart from the offices in the center, the IAMM had branch offices throughout the provinces. However, the number of officers in each branch varied according to the size and intensity of operations in that particular province. For instance, in the large provinces there were directors of the IAMM and in relatively small provinces there were only officials.

Table 2. General Directorate for the Settlement of Tribes and Refugees: Provincial Organization

Directorates of IAMM in 1st Class Provinces	Directorates of IAMM in 2nd Class Provinces
Director	**Director**
Accounts' Officer	Accounts' Officer
Number of Clerks (3)	Number of Clerks (2)
Officer in Charge of Deportations	n.a.
Officer in Charge of Agriculture	Officer in Charge of Agriculture
Officer in Charge of Settlement	Officer in Charge of Settlement
Offices of IAMM in 1st Class Towns	**Offices of IAMM in 2nd Class Towns**
Officer	Officer
Accounts' Officer	n.a.
Clerk	Clerk
Officer in Charge of Deportations	Officer in Charge of Deportations
Officer in Charge of Agriculture	Officer in Charge of Agriculture

The organizational blueprint given above was not static. In cases of emergency, some extra personnel would be hired in part-time positions. According to principles laid down in the Refugee Regulation (*Mülteci Talimatnamesi*), these part-time personnel were to be selected from incoming refugees from Eastern Anatolia fleeing the Russian invasion. They were supposed to be paid a *per diem*. If there were state officers among the refugees, they would be expected to work on a voluntary basis.

Funding Deportations: The Special Budget of the IAMM

The IAMM had a special budget separate from the Ministry of the Interior. For the year of 1916-1917 it was 15,798,000 *kuruş*. Nearly 30 per cent of this budget was allocated to the salaries of the officials, *per diem* paid to the personnel, and other bureaucratic expenditures. In the beginning, 10,000,000 *kuruş* was reserved for expenses related to settlement.[24] Here, the terminology is rather blurred. By the term settlement (*iskan*), I am sure they meant not only the actual settlement of individuals to a particular location, but also the deportation or "shipment" of Armenian population to deserts in Syria. Otherwise, we cannot find a plausible explanation for shifting extra funds for so-called "settlement/shipment" expenses. In the same budgetary year of 1916, five different transfers were made in order to cover the deficit: first 25,000,000 *kuruş* on 28th of March 1916; second 30,000,000 *kuruş* on 6th of June 1916; third 45,000,000 *kuruş* on 16th of August 1916; fourth 50,000,000 *kuruş* on 6th of November 1916 and fifth 50,000,000 *kuruş* was allocated to expenses related to Armenian deportations. The budget of financial year of 1916 was finalized at 210,000,000 *kuruş* for settlement expenses.[25]

Taking their lesson from the budget of 1916, the finance officers who prepared the following year's budget had allocated 205,700,440 *kuruş* from the outset for the total expenditure of IAMM in 1917. But this amount did not suffice either. They had to allocate 160,000,000 *kuruş* more within 1917. Thinking about the movement of Armenian masses, we know that in 1917 there were no more convoys travelling in the Anatolian inland. The majority of Armenians either massacred by locally formed bands (*çete*) or the Special Organization bands (*Teşkilat-ı Mahsusa*) on the road. Surviving ones had already reached their destinations of settlement in Syria. These sharp increases in the expenditures must be related to two different developments:

First, we know that masses of Muslim refugees had moved west, because gradually the eastern provinces fell under Russian occupation.

---

[24] Nedim İpek, *ibid*, 149.
[25] *Ibid*, 150.

After the catastrophic defeat at Sarıkamış front in the East in January 1915, the Russian counter-attack continued in April 1915. Starting with the fall of Doğu Beyazid and Van in May 1915, the Russian forces gradually occupied most of eastern Anatolia, including the strategic port of Trabzon on the Black Sea coast in the spring of 1916. According to the records of the IAMM, the total number of Muslim refugees who fled eastern Anatolia was 707,504 and the distribution of incoming population in different administrative units were as follows (Table 2).

Since these figures were put together by the IAMM, they concern Moslem refugees mostly Kurdish people receiving help from the IAMM provincial branches. The Director of the IAMM Hamdi Bey made a speech in the upper house of the Ottoman parliament in 24 March 1918 and mentioned that "adding the unrecorded refugees to the figures above, the total number of refugees in reality is around 1,500,000"[26]

Table 2. Distribution of the Muslim refugees from Eastern Anatolia in the spring of 1916 [27]

Adana Vilayeti	13,168	Urfa Sancağı	40,133
Ankara Vilayeti	108,042	İzmit Sancağı	699
Halep Vilayeti	26,315	İçel Sancağı	426
Diyarbakır Vilayeti	84,000	Eskişehir Sancağı	2,316
Sıvas Vilayeti	116,000	Bolu Sancağı	2,500
Kastamonu Vilayeti	10,104	Canik Sancağı	36,000
Konya Vilayeti	4,346	Kayseri Sancağı	30,000
Ma'muret-ül Aziz Vilayeti	5,088	Karahisar-I Sahip Sancağı	616
Trabzon Vilayeti	60,000	Maraş Sancağı	6,666
Musul Vilayeti	150,000	Niğde Sancağı	5,635

Under these conditions we can conclude that only a small fraction of the funds consumed by the IAMM were really spent on assisting the Ottoman Armenians. There are limited examples indicating that the IAMM had distributed meagre funds to the surviving Armenian refugees in Syria. For instance, in his memoir Vahram Dadrian - who was deported

---

[26] *Ibid*, 39.
[27] BOA.DH.İ.UM, Dos. No: E-15, Belge no. 54 cited in Tuncay Öğün, *Unutulmuş bir göç trajedisi Vilayât-i Şarkiye Mültecileri, (1915-1923)* (Ankara: Babil, 2004), 37.

from Çorum and managed to reach Jeresh and settled there - mentions the arrival of an IAMM official to that remote place in the middle of the desert: [28]

> [On 19th of February 1917] Mumtaz Bey, the inspector of refugees, has come to distribute things to help poor refugees... According to our list there are now 208 Armenian families in our village: a total of 743 people, of whom 500 are in need of their daily bread. Late this afternoon Mumtaz Bey distributed 50 banknotes to those in dire need. It was something to see the joy of these Armenians, as they grabbed their money and ran to the bakeries or other stores to shop. Some of them have been feeding themselves on grass for the past two months and haven't tasted any sweets for a year and half.[29]

Second, the high figures in meeting the expenses in relation to "settlement activities" should be related to the high rate of inflation in Turkey during war years. Especially in the big cities, the urban populations experienced a catastrophic wave of inflation. It is a universal phenomenon that in inflationary economies the middle-classes who have fixed incomes and salaries suffers considerably by the increases of the cost of goods and services. Using the data collected by the Ottoman Public Debt Administration (*Duyûn-u Umumiye İdaresi*), Zafer Toprak calculated that the "general consumer's price index" increased 18 fold in the Ottoman Empire during the war: "If we take 1914 prices as the base (100), it reached to 212 in 1916. Next year, it was 846 and in 1918 it had increased to 1823. This was the highest annual price increase in the world up to that time."[30]

At this point it is necessary to state the fact that these data collected by the Ottoman Public Debt Administration mostly reflected the economic situation in big cities. We know that it was very difficult to transport foodstuffs from the countryside to the urban centers. Due to war conditions the Ottoman railways were busy carrying soldiers, military vehicles and ammunitions to the front. Anyone who had good connections in the high command of the army could have been enriched himself by obtaining permission to transport his purchase of foodstuffs in the provinces to the urban centers. Using this opportunity, many businessmen and merchants coming from a Turkish/Muslim background had become rich overnight. However, the wave of inflation must have

[28] Jeresh is a small town nearby the ancient Greco-Roman settlement in today's Jordan. It is only 48 km north of Amman, famous for its archeological ruins.
[29] Vahram Dadrian, *To the Desert: Pages from My Diary* (London: Taderon Press, 2006), 196.
[30] Zafer Toprak, *İttihad - Terakki ve cihan harbi: savaş ekonomisi ve Türkiye'de devletçilik ; 1914-1918* (İstanbul: Homer Kitabevi, 2003), 197.

also been felt in the provinces. The sharp rise in the expenditures of the IAMM must therefore also be related to war-inflation.

The Ministry of the Interior and the CUP: Bribery, Corruption and Nepotism

Up to now, I have tried to explain novelties the Young Turks introduced to the late Ottoman state apparatus in the beginning of the 20th century. Especially after the *coup* of January 1913, the CUP established its dictatorship. The party eliminated all the opposition – practically exiled them to Black Sea port city Sinop and other remote towns in Anatolia - and ruled the country unchallenged until the summer of 1918.

On the eve of war in 1914, Talat Pasha and his friends exercised complete control over the Ministry of the Interior. They had passed the necessary laws in the parliament to purge the remnants of the Hamidian regime and formed crucial administrative tools to create a Turkish nation by reducing the ratio of non-Muslim minorities within the population by implementing deportations and massacres. In this part of the article, I shall try to illustrate structural characteristics of the period in terms of obstacles in realizing their political aspirations and also underlining the powers and the functioning of the CUP as a political organization in the provinces.

Although Talat Pasha had replaced nearly all high level bureaucrats in the Ministry of the Interior and appointed "young and vigorous" Turkish nationalists, the personnel in the lower echelons of the ministry remained intact. These petty officials had the centuries old habit of receiving bribes and grafting. These corrupt officials were especially abundant in the police-corps: The night guards, policemen and their immediate superiors in the police stations in Istanbul neighborhoods perceived public employment as a lucrative business.

Ali Rıza Öge was a nationalist police officer employed in the newly formed "2nd Bureau – Political Affairs" (*Siyasi Şube*) by the Unionist Director of Istanbul Police corps, Cemal Azmi Bey. After the appointment of Cemal Azmi to the governorship of Aleppo, the notorious Bedri Bey replaced him. Due to his good command of the Armenian language, Mustafa Reşat Bey was later appointed as the Chief of the Section of Political Affairs. As a dedicated police officer, Ali Rıza was promoted to the rank of superintendent, and he was in charge of the rounding up the Armenian revolutionaries and intellectuals on 24th of April 1915.

In his memoirs, Ali Rıza gives a good description of how he arranged the police squads to raid the Armenian homes and arrest them in order to be deported to Çankırı and Ayaş.[31] It is interesting to note that apart from intellectuals and the political elite, the police forces went after the Anatolian Armenians who came to work in Istanbul before the war. Especially non-married Armenian men who were not born in Istanbul were rounded up and deported to Syria.[32]

During the war, Ali Rıza promoted to the head of the "Armenian desk" pursued the affluent Armenian merchants from Anatolian towns that had found a way to reach Istanbul by bribing deportation officers. The story of the Kamburian brothers from Ankara is quite revealing. When Kamburian brothers were arrested, it was discovered that they had 52,000 Liras in cash, which offered to Ali Rıza who refused to accept the bribe. However, in the Haydarpasa train-station the deportation officers and attached gendarme guards were not that fastidious. Kamburian brothers have paid a very a small amount of cash and vanished into thin air.

Corrupt officials were everywhere. Even the Armenian elite deported to Çankırı and Ayaş had managed to find ways to bribe officials. Father Grigoris Balakian gives a vivid description of the attitudes of deported Armenians. Some of them were sending long telegrams to Istanbul and demanding justice in the name of the Ottoman constitution, but others were looking for influential contacts. He mentioned "over the course of one month, as in Chankiri, thirteen lucky ones succeeded in returning to Constantinople, thanks to powerful interventions and generous bribes."[33] Survivors' memoirs are full of passages where they describe how they paid different amounts of bribes to deportation officers, gendarme sergeants escorting the convoys and other minor officials in the provinces. For instance, Vahram Dadrian's family travelled all the way from Çorum to Aleppo by bribing gendarme escorts and converting them into their bodyguards. In his diary entry on 16th September, 1915 he states the following:

> We made it from Chorum all the way here thanks to our money and my mother's jewellery. Now we spent all the money; from now on we have to use the jewellery. We began to sell it, but no one pays its true value. Fortunately, in answer to our request, my father's Armenian and Greek friends in Samsun and Constantinople cabled us 100 Turkish pounds.[34]

---

[31] Ali Rıza Öge, Meşrutiyetten Cumhuriyete Bir Polis Şefinin Gerçek Anıları (Bursa, 1982), 213-266.

[32] Ibid, 233.

[33] Grigoris Balakian, Armenian Golgotha: A memoir of the Armenian genocide, 1915-1918 (New York: Knopf, 2009), 90.

[34] Dadrian, *ibid*, 60.

Bribery and nepotism interfered at different stages of the deportation process. In some cases, survivors bribed the officials just in the beginning; hence they were not deported at all. For example, Grigoris Balakian mentions the Armenian "master-cabinet maker born in Constantinople but long since settled with his family in Mersin - he had through bribery, succeeded in remaining in Adana during deportations."[35] Reading all these cases from survivors' memoires, we can conclude that the process of deportations leading to massacres or death due to hunger, fatigue and illness had affected the poor and working classes more than the wealthy and privileged Armenians. The ones who had the financial means and social connections were likely to find a way out within the system.

Ottoman Archives in Istanbul have a sufficient number of documents, especially in the correspondence between the Council of State (*Şurâ-yı Devlet*) and the Ministry of the Interior in relation to the trial and dismissal of corrupt bureaucrats. Another set of documents that reveal cases of corruption are the internal correspondence within the Ministry of the Interior.

Ministry of the Interior presented the cases of corrupt bureaucrats to the Council of State to decide whether they needed further prosecution or not. For example, on the 26th of March 1916 the local governor (*Kaymakam*) Cemal, local financial officer (*Mal Müdürü*) Ahmed Hilmi and the Mayor (*Belediye Reisi*) Recep in Viranşehir, Urfa had put on trial by the Administrative Council of the Sancak of Siverek. Their crimes were related to the embezzlement of certain goods and products (cows, oxen, grain, butter, household utensils) collected from the deported Armenians. Apart from these, it is stated in the document that "the Chief Cashier (*Sanduk Emini*) Ziya Efendi who was appointed *to seize the unnecessary items from the deported Armenians* in convoys had collected *one bagful of cash and jewellery* ... and turned those over to the Local Governor Cemal and Financial Officer Ahmet Hilmi... However, in the process of the official registration, the amount of jewellery had been underrated." [36] On the 29th of March 1916 the Council of State examined the appeal of the Administrative Council of Siverek and decided that those three officials must be put on trial in Diyarbakır.

It is quite obvious from this document that these three bureaucrats worked together and tried to appropriate cash and jewellery that was already collected from deported Armenians. I presume that the initial informer who had passed their names is likely to be related to the local branch of the CUP. In this respect, the decision to put these three

---

[35] Balakian, *ibid*, 80.
[36] BOA.ŞD.MLK 1500/14, Statement of the Administrative Council of the Sancak of Siverek in relation to the case of corruption in Viranşehir dated May 1, 1916 (Italics are mine! AA).

bureaucrats on trial must be related to Talat Pasha's determination to punish minor officials who were enriching themselves by stealing the cash collected from Armenians that was supposed to be transferred to local treasury. Petty officials here perceived as criminals stealing state's funds!

Talat Pasha's attempt to form a Vocational School for minor officials

The corruption cases must have been abundant during the war. It was quite obvious that the bureaucratic cleansing realized in the post-1908 period had not attained the desired level of efficiency. Corruption, fraud, bribery and nepotism were the essential ingredients of the Ottoman administrative culture.

The final attempt of Talat Pasha to create a more efficient bureaucracy could be observed in his proposal to form a special school for minor officials within the Ministry of the Interior. In his long statement explaining the *raison d'être* of the "Vocational School for the Officials within the Interior Ministry" [*Memurîn-i Dahiliye Tatbikat Mektebi*], he argued that the Imperial Academy of Administration [*Mekteb-i Mülkiyye*], and the School of Law at Istanbul University [*Mekteb-i Hukuk*] did not produce a sufficient number of personnel to be employed in the ministry. Talat Pasha also argued they were rather over-qualified for certain positions. He was proposing and also asking permission from the Council of the State [*Şurâ-yı Devlet*] to open up a school where students would follow courses for three semesters only. After this formal teaching they would spend a period of internship in the ministry and later they would get appointed as officials in the provinces.[37]

The Council of the State examined the proposal and answered on the 17th of January 1918 by recommending that Talat Pasha first modify the law in the parliament in relation to training and employment of the state officials. In other words, the Ottoman Council of the State politely told Talat Pasha that their consent would not be sufficient to realize this project. We do not have further evidence about the future of this project. Probably due to the adverse conditions in the Ottoman war effort, this proposal was left to oblivion. However, if Talat Pasha had succeeded in opening this school, we can argue that the students would have been selected from among the CUP hard-liners. It is very probable that the youngsters who were active in the branches of widespread nationalist organizations, for instance the members of *Türk Ocakları* [Turkish Hearths], would have been the possible candidates for this vocational

---

[37] BOA.ŞD.HU 47/13, Formal letter and the attached text of the *raison d'être* from the Minister of the Interior to the Council of the State, dated September 17, 1917.

school attached to the Ministry of the Interior.

The CUP becomes the extension of the State Apparatus under Unionist Dictatorship.

When the CUP forced Abdülhamid II to re-establish the Constitution in July 1908, in terms of cadres and organization the CUP was very weak. Kazım Karabekir (born 1882) states that the number of sworn members of the CUP before the revolution in Istanbul was only 72 persons.[38] One of the first actions of the CUP Istanbul branch was to ask support from the headquarters in Salonica in order to control daily matters.

During 1908 and until the spring of 1909 the CUP preferred to remain behind the scenes. They had intervened only when there was a clear-cut threat to the revolution. For instance, if there were governors still loyal to Abdülhamid II or army units suspected of counter-revolutionary activity, then, they asked them to be dismissed. From July 1908 to May 1909, the CUP had acted as a control mechanism for daily matters of the government, but only indirectly. However beginning with the appointment of Talat Pasha as the Minister of the Interior in August 1909, the CUP started to exercise direct control over some important ministries. Finally, starting from the *coup* of 26 January 1913 they established their dictatorship which resulted in their domination over the state apparatus.

Within a short period of time after July 1908, the CUP had transformed itself into a mass political party. Şükrü Hanioğlu explains the process as follows:

> As the doors of access to the lower levels of the organization were thrown open to mass membership, notables and merchants flocked to join the proliferating local branches of the CUP across the empire. Overwhelmed by a flood of applications for membership, the CUP centre tended to approve petitions for the establishment of local branches on the basis of superficial information concerning their members. By late 1909, the number of CUP branches across the empire had multiplied from 83 on the eve of revolution (several of them minor cells) to 360, while membership had grown roughly from 2,250 to 850,000.[39]

The rapid growth of membership had pushed the CUP central committee to develop certain rules and regulations to run such a mass party. Beginning in December 1908, the CUP organized several party congresses, during which the organizational chart of the party, its

---

[38] Kâzım Karabekir, *İttihat ve Terakki Cemiyeti* (Istanbul: YKY, 2007), 201.
[39] Hanioğlu, *ibid*, 160. Hanioğlu quotes the CUP's membership figures from *Haftalık Şûra-yı Ümmet*, no. 203 [23 January 1909].

hierarchical structure, financial responsibilities of the branches in the provinces and the rules of conduct of its auxiliary organizations - for instance the "Unionist Clubs"- were neatly defined.[40] Accordingly throughout the annual congresses between 1908 and 1913, the party and its organizational structure changed considerably.

The CUP organization in the provinces reached its perfection in the 1913 congress. The position of the Responsible Secretary (*Kâtib-i Mes'ul*) was mentioned for the first time, in the rules of conduct adopted in this congress. Apart from the 'Responsible Secretaries' in the provinces, there were assistants (*Muavin*) and reporters/informers (*Muhabir*) functioning at the level of districts or neighborhoods situated between the local CUP organization and its members.[41] Reading the 1913 party regulations and the rules of conduct, we can clearly conclude that the CUP had transformed itself into an excessively centralized organization with relatively high level of penetration among the masses.

During the deportations and massacres of the Armenians, this party organization worked parallel to the state apparatus. The architect of Armenian genocide, Talat Pasha had manipulated both the party and the Ministry of the Interior in order to uproot more than one million Armenians. Details and the structural characteristics of deportations were debated in the Ottoman parliament during November 1918, when Istanbul was under allied occupation.[42] For instance, on the 21st of November 1918, when the upper House of Ottoman Parliament (*Meclis-i Âyan*) debated the Armenian massacres, the former governor and Minister of Interior, Reşit Akif Pasha, took the floor and made a very important speech. He had served in Ahmet İzzet Pasha's cabinet as the head of *Şura-i Devlet*, the Ottoman Council of State. This short-lived cabinet ruled the country less than a month and signed the Mudros Armistice with Britain on the 30th of October 1918. Within this short period of time Reşit Akif Pasha conducted an administrative investigation into the organization of Armenian deportations and massacres in 1915. In spite of the fact that the scope of his research was limited, his findings were crucial to understanding the mechanisms behind this extensive deportation and massacre of the Ottoman Armenians. Reşit Akif Pasha summarized his findings in his speech:

> There are certain confidential things that I learned during my public service, which did not last more than 25 to 30 days, in the

---

[40] For the consecutive congresses of the CUP, see Tarık Zafer Tunaya, *Türkiye'de Siyasal Partiler, Cilt III. İttihat ve Terakki: Bir Çağın, Bir Kuşağın, Bir Partinin Tarihi*. (Istanbul: Hürriyet Vakfı, 1989), 200-214.

[41] For the full text of Rules of Conduct and the CUP Party Regulations, see Tarık Zafer Tunaya, *Türkiye'de Siyasi Partiler: 1859-1952*. Istanbul: Doğan Kardeş Basımevi, 1952, pp. 218-225

[42] Ayhan Aktar, "Debating the Armenian Massacres in the Last Ottoman Parliament, November – December 1918," *History Workshop Journal* 64, no. 1 (2007): 240–70.

Ahmet İzzet Pasha cabinet. In that respect, I encountered something quite strange. These orders of deportation had been given by the well-known Minister of the Interior [Talat Pasha] and officially communicated to [the governors in] the provinces. Following these official communiqués, the Central Committee [of the CUP] sent orders everywhere in order to secure the gangs to complete their devilish duty. Therefore, as the gangs became gradually more brutal, mutual killings took place. Here, [the activities of] this assembly known as the Central Committee [of the CUP] - that cruel and ruthless group which was solely responsible for these massacres and the countless troubles which we inflicted on the [Ottoman] State and an innocent nation - was more effectual than official orders. In my opinion, it is crucial to be able to decipher the soul of the matter when sufficient research and investigation are conducted. For ten years - not four! - there has been a treacherous group of people destroying not only the Islamic world but all of humanity. This [group] must be identified and disclosed to the public. If this is done properly, the whole truth will be revealed in its clarity and it will later serve as a terrible lesson to our children and to the next generations.[43]

From this sincere and powerful speech of Reşit Akif Pasha, we can argue that Talat Pasha first had sent the official orders of deportation to governors and local officials in the provinces in his capacity as the Ministry of the Interior. At the same time, as the head of the Central Committee, he cabled another set of orders to the "Responsible Secretaries" of the CUP "in order to secure the gangs to complete their devilish duty."

We know that Talat Pasha had functioned as a post-office clerk before the Young Turk Revolution of 1908 and that he had a telegraph device installed in his residence in Istanbul from where these "special orders" could have been sent.[44] His wife, Hayriye Hanım has also mentioned in an interview to a reporter that Talat Pasha used to send telegrams to the provinces from his residence.[45] While Talat Pasha organized the deportation of Armenians by utilizing the IAMM staff in the provinces attached to the Ministry of the Interior, he also mobilized the gangs formed at local level and the Special Organization (*Teşkilât-ı Mahsusa)* in order to initiate the massacres and plundering of Armenian property.

---

[43] *Meclis-i Ayan Zabıt Ceridesi* (Parliamentary Minutes of the Ottoman Upper House), 3rd Period, 5th Year of the Assembly, Volume 1, 1990, 123.

[44] Ambassador Morgenthau mentions that Talat Pasha had installed a telegraphic system in his residence: Henry Morgenthau, *Ambassador Morgenthau's Story* (Michigan: Ann Arbor, 2000), 93-96.

[45] Murat Bardakçı, *Talât Paşa'nın evrak-ı metrûkesi: Sadrazam Talât Paşa'nın özel arşivinde bulunan Ermeni tehciri konusundaki belgeler ve hususî yazışmalar* (İstanbul: Everest Yayınları, 2008), 211.

From the speech of Reşit Akif Pasha we can conclude, therefore, that the system worked efficiently, while many of the CUP members in Istanbul, probably knew very little about the massacres unless they themselves travelled to Anatolia, which was extremely difficult due to war conditions. For instance, Hüseyin Cahit (Yalçın) who was a prominent journalist and member of the CUP mentions in his memoirs that he first heard about deportations and massacres from an officer working the Public Debt Administration as a tax inspector who travelled in Anatolia in the spring of 1915. He underlines the fact that nobody talked about the deportations and massacres of Armenians in public in Istanbul.[46] There is no doubt that the communications system developed by the Minister of the Interior Talat Pasha enabled the whole operation to be conducted in a discrete manner.

Members of the CUP acting as Informers: Letters from Uşak, Kütahya and Aleppo

It has been nearly a decade that classification of the General Directorate of Internal Security - 5th Branch (EUM) in the Ministry of the Interior has been opened to the researchers in the Ottoman Archives (BOA) in Istanbul. It is interesting to note that informers' letters written by local party members in the provinces were registered under this classification.

On the 25th of August 1915, the Steering Committee of Uşak CUP Club sent an official letter with its rubber stamp of the CUP to its Central Committee (*Merkez-i Umumi*) in Istanbul.[47] The letter openly informs that the local Armenian community was under the command of their committee (Armenian Revolutionary Federation). The informer was sure from the way they were acting it is obvious that they receiving orders from this clandestine organization. For instance, the letter states that Armenians did not participate in the 1914 elections. It also underlines the fact that "they had not received any order from above, hence they could not participate in the elections." The letter also informs the Central Committee that two sons of the Priest Artin (?) in the town had fled to Russia during the Balkan Wars of 1912 to join the [Armenian] gangs in Russia. The letter finally comes to point out that although neighboring towns like Eskişehir and Afyon Karahisar have already deported their Armenians, in Uşak the "head of the town" - meaning local governor - protects the Armenians. The letter finally recommends that the central government immediately send official orders and put pressure on this

---

[46] Hüseyin Cahit Yalçın, *Siyasal Anılar* ed. by Rauf Mutluay (İstanbul: Türkiye İş Bankası Kültür Yayınları, 1976), 234.

[47] BOA.DH.EUM 5 Şb. 16/21 Letter sent from the Steering Committee of Uşak Ittihadist Club to the Central Committee of the CUP in Istanbul, dated 25 August 1915.

local governor.

We know that the Armenians of Eskişehir were deported on the 14th of August 1915 and the Armenians of Afyon Karahisar had shared the same destiny the next day.[48] However, we also know that the Armenian community of Kütahya was not deported at all due to the honorable resistance of Fâik Alî [Ozansoy] Bey in spite of the repeated deportation orders sent by Talat Pasa.[49] In those days, Uşak was also under the jurisdiction of Fâik Alî Bey. This letter was written ten days after the deportation of Eskişehir and Afyon Karahisar Armenians. It is informing on the developments in the province and trying to push the Ministry of the Interior via the Central Committee of the CUP. It is quite indicative to observe that at the end of the letter there is a short note written by the Responsible Secretary of the Central Committee, Mithat Şükrü [Bleda] Bey: "This is to present to the attention of our brother Aziz Mithat Bey - who was the Deputy Director of the General Directorate of Internal Security - 28th of August 1915." As the Responsible Secretary of the CUP, Mithat Şükrü Bey received this information from the CUP's provincial organization, but he immediately passes this letter to the attention of the Deputy Director of the General Directorate of Internal Security to be dealt accordingly. This correspondence is one of the few instances and a meaningful example on how the central bureaucracy and party cadres were united and acting together.

The second set of letters was sent from Eskişehir and dealt with the same matter: they criticized the protective attitude of the local governor Fâik Alî Bey towards the Armenian community. But the set also had an attachment that contained some "patriotic tall-tales." Let us examine this correspondence more closely.

On the 6th of December 1915, the Deputy Responsible Secretary in Kütahya, Nazmi Bey, writes to the CUP Inspector Nail Bey, who was at that time in Eskişehir. Nazmi Bey begins as "Dear Brother" and informs him that "five young Armenian men organized an orgy with a Muslim woman whose husband was drafted to the army. The neighbors complained about it and police raided the premises. All of them were arrested. The above-mentioned woman confessed that she was forced to accept prostitution under severe pressure and *Mutasarrıf* [Fâik Alî Bey] felt extremely sorry about it, and decided to put these youngsters on trial by the military court."[50] At this point the Gendarmerie Major intervened and two of the Armenians were exempted from trial. Nazmi Bey, extremely

---

[48] Raymond H Kévorkian, *Le génocide des Arméniens* (Paris: Odile Jacob, 2006), 703-704.

[49] Sarkis Seropyan, 'Vicdanlı Türk Vâlisi Fâik Ali Ozansoy' *Toplumsal Tarih*, 23, Kasım 1995, 46-50.

[50] BOA.DH.KMS 35/53, Letter from M. Faik who is Responsible Secretary of the CUP at Kütahya to the CUP Inspector Nail Bey in Eskişehir, dated 10 December 1915.

furious argues that "the negative attitude of this Major had no limits!"

Nazmi Bey also adds that an Armenian, Nishan (?), was still in the town and he probably had a meeting with the Deputy of Musul, Ibrahim Bey who stayed in the residence of Mutasarrıf [Fâik Alî Bey] for few days. Nazmi Bey mentions "Nishan had a legal document prepared in the local court mandating that all of his cash in the bank be transferred to the Deputy of Musul, Ibrahim Bey. Nishan also appointed Ibrahim Bey as the sole legal representative to sell all of his moveable and immovable property." Nazmi Bey adds "he cannot stop being astounded by such audacity."

This letter was an attachment to another letter written by M. Faik, who was the CUP Responsible Secretary in Eskişehir, and addressed to the CUP Responsible Secretary of the Central Committee in Istanbul on the 10th of December 1915. M. Faik begins his letter "Esteemed Brothers" and accuses the Mutasarrıf of Kütahya [Fâik Alî Bey] in the following manner:

> Under these conditions, I say 'no more' to the one who is still treating Armenians in a compassionate and benevolent manner. This person does not have the least amount of the national ideal - or to tell the truth (!) - he does not even have a single drop of Turkish blood in his veins. If the *Mutasarrıf* had the national ideal, he could have deported all the Armenians using the latest events as a pretext. Later, if anyone were to question [the deportations], he could defend his decision by saying that the Armenians had lacked gratitude.

The CUP circle in the town must have been working hard to have Fâik Alî Bey dismissed. From the quote above, we can conclude that they were referring to Fâik Alî's Kurdish background by saying that he did not have "a single drop of Turkish blood in his veins." Fâik Alî Bey was from a prominent Kurdish family of Diyarbakır. On the 19th of June 1919, he was appointed the governor of Diyarbakır only for a short period of time.[51]

All efforts of the informers working in Kütahya and Eskişehir created the expected results. On the 18th of December 1915, the Ministry of the Interior finally did send a letter from Istanbul and ordered an investigation of all the claims of the informants in Kütahya. However, we cannot follow the trail of this correspondence any further.

From the correspondence in the Ottoman Archives we learn that the CUP cadres were acting like control mechanism over the governors in the

---

[51] BOA.DH.KMS 53-1/71.

provinces. They monitored the deportation of the Armenians, sales of their property and did their best in enriching themselves.

Third set of correspondence is from Aleppo. During the war, Aleppo turned out to be a center of recreation and amusement for the Ottoman and German officer corps. As Lieutenant Abidin (Ege) mentions his memoirs, the prostitution was extensive in the city. Young officers seeking for female company were enjoying themselves at the theatres, cinemas, restaurants, café-chantants and certain type of houses with prostitutes. Lieutenant Abidin states the fact that during the war "Aleppo transformed into a bordello of lavish squandering and extravagance."[52]

The friends of survivor Yervand Odian in Adana and Islahiye recommended him to see Hovannes Mazlumian, the owner of the notorious Baron Hotel in Aleppo. At the end of 1915, when Yervand Odian reached Aleppo, the first thing he did was to visit Mazlumian Efendi, so-called the Baron. Naturally Odian was trying to avoid being deported to Der Zor, and he asked Mazlumian's help to secure his stay in Aleppo. [53] Apparently Mazlumian had good friends among the deportation officials and other Ottoman bureaucrats. In the first days of 1916, the Baron must have pulled certain strings so that Odian could go to Hama where the police would not disturb him. Yervand Odian stayed in Hama more than nine months. In relation to the Baron, Odian tells the following:

> At the end of 1916 the owner of Baron Hotel, Hovannes Efendi Mazlumian and his brother had been deported from Aleppo to Lebanon... They were deported to the place in Lebanon with the best climate, Zahleh, where the governor lived and which was regarded as the capital of Lebanon. Aram [Mazlumian] wrote two letters to me from there and, on behalf of the Baron, invited me to stay in Zahleh for few months.[54]

Unfortunately, Yervand Odian could not obtain a travel permit to go to Zahleh; instead he was first sent back to Aleppo and later to Der Zor.

On the 20th of June 1916, a letter from Allepo signed by Major Aziz was sent to Istanbul. Starting his letter with a spirit of brotherhood, Major Aziz stated the following:

> My dear brother, take my words very seriously. There is an Armenian center [of activity] in Aleppo that is important and functioning in perfect condition. Rich Armenians who were sent

---

[52] Abidin Ege, *Çanakkale, Irak ve İran Cephelerinden Harp Günlükleri* (İstanbul: Türkiye İş Bankası Kültür yayınları, 2011), 591.
[53] Odian, *ibid*, 94-95.
[54] *Ibid*, 121.

from Anatolia managed to remain in Aleppo. Today there are about 15,000 Armenian deserters and refugees staying in Aleppo. Believe in this! The ones who are dispatched to Der Zor and Syria are the poor and helpless ones. Believe in this with all your heart: except for the Governor [of Aleppo], all officials are receiving ample amount of money [as bribes]... Even our most trusted friends and others we do not know, [in short] every individual is stealing money. There is no need to write their names. There is only an honest governor Şevki Pasha who is not much occupied with his job and remains uncorrupted, that's all. Apart from those two, anyone who is dealing with Armenian matters is totally corrupted. I heard all these things from the Armenians in Aleppo... The new Armenian organization in Aleppo is located in the Baron Hotel. Therefore, all these men, inspectors, directors etc. are enjoying themselves in this Hotel... Recently the Baron asked for donations from the people for Armenian committees. [Later, they sent the Baron to military court to be put on trial for this] and the court decided all these funds were collected for schools! What schools? Where are we now? [55]

The informer Aziz goes on in the same style for two more pages. However, in the letter Aziz mentions that he went to the Baron Hotel with the recently appointed Mutasarrıf of Der Zor, [Salih] Zeki Bey, who was appointed from Everek - Kayseri in July 1916. Zeki Bey was notorious for his cruelty against the Armenian population in Kayseri.[56] Informer Aziz actually introduced the newly appointed Zeki Bey to Hovannes Mazloumian, the Baron. In that meeting, the Baron uttered some positive remarks about the former Mutasarrıf of Der Zor, namely Ali Suad Bey.[57] Naturally this was not received well by the informer Aziz who concluded that the Baron thought Ali Suad Bey was dismissed because he used to treat Armenians favorably! This is the general tone of the letter that is full of contempt and hatred against Armenians.

This letter must have been taken very seriously in Istanbul. On the 9th of July 1916 the Ministry of Interior sends a special order to the Governor

---

[55] BOA.DH.EUM 2.Şb 26/9. From Major Aziz in Aleppo to the 'presence of brothers' in Istanbul. Dated 20 June 1916.

[56] For Salih Zeki's atrocities in Everek - Kayseri see, Captain Sarkis Torossian, *From Dardanelles to Palestine* (Boston: Meador, 1947), 103-114.

[57] In the autumn of 1918, a criminal investigation commenced in Istanbul in relation to the state officials who committed atrocities against Armenians. In this respect, the police were looking for the former Mutasarrıf of Der Zor, Salih Zeki Bey. In those days it was heard that he was hiding somewhere in Kastamonu or Bursa. The Ministry of the Interior had send special orders to the governors of Canik and Hüdavendigar giving physical description of Salih Zeki and asking for his arrest. For the order to the Mutasarrıf of Canik, see DH. ŞFR 94/155 dated 16 December 1918. And for the order to the Vali of Hudavendigar see BOA.DH.ŞFR 94/215 dated 22 December 1918.

of Aleppo, Mustafa Abdülhalik [later adopted the surname Renda] that the case of the Baron must be investigated. Only five days later, on the 27th of July the Governor of Aleppo, Mustafa Abdülhalik answers back as follows:

> The intelligence about the Baron is correct ... He is a fanatic Armenian. He never misses any opportunity to do good for the Armenian people... My humble opinion [about the Baron] is the following: From the point of political and ethical considerations, this go-between [person] has to be kicked out and subjugated. However, his hotel being the best one in Aleppo has to go on providing its services under the new management of a Muslim hotel-owner somehow brought in from Istanbul or anywhere else. This must be done before the Baron's deportation... Any official who cannot resist women and gambling becomes the Baron's friend at the end. Nowadays, the Baron's best friend is the police chief of Aleppo... If you can find a police chief with an inflexible nature and appropriate political convictions who could also resist those two bewitching things, i.e. women and gambling; then I can add as a further opinion that it is advisable to replace the existing one in here.[58]

After receiving this letter, on the 9th of August 1916, Talat Pasha personally wrote to Cemal Pasha - the commander of the 4th Army Corps and the General Governor of Syria - and asked his opinion about the Baron's deportation from Aleppo. On the 12th of August, Cemal Pasha wrote back to Talat Pasha and his answer is interesting:

> In terms of being a gambling-house and brothel, the Baron Hotel is not much different from the other hotels in Aleppo. Şükrü Bey who is the General Director of IAMM knows the Baron personally and he has reliable personal information about the nature of his activities.[59] I prefer to be cautious by not expressing any opinion as to whether Baron should be deported or not. I kindly ask this matter to be decided by Mustafa Abdülhalik Bey, the Governor of Aleppo, whose conscience, honesty and judgement of opinion I am assured of.

Finally on August 16th 1916, Talat Pasha writes to the Governor of Aleppo Mustafa Abdülhalik Bey and orders the following: "as you have communicated before, it is appropriate to deport Baron the hotel-owner

---

[58] Ibid.
[59] Here, I suppose, Cemal Pasha is referring to Şükrü Bey's earlier visit to Aleppo in 1915. During his visit it is very probable that Şükrü Bey had stayed at Baron Hotel. This must be the basis of Şükrü Bey's personal information (!) about the Baron. For Talat Pasha's telegraph informing the Governor of Aleppo about the inspection tour of Şükrü Bey, see BOA.DH.ŞFR. 55-A/240 dated 13 September 1915.

to the interior."[60] During these exchanges between Aleppo, Jerusalem and Istanbul the owner of the Baron Hotel, Hovannes Mazloumian, must have sensed something. Perhaps informed by his friends among the police about the impending catastrophe, Mazloumian fled to Zahleh in Lebanon.

Concluding Remarks and Methodological Considerations on Sources

1. If the correspondence between the Unionists in the provinces and their Central Committee in Istanbul are taken as a point of departure, we can argue that the CUP rank and file acted as a pressure group on the governors in the provinces. They not only put pressure on local governors to deport the Armenian population to the deserts of Syria, in order to appropriate Armenians' property, but they also tried to mobilize the ministry by sending letters directly to the CUP top brass. Reading the special notes written at the end of every letter by the Responsible Secretary of the Central Committee, Mithat Şükrü Bey in Istanbul, we can say that these letters were taken quite seriously and the ministry acted without delay.

In the case of Fâik Alî Bey, the Mutasarrıf of Kütahya, these pressures did not create the expected results at once. This must be related to the personal qualities of Fâik Alî Bey and the type of relationship he had developed with the local notables of Kütahya. In Kütahya, we know that the local notables Germiyanzâde family and Hocazâde Ragıp [Soysal] supported Fâik Alî Bey and opposed Unionists who were utilizing all their means to deport the Armenians of Kütahya and Uşak.[61] Apart from that, Fâik Alî Bey was the younger brother of Süleyman Nazif, who himself was the governor of Bagdad. Both brothers were poets and quite well known within the literary circles of Istanbul.

2. The case of the Baron in Aleppo is quite revealing indeed. First of all, it demonstrates the degree of corruption of the Ottoman bureaucracy in the provinces. Using Yervant Odian's terminology, the appointment of "dyed-in-the-wool Ittihadists" to all critical positions did not change the centuries-old habit of receiving bribes and corruption. Contrary to the expectations of Talat Pasha and his friends, the CUP cadres were not immune to corruption either. The Young Turk regime turned out to be a total failure in terms of transforming Ottoman "bureaucratic culture." Bribery, corruption and other illegal practices not only remained intact, this bureaucratic culture also seduced the newcomers considerably. However, the very bureaucratic culture based upon receiving bribes made

---

[60] Ibid.
[61] Kévorkian, *ibid*, 702

a big difference to certain Armenians. The rich and well-connected ones found "ways to stay alive and survive." The poor Armenians coming from rural backgrounds paid a heavier price, since they did not have the means to bribe the officials and prevent their personal destruction, they were sent to death marches.

3. There is no doubt that the CUP cadres in the provinces acted as the extension of the Ottoman state between 1915 and 1918. By quoting the long speech of Reşit Akif Pasha in the Ottoman parliament in 1918, I tried to illustrate how the CUP leadership united the powers of the centralized state apparatus with the CUP network in the provinces. In this interaction, the driving force behind the local Ittihadists' actions was not only nationalist ideology, unsubstantiated feelings of betrayal or negative features attributed to non-Muslims in general. Perhaps the resentful local notables who rushed into the CUP after 1909 and increased its "roster of membership" to 850,000 persons were also jealous of the modern life-style of the Armenians and their conspicuous consumption habits in the urban centers. The social change, commercialization of agriculture and flooding in of imported goods in the second half of the 19th century in the Ottoman lands must have enriched the urbanized Armenians who were mostly active in trade, working as artisans or as owners of small workshops.

In his memoir, the famous Turkish industrialist Vehbi Koç (1901-1996) gives a vivid description of the non-Muslim minorities in Ankara before the First World War. It is interesting to note that the feelings of jealousy towards non-Muslims made young Koç drop out school and enter business life to become a prominent businessman in the nascent Turkish republic. This long passage is worth quoting:

> The Armenians, Greeks and Jews were dominant in the commercial life of Ankara. Although the Muslim Turks were the [real] owners of the country, they were mostly working under these social groups and leading a simple life. The best houses, best shops and best summer residences belonged to non-Muslims. They used to put their best dresses on Sundays, enjoy good food and drinks. They were also going out to have fun. On Sundays, the large streets of Ankara would be packed with the Christian and Jewish families in their best attire, strolling up and down in the spring and autumn months... Going to the countryside during the summer was an old tradition in Ankara... According to their wealth, some people had carriages with two horses, some with one horse. Some of them did not have carriages at all. They used to ride a horse or a donkey to commute to their country houses. Like the other Muslims of Ankara, our country house was in a place

called Çoraklık. It was next to Keçiören where most of the Catholic Armenians had their summer residences. Their well-kept vineyards, houses and gardens always attracted our attention... I used to play with the other kids by the road and look around. I used to feel jealous of the Christians when they were going to their summer residences. They had beautiful carriages pulled by the well-fed horses. I wanted to be like them... Then I decided to enter commercial life, I dropped out of school at the age of fifteen.[62]

Fortunately young Vehbi Koç and his family did not choose the easy way: participation in the massacres of the Armenians of Ankara and plundering of their fortunes. Instead, they preferred to build their fortune in the proper way, like their Christian neighbors had done before them.

I would argue that without taking into consideration the "accumulated envy" of the Turkish and Kurdish urban notables, we could not explain the motives behind the Ittihadists' sudden active support of Armenian deportations and massacres in the provinces. Arguably among the devilish genocidal calculations of Talat Pasha and his friends, this resentment and envy was the most reliable factor in the annihilation process of Ottoman Armenians.

4. In my opinion, politics of the Turkish state based upon "complete denial" has shaped the historiography on 1915. The 'politics of genocide recognition' contributed to this as well. As a reaction to the denialist position, the first scholarly works on the annihilation of the Ottoman Armenians had to rely on so-called "neutral" sources, such as the testimonies of American missionaries or the archive material coming from the neutral states in the First World War. For instance, the explanatory value of a diary of a Scandinavian missionary who was trapped in a small Anatolian town was thought to be more valuable than the account of an Armenian survivor who was deported from Çorum and went as far as Der Zor. The memoirs of the survivors were not considered reliable sources, since they were written by Armenian authors, and were hence considered biased by definition not only by the historians of the Turkish state but also by Armenian historians themselves. Exploring the survivors' accounts and quoting extensively from these memoirs meant the academic work would be branded "simple propaganda" by "the other side." However, by avoiding survivors' accounts historians have unfortunately ignored the intriguingly complex relations in the provinces.

In this respect, it was a revealing experience to read Grigoris Balakian's *Armenian Golgotha* finally published in English in 2009. Father Balakian

---

[62] Vehbi Koç, *Özel arşivinden belgeler ve anılarıyla Vehbi Koç* Can Dündar (ed.) (İstanbul: Doğan Kitap, 2006), 21-22.

not only masterfully narrates his painful journey from Istanbul to the north of Syria and his return. He also describes the feelings of the victims, perpetrators and the usual spectators. He not only tells us the dreadful stories of the massacres, but also describes the feelings, aspirations, motives and dreams of the different parties. Any historiography missing these infinitely 'grey areas' of human conduct cannot stand on its feet for long, I reckon.

Until recently, even the Ottoman archive documents used to be regarded as "unfit for historical explanation." Thanks due to the efforts of Taner Akçam who proved the Ottoman archives could be used along with German, French and American archives.[63] I would like to finish by saying that the future work on the destruction of Anatolian Armenians in 1915 must rely on Turkish and Armenian material first and foremost. I do not think that we could afford to avoid the basic sources in Armenian and Turkish for the sake of so-called "neutrality."

Bibliography

Archive documents

Prime Ministerial Ottoman Archive - Başbakanlık Osmanlı Arşivi (BOA).
Council of State - Şurâ-yı Devlet (ŞD).
Ministry of the Interior - Dahiliye Nezareti (DH).
Record Office of the Private Secretariat - Dahiliye, Kalem-i Mahsus Evrakı (DH.KMS)
Department of General Security - Dahiliye Nezareti, Emniyet-i Umumiye (DH.EUM)
Ministry of the Interior, Cipher Office - Dahiliye Nezareti, Şifre Kalemi (DH.ŞFR)

Academic Works and Memoirs

Akbayar, Nuri. (Ed.) II. Meşrutiyet'in ilk yılı: 23 Temmuz 1908-23 Temmuz 1909. İstanbul: Aygaz /YKY, 2008.

Akçam, Taner. Young Turks' Crime against Humanity - the Armenian Genocide and Ethnic Cleansing in the Ottoman Empire. Princeton: Princeton University Press, 2013.

Akşin, Sina, Sarp Balcı, Barış Ünlü (eds.) *100. yılında Jön Türk devrimi*. İstanbul: Türkiye İş Bankası Kültür Yayınları, 2010.

Aktar, Ayhan 'Homogenizing the Nation,Turkifying the Economy: Turkish Experience of Populations Exchange Reconsidered' in Renée Hirshon (ed.) *Crossing the Aegean: An Appraisal of the 1923 Compulsory Population Exchange between Greece and Turkey*. New York: Berghahn Books, 2004: 79-95.

———. "Debating the Armenian Massacres in the Last Ottoman Parliament, November – December 1918." *History Workshop Journal* 64, no. 1 (2007): 240–70.

Balakian, Grigoris. Armenian Golgotha: A memoir of the Armenian genocide, 1915-1918. New York: Knopf, 2009.

Bardakçı, Murat. Talât Paşa'nın evrak-ı metrûkesi: sadrazam Talât Paşa'nın özel arşivinde bulunan Ermeni tehciri konusundaki belgeler ve hususî yazışmalar. İstanbul: Everest Yayınları, 2008.

---

[63] Taner Akçam, *ibid*. See especially Chapter 1.

Birinci, Ali. Hürriyet ve İtilâf Fırkası: II. Meşrutiyet Devrinde İttihat ve Terraki'ye Karşı çıkanlar. İstanbul: Dergâh Yayınları, 1990.

Dadrian, Vahram. *To the Desert: Pages from My Diary.* London: Taderon Press, 2006.

Deringil, Selim. The Well-Protected Domains: Ideology and the Legitimation of Power in the Ottoman Empire, 1876-1909. London: I.B. Tauris, 2009.

Dündar, Fuat. 'The Settlement policy of the Committee Union and Progress: 1913-18.' Paper presented at the workshop titled as "Ideologies of Revolution, Nation and Empire: Political Ideas, Parties, and Practices at the End of the Ottoman Empire, 1878-1918, Salzburg, Austria, April 15-17, 2005.

————. İttihat ve Terakki'nin Müslümanları iskân politikası, 1913-1918. İstanbul: İletişim Yayınları, 2011.

Ege, Abidin. *Çanakkale, Irak ve İran Cephelerinden Harp Günlükleri.* İstanbul: Türkiye İş Bankası Kültür yayınları, 2011.

Emiroğlu, Kudret. Anadolu'da devrim günleri: İkinci Meşrutiyet'in ilanı, Temmuz - Ağustos 1908. Ankara: İmge Kitabevi, 1999.

Findley, Carter V. Bureaucratic Reform in the Ottoman Empire: The Sublime Porte, 1789-1922. Princeton: Princeton University Press, 1980.

Hanioğlu, Şükrü. *A Brief History of the Late Ottoman Empire.* Princeton: Princeton University Press, 2010.

İhsanoğlu, Ekmeleddin, and Mustafa Kaçar (eds.) Çağını yakalayan Osmanlı!: Osmanlı devletinde modern haberleşme ve ulaştırma teknikleri. İstanbul: IRCICA yayını, 1995.

İpek, Nedim. *İmparatorluktan Ulus devlete: göçler.* Trabzon: Serander, 2006.

Karabekir, Kâzım. *İttihat ve Terakki Cemiyeti.* İstanbul: Yapı Kredi Kültür Sanat Yayıncılık, 2009.

Kévorkian, Raymond H. *Le génocide des Arméniens.* Paris: Odile Jacob, 2006.

Koç, Vehbi. Özel arşivinden belgeler ve anılarıyla Vehbi Koç. İstanbul: Doğan Kitap, 2006.

Morgenthau, Henry. *Ambassador Morgenthau's Story.* Ann Arbor: Gomidas Institute, 2000.

Odian, Yervant. Accursed Years: My Exile and Return from Der Zor, 1914-1919. London: Gomidas Institute, 2009.

Öge, Ali Rıza. Meşrutiyetten cumhuriyete bir polis şefinin gerçek anıları. Bursa, 1982.

Öğün, Tuncay. Unutulmuş bir göç trajedisi: Vilayât-i Şarkiye Mültecileri, (1915-1923). Ankara: Babil, 2004.

Seropyan, Sarkis. 'Vicdanlı Türk Vâlisi Fâik Alî Ozansoy' *Toplumsal Tarih*, 23, (Kasım 1995): 46-50.

Toprak, Zafer. İttihad - Terakki ve cihan harbi: savaş ekonomisi ve Türkiye'de devletçilik ; 1914-1918. İstanbul: Homer Kitabevi, 2003.

Torossian, Sarkis. *From Dardanelles to Palestine.* Boston: Meador, 1947.

Toynbee, Arnold J. The Western Question in Greece and Turkey: A Study in the Contact of Civilizations. Boston: Houghton Mifflin Company, 1922.

Tunaya, Tarık Zafer. Türkiye'de siyasal partiler: İttihat veTerakki Bir Çağın, Bir Kuşağın, Bir Partinin Tarihi. Cilt III. İstanbul: Hürriyet Vakfı Yayınları, 1989.

Tural, Erkan. Son dönem Osmanlı bürokrasisi: II. Meşrutiyet dönemi'nde bürokratlar, İttihatçılar ve parlamenterler, Ankara: İmge, 2016.

Turfan, M. Naim. Rise of the Young Turks: Politics, the Military and Ottoman Collapse. London: I.B. Tauris, 2002.

Yaghiayan, Vartkes. *Malta Belgeleri.* Istanbul: Belge yayınları, 2007.

Yalçın, Hüseyin Cahit, and Rauf Mutluay. *Siyasal Anılar.* İstanbul: Türkiye İş Bankası Kültür Yayınları, 1976.

CHAPTER 3

HOMOGENIZING THE NATION, TURKIFYING THE ECONOMY: THE TURKISH EXPERIENCE OF POPULATION EXCHANGE RECONSIDERED

There is no greater sorrow on earth than the loss of one's native land.
Euripides, 431 B.C.

Introduction

Commenting in 1922 on the export of nationalism to Greek and Turkish societies, the British historian Arnold Toynbee noted that 'the inoculation of the East with nationalism has from the beginning brought in diminishing returns of happiness and prosperity.'[1] The compulsory exchange of populations between Greece and Turkey demonstrates this point. The forced migration of well over one million Greeks and Turks not only increased chaos and despair among the migrants, but also profoundly changed the social and political texture of both countries. Concentrating mainly on Turkey, I argue that the exchange reduced the possibility of foreign intervention in her domestic affairs by homogenizing the population along ethnic and religious lines, which in turn promoted the formation of a nation-state similar to western models. However, the exchange's effect on the economy of the new state was damaging, and necessitated many years of structural modification and readjustment.

A balance sheet: comparative advantages and disadvantages of the exchange of populations

The Ankara Convention of 10 June 1930, signed by Turkey and Greece, provided a solution to the problems still outstanding from the compulsory exchange of populations in 1923. A careful analysis of the U.S. archive documents of the period indicates that American diplomats had perceived the population exchange and its attendant problems as a great obstacle to restoring peace in the Balkans. Following the Ankara Convention, an extensive report on the population exchange prepared by Raymond Hare in October 1930 assessed the economic and political

---

[1] Arnold Toynbee, *The Western Question in Greece and Turkey* (Boston: Houghton Mifflin Company, 1922), 18.

consequences of the exchange: 'By the way of making a general summary of the situation, it might be said that Greece has gained economically and lost politically, and that Turkey has gained politically but lost economically.[2]

For Greece, the political losses came in the form of outside interference. Between 1922 and 1930, Greece had spent more than £10 million on the settlement of Anatolian refugees. Mostly financed by foreign loans, the cost to Greece of this expenditure was a yearly debt-servicing burden of approximately £2.9 million. Indeed, because of the cost of mobilization and the Asia Minor adventure, Greece had been in desperate need of foreign assistance from the beginning of the 1920s, as a direct result of which Greek politicians adopted a development strategy whereby in return for financial aid they accepted a certain amount of political interference by outside powers.[3] Acceptance of foreign intervention thus became a *modus vivendi* for the Greek political establishment.

Conversely, Turkey's major political gain was to rid her domestic affairs of interference from the Great Powers, a problem that had plagued the Ottoman Empire throughout the nineteenth century, for with the emptying of Anatolia of its non-Muslim minorities there was no longer a basis for such interference.[4] In addition, unlike Greece, Turkey did not receive any foreign assistance to facilitate the integration of the Rumelian[5] refugees into the national economy. Although Turkey was economically shattered and the government could not even spend £1 million on settlement and other refugee-related programs, the advantage for Turkey was that it incurred no financially and politically crippling debts to the Powers. Combined with strong economic protectionism and clearly asserted neutrality in inter- national relations, the consequent level of non-intervention that the Turkish political elite was able to enjoy is arguably the most important achievement of the Kemalist regime.

---

[2] Special report prepared by Raymond Hare on 'The Origin and Development of the Greco- Turkish Exchange of Populations Question' dated 15 October 1930. Document no.767.68115/143, p. 132 classified in US National Archives, Records of the Department of State relating to the Political Relations of Turkey, Greece and the Balkan States, 1930 – 1939. Raymond Hare later served as the U.S. Ambassador in Ankara between 1961 and 1964.

[3] J. A. Petropoulos, "The Compulsory Exchange of Populations: Greek - Turkish Peacemaking 1922 - 1930," *Byzantine and Modern Greek Studies* 2 (1976): 160.

[4] However, issues surrounding the Greek minorities in Istanbul and the Aegean islands continued to pose problems for decades. See, Baskın Oran, 'The Story of Those Who Stayed: Lessons From Articles 1 and 2 of the 1923 Convention' and Alexis Alexandris, 'Religion or Ethnicity: The Identity Issue of the Minorities in Greece and Turkey' in Renee Hirschon (ed), *Crossing the Aegean: An Appraisal of the 1923 Compulsory Population Exchange between Greece and Turkey* (New York: Berghahn Books, 2003).

[5] 'Rumelia' denotes Ottoman or former Ottoman domains west of the Straits, including Aegean possessions.

Transformation of the social fabric: a search for ethnic homogeneity in both countries

In the post-Lausanne period, Turkey and Greece were occupied with building nation-states, the distinctive feature of which was the emphasis on an ethnically homogenous population. In a long speech given to the Greek Parliament on 17 June 1930, Prime Minister Venizelos urged ratification of the Ankara Convention. In so doing, he analyzed the dominant political tendencies of both countries as follows:

> Turkey herself – new Turkey – is the greatest enemy of the idea of the Ottoman Empire. New Turkey does not wish to hear anything about an Ottoman Empire. She proceeds with the development of a homogeneous Turkish national state. But we also, since the catastrophe of Asia Minor, and since almost all of our nationals from Turkey have come over to Greek territory, are occupied with a similar task.[6]

The fact that both political leaderships were busy completing 'a similar task' within their respective domains provided the objective basis of rapprochement between the two countries in the 1930s.

However, the process of forming ethnically homogeneous nation-states did not take place all at once, nor was it mainly the result of the compulsory exchange of populations between Greece and Turkey themselves. For Turkey, it was the result of the ten years of war between 1912 and 1922 (the Balkan Wars, the First World War and the War of Independence). The first examples of population exchanges between Turkey, Greece and Bulgaria took place just after the Balkan Wars of 1912/13. Then, during the First World War, the Armenians of Anatolia were forced into migration or worse, massacred.

The Ottoman population census of 1906 indicates that within the borders of present-day Turkey the population at that time was 15 million. However, the first Turkish population census to be conducted under the republican regime, in 1927, indicates that the population of the country had decreased to 3.6 million. McCarthy calculates that nearly 18 percent of the Muslims in Anatolia perished during the ten years of war.[7] Changes in the ethnic and religious composition of the population were also dramatic: Keyder states that before the First World War, 'one out of every five persons [20 %] living in present-day Turkey was non-Muslim, after the war,

---

[6] Official translation of Venizelos's speech is attached to Robert Skinner's dispatch sent from Athens to the U.S. Secretary of State, Washington, 20 June 1930. Document no. 767.68115/136. *Records of the Department of State Relating to the Political Relations of Turkey, Greece and the Balkan States, 1930–1939.*
[7] Justin McCarthy, *Muslims and Minorities: The Population of Ottoman Anatolia and the End of the Empire* (New York: New York University Press, 1983), 133.

only one out of forty persons [2.5 %] was non-Muslim.'[8]

This drastic decline in the number of non-Muslims had severe economic consequences for Turkey. Observers of the period have noted the decisive role of Greeks and Armenians not only in petty trade and credit activities, but also in wholesale internal trade, in import and export, and in the overall financial structure of Turkey. As a careful observer of the pre-war period, Sussnitzki presents the fact that: 'The Greeks and Armenians are preponderant almost everywhere. Neither the Arabs and Persians, who are able traders, nor by and large the Jews can compete with them.'[9] The departure of the Greeks and Armenians from Turkey meant that the most productive elements of the population, and a good deal of the entrepreneurial know-how, had left the country for good. Thus, when the republic was formed, the bureaucracy found itself largely unchallenged, enabling the Kemalists to implement policies of Turkification in the early years of the republic without much opposition.[10]

For Greece, however, while the Muslims that left Rumelia were mostly peasants, the incoming Anatolian Greeks were mostly urban artisans or from the commercial classes. Indeed, the influx of refugees from Turkey had positive repercussions on the commercial and industrial life of Greece, and was in fact responsible for a short-term economic boom in the post-Lausanne period. As Giannakopoulos clearly argues: 'the urban refugee population was a source of cheap labor as well as skilled craftsmen. The country was enriched by men of proven business competence and experience.'[11] According to the survey conducted by the League of Nations in 1926: 'Of the 7,000 merchants and industrialists enrolled in the Athens Chamber of Commerce, 1,000 were refugees, while the proportion was even higher in Piraeus. In 1961, 20 percent of Greek industrialists had been born in Asia Minor and Eastern Thrace.'[12] Commenting on the economic prosperity that Greece experienced in the 1920s, one foreign observer made the following comparisons: 'Thus, we may expect the Asiatic Greeks to bring to Greece the same kind of stimulus that England and America received from Huguenots expelled from France in the seventeenth century, and that Turkey benefited by when she welcomed the Jews exiled from Spain [in 1492].'[13]

[8] Çağlar Keyder, *State and Class in Turkey: A Study in Capitalism Development* (London ; New York: Verso, 1987), 79.
[9] A. J. Sussnitzki, 'Ethnic Division of Labor' in Charles Philip Issawi, (ed) *The Economic History of the Middle East, 1800-1914: A Book of Readings* (Chicago: University of Chicago Press, 1966), 120-121.
[10] Keyder, *ibid*, 79.
[11] Giorgos A. Giannakopoulos, *Prosphygikē Hellada - Refugee Greece: phōtographies apo to Archeio tou Kentrou Mikrasiatikōn Spoudōn* (Athēna: Kentro Mikrasiatikōn Spoudōn, 1992), 42.
[12] Ibid.
[13] Eliot Grinnell Mears, Greece Today; the Aftermath of the Refugee Impact (Stanford: Stanford University Press, 1929).

The influx of Anatolian Greeks and the departure of Muslim peasants greatly contributed to the realization of ethnic homogeneity in Greece. As the Greek member of the Refugee Settlement Committee, A. A. Pallis, stated in a report that was summarized in a U.S. diplomatic dispatch, '[Greece] has been rendered racially more homogenous by the exchange, its minority population now amounting to only six percent of the total population as compared to 20 percent in 1920.'[14] This was no doubt a considerable achievement, and very similar to the Turkish one.

Setting the stage for the final exchange: the Balkan Wars and their aftermath

A full dress rehearsal of the population exchange of 1923 was staged in 1912 when the Ottoman army was defeated in the first Balkan War, and Turkish territory overrun by troops from the Balkan states. The first group to suffer was the Rumelian Muslims living in the war zone. When the advancing Bulgarian army was halted just sixty-five kilometers from Istanbul, nearly 250,000 Muslim refugees who were fleeing ahead of the army spilled into the imperial capital.[15] In Istanbul, all the mosques, including the Hagia Sophia, had to be converted into shelters for the homeless refugees. The tragic consequences of the Balkan Wars on the Rumelian refugees had important repercussions on the collective consciousness of the Anatolian Greeks too. As Toynbee rightly observed, 'The arrival of the Rumelian refugees from the end of 1912 onwards produced an unexampled tension of feeling in Anatolia and a desire for revenge; and so the Balkan War had two harvests of victims: first, the Rumeli Turks on the one side, and then the Anatolian Greeks on the other.'[16]

With the tension manifesting itself in hostile mob behavior and a more nationalistic state bureaucracy, Greeks started to migrate from the western coast of Turkey towards the Aegean islands. At this point, Galip Kemali [Söylemezoğlu], the Turkish Minister in Athens, unofficially proposed 'an exchange of the rural Greek population of the Izmir province for the Muslims in Macedonia.'[17] This proposal was subsequently approved by the Greek administration on the condition that the exchange not to be compulsory. In the post-Lausanne period, this decision faced severe criticism. In particular, Prime Minister Venizelos was accused of being the first perpetrator of a population exchange that uprooted hundreds of thousands of Anatolian Greeks. Nearly sixteen years later, in June 1930, Venizelos felt

---

[14] Raymond Hare, ibid, 94.
[15] Toynbee, ibid, 138.
[16] Ibid, 139.
[17] Galip Kemali Söylemezoğlu, *Hatıraları, Atina sefareti, 1913-1916*, Canlı tarihler ; [5] (Istanbul: Türkiye Yayınevi, 1946), 102-132.

the need to justify his position in his speech to the Greek Parliament:

> Finding myself, after the Balkan Wars, faced by the beginning of the expulsion of the Greek element in Turkey, I sought by every means to evade throwing the country into war. I sought, therefore, to come to an agreement with Turkey upon the following basis: let it recognize the secession of the islands to Greece and I would agree, that is to say the Hellenic Government would consider itself morally bound, to advise a part of the Greeks in Turkey, whose presence in Turkey was considered as dangerous by the Turkish government, to consent, if possible, to exchange their homes in return for those of Turks in Greece.[18]

Although, due to the outbreak of war in October 1914, the exchange was not officially implemented, approximately 150,000 to 200,000 Greeks living within Ottoman borders had already left their homes and migrated to Greece.[19]

Unfortunately, there are very few mentions in the memoirs of Turkish statesmen of how the exchange of populations took place during these years. However, Hilmi Uran is an exception. Uran was appointed the local governor of a small town, Çeşme, in May 1914, only a few months before the outbreak of the First World War.

The Greek community of Çeşme had been formed largely by late-eighteenth-century Greek migrants from Chios hoping to take advantage of changing trade patterns and the growing economic importance of Izmir at the expense of Salonica.[20] In the nineteenth century, this community rented strips of land from local Turkish notables, which they then converted into vineyards. Subsequently, vines were supplemented by the production of cash crops, such as tobacco and aniseed. This agricultural commercialization had generated a level of wealth and living standards that impressed the newly appointed local governor, but upon his arrival in Çeşme, Uran was confronted with innumerable legal disputes between Turkish landlords and Greek tenants.[21] He goes on to describe how just a few days after his arrival, the Greek community in and around Çeşme started to panic and arranged the means of transport to the nearest island, Chios. Nearly forty thousand Greeks migrated in two weeks.[22]

[18] See Skinner's dispatch sent from Athens to the U.S. Secretary of State, Washington, dated 20 June 1930, 767/68115/136. *Records of the Department of State Relating to the Political Relations of Turkey, Greece and the Balkan States, 1930–1939.*
[19] Hare, *ibid*, 31.
[20] Gerasimos Augustinos, *The Greeks of Asia Minor: Confession, Community, and Ethnicity in the Nineteenth Century* (Kent, Ohio: Kent State University Press, 1992), 92.
[21] Hilmi Uran, *Hâtıralarım* (Ankara: Ayyıldız Matbaası, 1959), 67.
[22] *Ibid.*, 69-71.

Çeşme's Greek community migrated to Chios in such haste that they left their homes and most of their personal belongings intact. One of Uran's most important responsibilities as governor thus became the protection and proper re-distribution of Greek moveable property. Soon, however, all his efforts became futile and the abandoned Greek property was plundered either by the local population or by Rumelian refugees arriving from Salonica.

These refugees were mostly wheat-growing peasants from the highlands of Macedonia. As Uran complained in his memoirs: 'these were people who could not adjust either to Çeşme's climate, or to its agricultural character; as a matter of fact, they did not. For instance, there were among them those who saw aniseed for the first time in their lives and, because of their ignorance, tried to use it as animal feed'[23] (ibid.: 72). Some of the refugees even wore the clothing left by the Greeks. For instance, there is a humorous account in Uran's memoirs of a couple of refugees who, upon being assigned a house originally owned by a Greek priest, proudly took to the streets unwittingly promenading in their newly acquired robes, those of a Greek priest. Uran mentions that these 'men in black' must have created some suspicion among the local officers as to whether Greeks had returned to town. Some other refugees, not accustomed to the warm weather, used the black umbrellas they found to protect themselves from the sun. Uran was also very amused watching the refugees work their land holding fancy lacy umbrellas formerly belonging to urban Greek women.

Criticising the incompetence and lack of information in government circles with respect to refugee settlement, Uran also made embittered remarks about the transformation of the city:

> As a matter of fact the majority of the refugees who were sent to a place like Çeşme in that period did not even know the details of wheat production. They were Bosnian peasants who were very poor, very ignorant and quite primitive and did not even speak Turkish... They were by no means suited to the advanced living standards which they had encountered in Çeşme. Finally, they did their best to reduce Çeşme to their own standards in a very short period of time.[24]

This instance of settling Rumelian refugees in Çeşme provides the first example of the human tragedies that were to be experienced in abundance after 1923. Unfortunately, the Lausanne exchange was more complicated and painful due to the severe post-war conditions Turkey faced, making the settlement of refugees even more problematic.

---

[23] *Ibid*, 76
[24] *Ibid*, 75.

Obstacles to refugee settlement in post-Lausanne Turkey

The prevailing view in most publications on the Lausanne population exchange is that the task of the Turkish Government was far easier than that of the Greek one. For instance, Stephen P. Ladas argues that the settlement problem in Turkey was easy enough to solve because of the abundance of land in that country.[25] One can conjecture that this dominant theme emerges among Greek scholars working on the topic due to the fact that in the post-1922 period the number of exchanged Anatolian Greeks was substantially more than that of the Rumelian Muslims. However, the housing problem in Turkey was already serious before considering the needs of incoming Rumelian refugees. Since the western part of Turkey had been a theatre of war between 1919 and 1922, and was further ravaged by the retreating Greek army, there were actually thousands of homeless *local* Turks, who were trying to survive in properties that had been burned down during the military operations.

In order to administer the exchange, on 8 November 1923, the Turkish Parliament created the 'Ministry of Reconstruction, Exchange and Settlement.'[26] During the parliamentary discussions, some deputies proposed that the properties remaining after refugee land distribution should be given to homeless locals.[27] Indeed, four months later, after one deputy's argument on 3 March 1924 that 'the true sons of this country whose homes were destroyed and razed to the ground and who are in real need of housing and shelter should be given homes after the refugees', the proposal was accepted and the law modified on 13 March 1924.[28]

The Anatolian Greeks, on the other hand, had started pouring into main-land Greece between the fall of Izmir on 9 September 1922 and the armistice signed in Mudanya on 11 October 1922. Hence, by the opening of the Lausanne peace talks on 1 December 1922, most of the exchangeable Greeks had already left Turkey. Ambassador Morgenthau, who travelled to Greece at that time, commented on the nature of their departure when he wrote, 'Within a few weeks 750,000 people were dumped like cattle at the ports of Salonica and Athens, and upon the larger Greek islands.'[29] This helps us to understand why the Greek delegation in Lausanne had to argue that the population exchange be compulsory. Only by the compulsory removal of the Muslim minority would their land be

[25] Stephen P. Ladas, *The Exchange of Minorities; Bulgaria, Greece and Turkey*, (New York: The Macmillan Company, 1932), 708.

[26] Kemal Arı, *Büyük mübadele: Türkiye'ye zorunlu göç, 1923-1925*, Türkiye araştırmaları ; 17 (İstanbul: Tarih Vakfı Yurt Yayınları, 1995), 33.

[27] *Türkiye Büyük Millet Meclisi - Zabıt Ceridesi*, Devre 2, vol. 3, [Turkish Grand National Assembly - Record of Minutes] (Ankara, TBMM Matbaası, 1975): 303.

[28] *TBMM - Zabıt Ceridesi*, Devre 2, vol. 7: 414.

[29] Henry Morgenthau, *I Was Sent to Athens*, (N.Y.: Doubleday, Doran & Company, 1929), 48.

freed up for the thousands of Asia Minor refugees, and only by their compulsory removal could Greece itself achieve the level of homogeneity to which it aspired.[30][7]

The Muslim minority in Greece remained on their land for another year before being deported. However, Anatolian Greeks had already started to be settled in towns and villages throughout Greece with the result that during this transition period they often had to coexist in the same villages as the Rumelian Muslims. It is very significant that there are no records of serious inter-communal strife during this period, even though the Greek state confiscated some of the Rumelian Muslims' property and livestock and distributed it among the newcomers.[31]

Muslims of Kavala on the move to Turkey, 1924

At Lausanne, 1 May 1923 was set as the commencement date of the exchange, but according to the records of the Turkish Red Crescent, which was responsible for the transfer of the Rumelian refugees to Turkey, the

---

[30] As Dimitri Pentzopoulos rightly argues, the agreement reached in Lausanne indeed alleviated some of the problems of refugee settlement in Greece. As the Greek government had already confiscated and distributed the lands that formerly belonged to Rumelian Turks, Pentzopoulos suggests that: 'The remaining 350,000 hectares were to be land [sic] left behind by the exchanged Turks and Bulgarians. This figure shows the tremendous importance of the transfer of populations in the settlement of the Greek refugees. It is obvious that without the vacated Moslem properties the solution of the refugee program through an agricultural settlement would have been very difficult indeed.' See, Dimitri Pentzopoulos, *The Balkan Exchange of Minorities and Its Impact upon Greece*, (Paris: Mouton, 1962), 104.

[31] See, Yalçın, *Emanet çeyiz*.

refugees started to leave Greece much later. The first ship sailed from Salonica to Turkey on 19 December 1923, while the major influx of Rumelian Muslims to Turkey actually took place later, during the first eight months of 1924.[32] During the same period, the remaining Greeks in central Anatolia were transported to Greece, albeit in considerably lower numbers than the Rumelian Muslims. The official figures of the Mixed Commission for the exchange state that 354,647 Muslims were exchanged for 192,356 Greeks but, as noted, the bulk of Greek refugees (well over one million) had already left Turkey.[33]

Between September 1922 and the middle of 1924, most of the abandoned property belonging to the Greeks in Turkey was either looted or occupied, or both. The following telegraph of Dr. Bahtiyar, the president of the Association of Settlement and Mutual Assistance in Izmir, was read in Parliament on 26 October 1924:

> In spite of the fact that the settlement regulations of Balkan War refugees were well-defined and obvious enough, some deputies, state officials from various ranks, army officers, local notables and homeless individuals – but not the ones who deserved assistance! – occupied the abandoned properties that originally belonged to the Greeks. Under the guise of being homeless due to fire, the unlawful occupation of abandoned Greek property has increased the feelings of despair and weakness, further exacerbating the disorder among the refugees.[34]

The discrepancy between the early departure of Anatolian Greeks and the late arrival of Rumelian refugees had made this pillage easy. Building materials extracted from the so-called 'abandoned buildings' such as tiles, iron -bars, window frames and doors were either sold on the market or used in the construction and repair of the houses belonging to locals. For instance, Cavit Paşa, in his criticism of government incompetence, mentioned how the plundered tiles were sold in the market place in Samsun.[35] As a result, the houses given to most of the arriving refugees had nothing but bare walls.[36]

In a dispatch to the Secretary of State for Foreign Affairs, R. W. Urquhart, the British Consul in Izmir, described how the Turkish Government's decision to pay salaries 'in kind' encouraged the army

---

[32] Mehmet Çanlı, 'Yunanistan'daki Türklerin Anadolu'ya nakledilmesi,' *Tarih ve Toplum*, 130, (October, 1994): 51-59.

[33] Raymond Hare, *ibid*, 64.

[34] *TBMM - Zabıt Ceridesi*, Devre 2, vol. 9: 94.

[35] *TBMM - Zabıt Ceridesi*, Devre 2, vol. 10: 36.

[36] Kemal Yalçın's work contains valuable interviews conducted with ageing Greek and Turkish refugees on both sides of the Aegean. They both tell of their frustrations during the population exchange and most still complain about the miserable condition of the property assigned to them. See, Yalçın, *Emanet Çeyiz*.

officers to participate in an unusual form of commercial activity: 'The officers have received during the past ten months a certain small percentage of their pay in cash, but part of it has been paid by drafts on the *Commission de Liquidation des Biens abandonnés*, which are accepted by that commission in payment of goods in its hands; so they have become dealers in old furniture.'[37]

In October 1924, the deputies from the opposition benches criticized the government's misconduct of the refugee settlement by recounting the stories they had heard or the cases they had observed in their election districts, and demanded a parliamentary investigation of the Ministers of Reconstruction, Exchange and Settlement. A two-week long parliamentary discussion of issues related to the exchange of populations and the settlement of Rumelian refugees in Turkey followed. In these sessions, all three consecutive Ministers of Exchange took the floor and faced fierce criticism.

Turkish parliamentary debates on the population exchange

Turkish parliamentary debates provide an extremely useful source for under- standing the structural limitations that prevented a more successful implementation of refugee settlement in the post-Lausanne period, as well as its immediate political repercussions. For instance, the speech of Hasan [Saka] Bey, one of the representatives in Lausanne, on 1 January 1923, provides a narrative of the population exchange discussions in Lausanne. He stated that the Greek delegation had proposed the exchange of populations and that the Turks willingly accepted it; he also noted that both sides agreed to keep the Greeks of Istanbul excluded from the exchange.[38] Another significant discussion on the population exchange occurred two months later, on 3 March 1923, when Dr. Rıza Nur, the deputy-head of the Turkish delegation in Lausanne, specifically narrated the Turkish position on the issue of minorities. During the Lausanne peace talks, Dr. Nur personally led the debates at the sub-committee level where the legal position of the non-Muslim minorities in the newly forming Turkish republic was negotiated. This was a critical issue since the Great Powers often used the position of non-Muslim minorities as a pretext to intervene in the domestic affairs of the Ottoman Empire. Dr. Nur quite bluntly stated that the compulsory exchange of populations had already resolved this question: as there would be no minorities left in Anatolia, there would be no foreign intervention. Furthermore, he argued

---

[37] Dispatch sent from Acting Consul-General in Izmir to the Marquess Curzon in London: The National Archives (Kew, London), Foreign Office Correspondence, FO424: British Confidential Reports / Document dated 21 July 1923 / E 8317/19 9/44.

[38] *Türkiye Büyük Millet Meclisi - Gizli Celse Zabıtları* [Turkish Grand National Assembly - Closed Session Minutes], vol. 3, (Ankara: Türkiye İş Bankası Kültür Yayınları, 1985), 1173.

convincingly that Greeks who had already migrated would never be allowed to return to Anatolia. Dr. Nur articulated the reasoning behind this position later in his memoirs:

> The most important thing was the liberation of Turkey from the elements which through the centuries had weakened her either by organizing rebellions or by being the domestic extensions of foreign states. Hence the making of the country uniformly Turkish ... was a huge and unequalled responsibility. It would have been extremely difficult to make the Greeks agree to this or even to suggest this. Thank God, they were the ones to propose it.[39]

Dr. Rıza Nur's position on the achievement of ethnic homogeneity in Turkey was endorsed by nearly all of the deputies, who were unanimous in their support of the exchange of minorities. The deputies considered the existence of minorities in Anatolia a potential threat to the national security of the young republic in terms, not only of inter-communal strife, but also in relation to the possibility they presented for foreign intervention. Their minds were influenced by bitter memories of the late nineteenth and early twentieth centuries when consistent and repeated Great-Power interference occurred. For instance, Vehbi Bey, the deputy for Karesi, articulated these feelings when he stated on 5 November 1924, 'The arrival of every individual is a [source of] richness for us; and the departure of every individual who leaves is a blessing for us!'[40]

The parliamentary debates also illuminate the ideological concerns of the deputies in the execution of the exchange. The neglect of the linguistic criterion in the settlement process was one of the first criticisms the Ministers of Exchange had to face, especially from prominent nationalist deputies who criticized the settlement of the Albanian- or Greek-speaking Muslims on the western coast. For instance, the ardent nationalist Hamdullah Suphi [Tanrıöver] Bey brought the question to the attention of the Parliament in the following statement:

> They settled the Greek-speaking masses right across the sea from the islands. A grave mistake! Soon, when peace truly reigns and relations between the islands and our shores pick up and Greek islanders and the Greek-speaking masses reestablish contact, then it will be impossible ever to eradicate this foreign language.'[41]

Among other deputies who were more critical of the cultural consequences of the settlement, Ali Ş uuri Bey, the deputy of Karesi, complained: 'Among the refugees settled on the coast, the dominant dance is

---

[39] Rıza Nur, *Hayat ve Hatıratım*, vol. 3, (İstanbul: Altındağ Yayinevi, 1967), 1041.
[40] *TBMM - Zabıt Ceridesi*, Devre 2, vol. 10: 25.
[41] *TBMM - Zabıt Ceridesi*, Devre 2, vol. 9: 92.

the polka instead of our national dance; the dominant musical instruments are the mandolin and the bagpipe instead of our national instruments; the dominant language is Albanian and Bosnian instead of our national language!'[42] The concentration of Greek- or Albanian-speaking refugees in certain regions created further suspicion among the nationalists, who desired complete homogeneity of the population. For them, this was a clash between the 'ideal' and the 'real'. Instead of an imagined community they hoped would be similar to their own, they encountered, in their view, a group of people from a rural background, speaking foreign languages and with very different life styles. Needless to say, the Turkish nationalists were disturbed by the cultural discord created by the influx of refugees. Here the process of turkification worked in the opposite direction: it created distrust and suspicion among the ruling nationalist elite towards the repatriated masses. Bernard Lewis demonstrates the absurdity of the nationalists' expectations on both sides of Aegean as follows: 'A Western observer, accustomed to a different system of social and national classification, might even conclude that this was no repatriation at all, but two deportations into exile - of Christian Turks to Greece, and of Muslim Greeks to Turkey.'[43] The reactions of the Turkish nationalists were especially significant in that they came to constitute the backbone of the 1930s cultural xenophobia that eroded the cosmopolitanism of the late-Ottoman period.

The structural impediments to a better settlement: determining the material basis of chaos and despair

A careful analysis of the scholarly works on the compulsory exchange reveals that there was a substantial amount of ill-considered and inappropriate settlement in both Turkey and Greece. For instance, tobacco producers from both countries were resettled in regions where tobacco production was virtually impossible. Even worse, wheat-producing peasants were forced to settle in regions with olive groves. Unaccustomed to growing olives, the refugees simply cut down the trees and used them as wood for their stoves, planting wheat or barley in their place. These unfortunate events were naturally blamed on the governments.

The answers given by the Ministers of Exchange to the deputies' criticisms in the Turkish Parliament reveal the nature of the social and economic problems the young republic faced in its settlement efforts. The most important problem in the exchange was the contrast between the departing Anatolian Greeks and the incoming Rumelian Muslims. While the Anatolian Greeks were predominantly urban, the Rumelian Muslims

---

[42] *TBMM - Zabıt Ceridesi*, Devre 2, vol. 10: 28.
[43] Bernard Lewis, *The Emergence of Modern Turkey*, 2nd ed., (London: Oxford UP, 1968), 355.

were largely rural. Even if the armies had not burned down the villages during the war, even if the homeless locals had not occupied most of the abandoned property, this dissimilarity in populations would have complicated matters in and of itself. The Minister of Exchange, Mahmut Celal [Bayar] Bey therefore had to admit in Parliament that:

> The lifestyles and economic conditions of those arriving are not similar to those of the departing [Greeks]: those departing are mostly tradesmen or merchants. However, those arriving are generally farmers. Gentlemen, the overwhelming majority of those arriving are peasants; the overwhelming majority of those departing are urban dwellers! I leave it to your judgement to decide if it is at all possible to succeed in [the matter of] settlement under such irreconcilable conditions.[44]

The second structural limitation preventing a successful settlement of refugees was the lack of information. In the immediate post-Lausanne period, the government in Ankara lacked even the most basic information about the society it was trying to rule. Social statistics about the various forms of livelihood within the Turkish population were either non-existent or had become obsolete. Furthermore, the republican elite proved inefficient in gathering information about the country and developing a sense of control over its economic and social issues. Under these conditions, the settlement of refugees was conducted at best in an ad hoc manner. When the Ministers of Exchange were accused in Parliament of forcing people from plains to settle in valleys and vice versa, one minister, Refet [Canıtez] Bey, had to acknowledge the following:

> Gentlemen, how much of the land in the villages is in the plains and how much of it is in the highlands? What is the sum of arable land in the villages? How many persons could be engaged in cultivation? What is the actual level of agriculture? It is necessary to conduct extensive research on these issues. Yet it is impossible to obtain this information now. Since this type of information does not exist, it is necessary to progress in general terms and that is what we are undertaking now! [45]

Lacking any kind of scientific information like a population census, industrial and agricultural surveys or cadastral maps of Turkey, the government relied on the information gathered informally at ports during the arrival of the refugees. Their final destinations were decided on this scant information.

The third structural problem arose from the poor quality of the staff employed. Immediately after the formation of the Ministry of

---

[44] *TBMM - Zabıt Ceridesi*, Devre 2, vol. 10: 52.
[45] *TBMM - Zabıt Ceridesi*, Devre 2, vol. 10: 43.

Reconstruction, Exchange and Settlement on 8 November 1923, many of its positions were filled by retired army officers, and then by bureaucrats dismissed from their posts in other ministries. Indeed, references are frequently made in the parliamentary debates to the harsh, inflexible and irresponsible attitude of these state officials towards the refugees.

Collapsing system of communications: government support for the turkification of Anatolia

After the ten years of war between 1912 and 1922, not only was much of Turkey's agricultural land in a state of ruin, but homes and cities had been torched, leaving many people destitute. Moreover, at a time of such need, the country's reserves of entrepreneurial know-how and artisanship had been almost totally drained with the departure of Anatolia's minorities. The non- Muslim commercial bourgeoisie of relatively developed Anatolian cities such as Samsun, Trabzon, Erzurum, Adana and Gaziantep had been subjected either to forced migration and massacre – as in the case of the Armenians – or to exchange – as in the case of the Greeks – while artisans and craftsmen had found their way either to Europe or to neighboring countries. The newly emerging Turkish bourgeoisie and urban artisans could not replace the minorities in all sectors of economic and social life.

The loss of entrepreneurial know-how was critical in trade, especially in western Anatolia. Traditionally, Izmir had been an important center for the export of Turkish agricultural products. Basic agricultural goods exported from Izmir such as tobacco, sultanas, cotton, dried figs and hazelnuts had constituted nearly 60 percent of Turkish export revenues.[46] However, when the Greek, Armenian and Levantine merchants who had been acting as intermediaries between local producers and foreign buyers were removed, trade proved difficult. This is evidenced by the following correspondence received by the British Chamber of Commerce of Turkey from a dried-fruit importer in Bristol in October 1923:

> Owing to the recent troubles in Smyrna we have lost several of our old connections and shippers of sultanas, and this season and the last we have not been in a position to import, or to offer, on account of being unable to obtain offers of Smyrna fruits... We shall be very pleased if you will put [us] in touch with reputable houses and shippers, who will immediately forward us type samples ... We are [also] interested in dried plums and prunes, and [if] it is possible you may be able to put us in touch with a shipper.[47]

Soon the Turkish Government attempted to fill the vacuum with local

---

[46] Çağlar Keyder, *Dünya ekonomisi içinde Türkiye, 1923-1929*, (Ankara: Yurt Yayınevi, 1982), 109.
[47] [Letter to the Editor], *Journal of the British Chamber of Commerce of Turkey*, 11, no. 73, (October, 1923): 541.

Turkish merchants. Already, some local notables with good contacts in Ankara had profited from the distribution of abandoned Greek property, not only by occupying the most fertile agricultural holdings, but also by claiming the abandoned industrial establishments and workshops. Parliamentary debates reveal, for instance, that a deputy from Balıkesir had acquired for himself a house in the town center, a summer residence, thousands of olive trees and a soap factory around Ayvalık.[48] Even though this emerging group of Turkish businessmen had very limited experience in international trade and business transactions, they volunteered to replace the non-Muslim entrepreneurs. Although they lacked commercial expertise, they nevertheless had the advantage of government support from Ankara. This dependency on the state, however, ultimately limited their development as an independent bourgeoisie.

By the mid-1920s, the native commercial class was gradually beginning to fill the vacuum left by the departing minorities. For instance, in May 1925, a report written by Alaiyelizade Mahmut Bey, the president of the Izmir Chamber of Commerce, stated that many Turkish businessmen had settled in Izmir after the liberation, opening about fifty-four stores and selling mostly imported European textile products. Many companies specializing in the export of agricultural products were also formed in Izmir. Indeed, Mahmut Bey provided a detailed account of the levels of production reached for certain agricultural products such as sultanas, dried figs, tobacco, olive oil, cotton, and convincingly argued that thanks to the continuous support of the government in Ankara, pre-war production levels had already been reached.[49]

In contrast to these positive accounts of Mahmut Bey, however, the foreign diplomats stationed in Turkey presented an altogether different and dire picture of Turkish economic performance in their dispatches: all were highly critical of the turkification policies being implemented in the early years of the republic. For instance, in November 1929, British Ambassador Sir George Clerk evaluated the performance of the newly formed Turkish firms as 'incompetent', and continued with the following scathing assessment:

> This incompetence is repeated in the numerous Turkish firms of smaller importance which have endeavored to replace the Greek and Armenian middlemen who were always the backbone of Turkish commerce. Almost invariably these new Turkish firms start business as commission agents, but they have neither the patience [and] the experience nor the temperament to build up their

[48] *TBMM - Zabıt Ceridesi*, Devre 2, vol. 10: 36
[49] Murat Koraltürk, 'Mübadelenin İktisadi Sonuçları hakkında bir rapor [Report on the Economic Consequences of the Exchange] *Çağdaş Türkiye Araştırmaları Dergisi*, 2, no. 6-7, (1996-1997): 197.

fortunes slowly in the same way as their Christian predecessors. In most cases they drift to Ankara, to the neglect of their agency commitments, and endeavor to get rich quickly by dabbling into large contracts. Further, commercial morality here has declined of late years.[50]

Ambassador Clerk's remarks reveal that at least in some cases continuing sup- port from government circles had not been sufficient to create the desired outcome. Perhaps if the group replacing the minorities had received less protection and tutelage from Ankara, it might have been forced to develop its entrepreneurial capacities much more effectively and successfully. Mostly due to the lack of business skills of this emerging bourgeoisie, as well as the destructive effects of the Great Depression in 1929, the founders of the new Turkish state were forced in the 1930s to move towards a more protected and autarchic model of economic development. Subsequent growth in the size of the public sector and the newly formed state economic enterprises to compensate and eventually replace private initiative not only dwarfed the Turkish business elite in size, but also consolidated their immaturity. I personally view this as the most significant and negative outcome of the population exchange in Turkey.

The turkification policies implemented in Istanbul

By mutual agreement at Lausanne, the Greek community of Istanbul was excluded from the compulsory exchange. Nevertheless, especially in the second half of the 1920s, the remaining minority merchants and foreign companies were forced to suffer continuous pressures, the most significant of which came as a result of the emerging trend of nationalist economics. Under the dominant slogan of the period 'Turkey for the Turks', Muslim Turkish merchants organized themselves in the Chambers of Commerce that had previously been dominated by non-Muslims. With government support, they then identified themselves as 'national merchants' (*milli tüccar*) thereby implying that the minority businessmen who remained in Istanbul were not national, and therefore of suspect loyalty to the regime. In other words, the aim of the turkification schemes was not merely to create a nationalist bourgeoisie, but to do so at the expense of existing minorities and foreign-owned companies. The turkification program can thus be defined in practice as a set of policies aimed at establishing the unconditional supremacy of Turkish ethnic identity in nearly all aspects of social and economic life.

The policies implemented in the 1920s consisted of measures such as mandating that foreign companies must keep their books in Turkish,

---

[50] Dispatch sent from Sir George Clerk in Istanbul to Mr. A. Henderson in London: FO 371: Foreign Office Correspondence / Document dated 13 November 1929 / E 5984/89/44.

allocating certain professions and state employment exclusively to Muslim Turks, and ruling that foreign-owned companies should have Muslim Turks comprise at least three-quarters of their employees. In one dispatch to London, British Ambassador Sir R. Lindsay grumbled about the news that 'in the future only Turks would be allowed to act as chauffeurs.'[51] Similar pressures were also exerted on foreign concessionaire companies like the Izmir - Aydın railway company (The Ottoman Railway from Smyrna to Aidin). A representative of the company paid a visit to the British Ambassador on 18 March 1926 and mentioned that the Turks were demanding that the personnel of the railway should be entirely Turkish. The railway company was willing to employ Turks as far as possible, but could not find any suitable.[52] In this period firms, shopkeepers, companies and sometimes even the professionals such as doctors and lawyers were told to dismiss their non-Muslim employees and hire Muslim Turks instead. Perfect examples of the discrimination against non-Muslim minorities, most of these demands had neither a legal basis nor any constitutional justification; they were simply de facto pressures exerted by the Turkish bureaucracy.

In another of his dispatches, also in 1926, the British Ambassador Sir R. Lindsay examined the psychological factors behind the turkification programs:

> Imbued with a profound distrust of all non-Turkish elements, a distrust due to the policy of the Powers towards Turkey for more than a hundred years, the republic is resolved to surround itself with a Chinese wall of exclusiveness and reconstruct a State in which there shall be no room for the exercise of foreign influence even by individuals and traders. This policy is being pursued with remorseless pertinacity ... and it receives the cordial support of the whole population.[53]

The construction of the 'Chinese wall' would be completed in the next decade, with *étatist* development models and autarchic trade regimes forming its cornerstone. Moreover, while the turkification policies implemented in the 1920s had been de facto administrative policies, later policies eventually acquired legal force so that the discriminatory practices against the non-Muslim minorities became *de jure* expressions of nationalist ideology. The notorious law (number 2007) passed in 1932 'Restricting certain Professions and

---

[51] Dispatch sent from Sir R. Lindsay in Istanbul to Sir Austin Chamberlain in London: FO 371: Document dated 3 March 1926 / E 1571/373/44.

[52] Resume of the conversation between Sir R. Lindsay and Lord Howard of Glossop. FO 371: Document dated 18 March 1926 / E 1874/373/44.

[53] Dispatch sent from Sir R. Lindsay in Istanbul to Sir Austin Chamberlain in London: FO 371: Document dated 15 February 1926 / E 1072/373/44

Trades to Turkish Citizens only' is an example of this transformation.[54] As a result of its implementation, nearly nine thousand non-exchanged *établis* Greeks lost their jobs, and soon after migrated to Greece for good.[55] Indeed, there is no doubt that the policies of turkification were responsible for the hemorrhaging of non-Muslim communities from Istanbul during the early years of the republic, despite the clauses specifying minority rights in the Treaty of Lausanne.

A final note: the transformation of Turkish nationalism

It is widely accepted that Turkish nationalism was first formulated and codified by Ziya Gökalp (1876–1924) during the Balkan Wars. Unlike most formulations for national identity, which emphasize race and ethnicity, Gökalp's criteria for membership of the 'national community' were cultural and linguistic. Gökalp defined the nation as follows:

> [The] nation is not a racial, ethnic, geographical, political, or voluntary group or association. [The] nation is a group composed of men and women who have gone through the same education, who have received the same acquisitions in language, religion, morality and aesthetics ... Men want to live together, not with those who carry the same blood in their veins, but with those who share the same language and the same faith.[56]

It was the multiethnic and multi-religious nature of the Ottoman Empire that necessitated such criterion, an empire in which it was practically unreasonable to preach particularistic nationalism even during the Balkan Wars. In formulating the principles of Turkish nationalism, Gökalp inevitably had to recognize the significance of the *millet* system even if it had already disintegrated. Furthermore, for Gökalp, religion was significant only insofar as it was a factor of shared culture; he emphasized Islam only as a moral force that would help bring about social solidarity, and not as a necessary condition for being a Turkish nationalist. Gökalp's place for Islam might also help explain why Jewish intellectuals like Moise Cohen Tekinalp (1883–1961) and Abraham Galante (1873–1961) played an active part in the ideological kitchen of Turkish nationalism.[57]

Gökalp's conceptions of nation and nationalism were accepted until the second half of the 1920s, at which point an ideological break set in and the model underwent a radical reconstruction. Gökalp's idea of an individual's

---

[54] *Düstur*, Üçünü Tertip, Vol. 13: 519

[55] See my article titled as 'Turkification' Policies in the Early Republican Era' in this volume.

[56] Ziya Gökalp, *Turkish Nationalism and Western Civilization: Selected Essays. Ed. and tranlated by Niyazi Berkes* (New York: Columbia University Press, 1959), 137.

[57] See my article titled as 'Economic Nationalism in Turkey: The Formative Years, 1912–1925' in this volume.

ties to the national community being along cultural and therefore civic lines was superseded by an ethnic definition tailored by the republican elite. The formation of the rhetoric on nationalism can be traced through the Turkish parliamentary debates on the exchange and settlement. Earlier in this article, I noted that the Ministers of Exchange and Settlement were criticized because of their neglect of linguistic criterion. When Dr. Rıza Nur was especially harsh in criticizing the settlement of Albanians in and around Izmir, some deputies pointed out that he had been politically very accommodating to the Albanian deputies when he served in the Ottoman Parliament. His reaction was quite revealing:

> At that time the Albanians were part of the ingredients of this land. From Basra all the way to Iskodra [in Albania] there were fifteen to twenty national groups; under such conditions I could not possibly pursue the line of argument of Turkism. You know as well as I do that the 'Union of all Ottomans' was in fashion then. It was truly impossible to pursue any other policy. Later, I began on the path of Turkism [when it became politically viable].[58]

The majority of the republican political elite soon followed Dr. Nur in accepting this new understanding of nationalism, so much so that the republican version of ethnic nationalism soon became the mainstay of official Turkish ideology. In this context, the non-Muslim minorities – even though they were Turkish citizens – were clearly left out of the national community, and became technically impossible to incorporate. As a consequence, they started to be discriminated against and treated as outsiders in their own lands: ethnic nationalism thus became the archenemy of cosmopolitanism.

However, one has to concede that the new regime in Ankara, stripped of its imperial traditions and confined in its sovereignty to Anatolia alone, could not have responded otherwise. Already turkified human geography of Anatolia made it impossible for the republican elite to provide an umbrella sheltering Greek tinker, Armenian tailor and Turkish soldier all at once. The sociologically defined Gökalpian culture that functioned as a collective conscience to homogenize peoples of varying status, class, religion / sect and in some cases ethnicity was no longer meaningful. Gökalpian cultural unity was designed to mould a conglomerate of ethnically diverse individuals into one nation, but it became outdated. The political formulations of an ethnically and religiously heterogeneous empire had become antiquated in a mere ten years.

---

[58] *TBMM - Zabıt Ceridesi*, Devre 2, vol. 10: 152

Bibliography

US National Archives

Records of the Department of the State relating to the political relations of Turkey, Greece and the Balkan States 1930 – 1939, (Microfilm No: T1245).

British National Archives (Kew, London)

FO 371: Foreign Office Correspondence.
FO424: British Confidential Reports

Official Publications - Turkey

Düstur, Üçünü Tertip, Vol. 13.
Türkiye Büyük Millet Meclisi - Zabıt Ceridesi, Devre 2, [Turkish Grand National Assembly - Record of Minutes]. Ankara, TBMM Matbaası, 1975.
Türkiye Büyük Millet Meclisi - Gizli Celse Zabıtları [Turkish Grand National Assembly - Closed Session Minutes], 4 vols. Ankara: Türkiye İş Bankası Kültür Yayınları, 1985.

Other Academic Works and Memoirs

Alexandris, Alexis. 'Religion or Ethnicity: The Identity Issue of the Minorities in Greece and Turkey' in Renee Hirschon (ed), *Crossing the Aegean: An Appraisal of the 1923 Compulsory Population Exchange between Greece and Turkey* (New York: Berghahn Books, 2003).
Arı, Kemal. *Büyük mübadele: Türkiye'ye zorunlu göç, 1923-1925*. İstanbul: Tarih Vakfı Yurt Yayınları, 1995.
Augustinos, Gerasimos. The Greeks of Asia Minor: Confession, Community, and Ethnicity in the Nineteenth Century. Kent, Ohio: Kent State University Press, 1992.
Çanlı, Mehmet. 'Yunanistan'daki Türklerin Anadolu'ya nakledilmesi,' *Tarih ve Toplum*, 130, (October, 1994): 51-59.
Giannakopoulos, Giōrgos A. Prosphygikē Hellada [Refugee Greece]: phōtographies apo to Archeio tou Kentrou Mikrasiatikōn Spoudōn. Athēna: Hidryma A.G. Leventē : Kentro Mikrasiatikōn Spoudōn, 1992.
Gökalp, Ziya. Turkish Nationalism and Western Civilization: Selected Essays. New York: Columbia University Press, 1959.
Hirschon, Renee. Crossing the Aegean: An Appraisal of the 1923 Compulsory Population Exchange between Greece and Turkey. New York: Berghahn Books, 2008.
Issawi, Charles Philip. The Economic History of the Middle East, 1800-1914: A Book of Readings. Chicago: University of Chicago Press, 1966.
Justin McCarthy. Muslims and Minorities: The Population of Ottoman Anatolia and the End of the Empire. New York: New York University Press, 1983.
Keyder, Çağlar. *Dünya ekonomisi içinde Türkiye, 1923-1929*. Türkiye araştırmaları dizisi ; 3. Ankara: Yurt Yayınevi, 1982.
Keyder, Çağlar. State and Class in Turkey: A Study in Capitalism Development. London ; New York: Verso, 1987.
Koraltürk, Murat. 'Mübadelenin İktisadi Sonuçları hakkında bir rapor [Report on the Economic Consequences of the Exchange] *Çağdaş Türkiye Araştırmaları Dergisi*, 2, no. 6-7, (1996-1997): 183-198.
Ladas, Stephen P. *The Exchange of Minorities; Bulgaria, Greece and Turkey*. New York: The

Macmillan Company, 1932.

Lewis, Bernard. *The Emergence of Modern Turkey*. 2nd ed. London: Oxford UP, 1968.

McCarthy, Justin. Muslims and Minorities: The Population of Ottoman Anatolia and the End of the Empire. New York: New York University Press, 1983.

Mears, Eliot Grinnell. *Greece Today; the Aftermath of the Refugee Impact*. Stanford: Stanford University Press, 1929.

Morgenthau, Henry. *I Was Sent to Athens*. N.Y.: Doubleday, Doran & Company, 1929.

Oran, Baskın. 'The Story of Those Who Stayed: Lessons From Articles and 2 of the 1923 Convention' in Renee Hirschon (ed), *Crossing the Aegean: An Appraisal of the 1923 Compulsory Population Exchange between Greece and Turkey* (New York. Berghahn Books, 2003).

Pentzopoulos, Dimitri. The Balkan Exchange of Minorities and Its Impact upon Greece. Paris: Mouton, 1962.

Petropoulos, J. A. "The Compulsory Exchange of Populations: Greek - Turkish Peacemaking 1922 - 1930." *Byzantine and Modern Greek Studies* 2 (1976): 135–60.

Rıza Nur. *Hayat ve Hatiratim*. 4 vols. İstanbul: Altindağ Yayinevi, 1967.

Söylemezoğlu, Galip Kemali. *Hatıraları, Atina sefareti, 1913-1916*. Canlı tarihler ; [5]. [Istanbul]: Türkiye Yayınevi, 1946.

Sussnitzki, A. J. 'Ethnic Division of Labor' in Charles Philip Issawi, (ed) *The Economic History of the Middle East, 1800-1914: A Book of Readings*. Chicago: University of Chicago Press, 1966.

Toynbee, Arnold. *The Western Question in Greece and Turkey*. Boston: Houghton Mifflin Company, 1922.

Uran, Hilmi. *Hâtıralarım*. Ankara: Ayyıldız Matbaası, 1959.

Yalçın, Kemal. *Emanet çeyiz: Mübadele insanları*. İstanbul: Belge Uluslararası Yayıncılık, 1998.

CHAPTER 4

CONVERSION OF A 'COUNTRY' INTO A 'FATHERLAND': THE CASE OF TURKIFICATION EXAMINED, 1923–1934

On 1 March 2005, a well-known Turkish journalist, Yalçın Doğan, published an opinion piece titled 'Vulpes Vulpes Kurdistanicum' in the Turkish daily *Hürriyet* in which he criticized the United Nations Development Programme's (UNDP) activities in Turkey. We learned from Yalçın Doğan in particular of a UNDP project to promote the conservation, identification and naming of wildlife in the Ağrı region (Mount Ararat) of eastern Turkey. In this context the scientific name of the good old fox, locally known as *Kızıl Tilki* (Grey Fox), was cited as "*Vulpes Vulpes Kurdistanicum*" and this, according to Doğan, was a perfect example of clandestine operations conducted by the UNDP in eastern Turkey. Doğan's argumentation went as follows:

> This is precisely what I mean by the Kurdish Question! We want to settle this question among us, [I mean] with the Kurdish citizens of this country. But [foreigners] do not let us do so! On every occasion, there is a foreign intervention! Can you imagine, even an organization part of the United Nations performs a role in this plot. Weren't there foreign powers behind every Kurdish uprising that flourished at the end of the nineteenth century and repeated throughout the twentieth century? [1]

Yalçın Doğan continued his reasoning by giving another example of foreign powers' attempts to divide Turkey, this time using the name of undomesticated wild sheep, elsewhere referred to as 'Armenian sheep' (*Ovis Armeniana*) by the UNDP. Doğan concluded his piece as follows:

> By simply following the changes in the scientific names of those animals, it is possible to demonstrate two major problems which have recently turned out to be a headache for Turkey. [No doubt], the first one is the Kurdish question. The second one is the Armenian Question that has started to be discussed on international platforms in a sinister manner. Don't they ever let us live in peace? [2]

All of this led the Ministry of Environment and Forestry to make an official statement to the press in Ankara, where it was stated that the

---

[1] Yalçın Doğan, "Vulpes Vulpes Kurdistanicum," *Hürriyet* daily, 1 March 2005.
[2] Ibid.

process of naming local animals in eastern Turkey became a threat to the "unitary structure of the Turkish Republic."[3] The official declaration went on to state the fact that, unfortunately, foreign scientists approached the question with prejudices. General Director of National Parks Professor M. K. Yalınkılıç clearly stated in the press conference that

> Here there are certain traps set for Turkey. Certain individuals are travelling freely in Turkey. These individuals put these names [to the animals] in order to create the impression that once the Kurds and Armenians existed here! [4]

I believe this remarkable piece constitutes a starting point to ponder upon the nature of Turkish nationalism. Nearly a century has passed since the ideology of nationalism first flourished in the geographical territory known today as Turkey. This chapter sets out to make a general assessment of how the 'country of the Turks' was converted into a 'Turkish fatherland' in the early years of the Republic.

Ten years ago when I first published an article on the policies of Turkification in the early days of the Turkish Republic, I made the following assessment:

> The Turkification program could be defined in practice as a set of policies aimed at establishing the unconditional supremacy of Turkish ethnic identity in nearly all aspects of social and economic life ranging from the language spoken in the streets to the history teaching at schools; from regulating private matters of Turkish citizens by the civil code to the forced settlement of Turkish people in the particular regions of the country.[5]

After ten years, I find the definition remains correct, but quite simplistic in the light of recent scholarship arose in Turkey and elsewhere. Now, I believe one of the essential features of the 'Turkification process' is the conversion of the country into fatherland. This was made possible by attempting to create a feeling of 'authenticity' among the masses. In other words, one of the most important dimensions of Turkification policies was the aim to convert Turkish geographical territory into something exclusively Turkish. In order to achieve this, the Turkish nationalists declared a permanent ideological war against the 'other' ethnic, religious and linguistic groups who once lived in the

---

[3] "Bakanlıktan 'bölücü hayvan' operasyonu," *Hürriyet*, 5 March 2005
[4] *Ibid.* See also Suavi Aydın, "İsimler Milli Birliği nasıl bozar? Bak şu tilkinin ettiğine ...", *Toplumsal Tarih*, 143, (2005): 90-97.
[5] Ayhan Aktar, "Cumhuriyetin İlk Yıllarında Uygulanan 'Türkleştirme' Politikaları," *Tarih ve Toplum* 156, (1996): 4.

same geographical location.

In order to illustrate my argument, I would like to explain the stages of Turkification in an evolutionary perspective.

Homogenization of population by demographic engineering: 1913–1923

The first step in converting the country of the Turks into the Turkish fatherland was the demographic engineering that was implemented during the First World War and after. If we take 29 October 1923, the date of the promulgation of the Turkish Republic, and, later, the abolition of the Sultanate, as a turning point in the formation of the Turkish nation-state, then these ten years between (1913 and 1923) can be treated as a transition period towards this end. Having a small group of radical/nationalist officers, the Young Turks, in power and contextualized by the social and political turmoil created by defeats in the Balkan Wars and the First World War, it is obvious why a fertile ground for the implementation of policies towards homogenization by demographic engineering was possible.

The Young Turks, better known as the Committee of Union and Progress (hereafter the CUP), came to power through a *coup d'état* in January 1913. The Ottoman army had just been defeated in the first Balkan War and the Ottoman state had lost 83 per cent of its European territory and 69 per cent of its population living in Europe.[6] Simultaneously, eastern Thrace was under the occupation of the Bulgarian army. The first group to suffer from this calamity was the Muslim population living right at the heart of this theatre of war.[7] When the advancing Bulgarian army was halted on the outskirts of Istanbul, nearly 250,000 Turkish/Muslim refugees flooded the imperial capital.

It was the first time Istanbul had ever received such a large number of refugees in its history, and accordingly a special regulation titled 'Law for the Settlement of Immigrants', dated 13 May 1913, was enacted. This resulted with the formation of a bureaucratic organization called 'General Directorate for Settlement of Tribes and Refugees' (*İskân-ı Aşairin ve Muhacirîn Müdiriyeti, hereafter IAMM*) directly attached to Talat Pasha, Minister of the Interior – and later, planner of Armenian deportations and massacres in 1915. After the Balkan Wars, the CUP ordered the settlement of refugees from Macedonia in the towns on the Aegean coast. However,

---

[6] Stanford J Shaw and Ezel Kural Shaw, *History of the Ottoman Empire and Modern Turkey. Reform, Revolution, and Republic: The Rise of Modern Turkey, 1808-1975.* Vol. 2 (Cambridge: CUP, 1977), 298.
[7] Arnold J. Toynbee, *The Western Question in Greece and Turkey* (Boston: Houghton Mifflin Company, 1922), 138.

these were exasperated people who had lost their land and property, and now started to organize attacks on Anatolian Greeks. The local Greek population, especially along the western coast of Turkey, was understandably disturbed by the bands formed mostly Rumelian refugees and organized by the CUP on the one hand, and the CUP's increasingly discriminatory policies on the other. Soon thereafter, Greek migration started to flow from the western coast of Turkey towards the Aegean islands and mainland Greece, and before the outbreak of the First World War nearly 150,000 had relocated.

At this point too came the first pronouncement of the idea of an organized and official population exchange. A Turkish diplomat in Athens, Galip Kemali (Söylemezoğlu) Bey proposed a voluntary exchange between Muslims of Greek Macedonia and the Greek population of the Smyrna region. Greek Prime Minister Elefterios Venizelos tentatively agreed to implement this proposal; however, the war broke out in August 1914 and effectively put everything on hold. For a total and compulsory exchange, the Greek and Turkish nationalist elites would have to wait until 1922.

On 30 January 1923 the Greek and Turkish diplomatic delegations signed the convention to exchange their respective minorities at the Lausanne Peace Conference. In so doing, they formalized the existing status quo – there were 950,000 Anatolian Greeks already in Greek towns and islands – into a legal framework. This was the first diplomatically negotiated, and internationally endorsed, obligatory, ethnic cleansing of the twentieth century. Utilizing British Foreign Secretary Lord Curzon's terminology, the decision sought the "unmixing of populations" on both sides of the Aegean in order to minimize all future ethnic and religious conflicts. What resulted was the total migration of 1.2 million Anatolian Greeks and nearly 400,000 Rumelian Muslims, and this not only increased uncertainty, frustration and misery among the migrants, but also profoundly homogenized the demographic texture in Greece and Turkey.

Returning back to the days of the Balkan Wars, we have to acknowledge the fact that the homogenization of the population, and the conversion of the country into 'fatherland', did not take place overnight. Rather, recent research in the Ottoman Archives shows us that within the General Directorate for Settlement of Tribes and Refugees, a "scientific committee" (*Encümen-i İlmiye Heyeti*) had been formed to study the distribution of ethnic, linguistic and religious minorities in Anatolia from May 1913.[8] This committee had prepared a set of statistical tables and ethnographic maps of Anatolia by persuading local authorities to collect

---

[8] Fuat Dündar, "The Settlement Policy of the Committee of the Union and Progress: 1913-18," in Hans-Lukas Kieser, (ed.) *Turkey beyond Nationalism: Towards Post-Nationalist Identities* (London: I.B. Tauris , 2006), 39.

information all the way down to village level. The findings in Istanbul were collated and updated meticulously every three months, and changes in the ethnic and religious composition of the local population were recorded fastidiously. In any case, from the outbreak of war in 1914 until 1918, Ottoman subjects were banned from travelling within the country for business or pleasure, and the railway transportation system fell under the complete control of the military. Complete censorship of the press accompanied these moves with only the official communiqués, prepared by the CUP, published in the newspapers. Therefore, war conditions actually gave a free hand to the CUP to implement policies of long-term demographic engineering and Turkification on a massive scale.

For the CUP the basic principle of demographic engineering was quite simple:

1. It was decided that the ratio of non-Muslims (Greeks, Armenians, Jews) or non-Turkish minorities (Kurds, Bosnians, Arabs, Georgian Muslims, Albanians, Gypsies, etc.) within any of the provinces would not be more than 5 per cent. For example, if in one province the percentage of any kind of minorities in the total population was 15 per cent, then two-thirds of this community had to go elsewhere.

2. When the Anatolian Armenians were deported to a desert in Syria (Der Zor), their numbers were not allowed to be more than 10 per cent of the existing population in the region.

3. The houses and fields evacuated by the deported/massacred Armenians were distributed to incoming Balkan refugees.

Therefore, the basis of such demographic engineering in this period could be summarized as "mixing of the populations." The dream of the Young Turks was to unite Anatolian people to form a single national community. However, as in the case of Anatolian Armenians, whenever the policies of "mixing and melting" did not work out, then the policies of ethnic cleansing and massacres had to be initiated.

According to Fuat Dündar, the data accumulated in the IAMM shows that the CUP leadership carefully observed population movements in Anatolia.[9] Whenever necessary, the Minister of the Interior, Talat Pasha, issued orders from Istanbul to local governors on the settlement, forced migration and deportation of different communities throughout Anatolia. The underlying principle behind these orders was to create a fatherland where the Turkish/ Muslim majority would feel secure and where the collective claims of "national self-determination" coming from minorities

---

[9] Fuat Dündar, *İttihat ve Terakki'nin Müslümanları iskân politikası, 1913-1918* (İstanbul: İletişim Yayınları, 2011), 245-252.

could be crushed militarily at once. In essence, cultural and ideological loyalty to the political regime was to be secured by the strategic mixing and significant reshuffling of the entire Anatolian population.

Under the auspices of the Minister of the Interior, other committees were formed at a local level to rename villages, towns, mountains, plains and all other geographical entities in general. Conversion of the "country" into a "Turkish fatherland" through renaming had actually started immediately after the deportation of the Armenian population in the summer of 1915. In the following year (on 5 January 1916), and now well into the war, the Supreme Commander of the Ottoman army and the leader of the CUP, Enver Pasha, dispatched a circular to the local governors in the provinces and informed them that "it has been decided to change the names of the cities, towns, villages, mountains, rivers etc. in Ottoman lands – which have names taken from languages of the non-Muslim groups, like Armenian, Greek and Bulgarian – into Turkish". In the same circular it was also stated that new names should make reference to the glorious military history of the Turks, and commemorate, in particular, exemplary individuals who would inspire future generations by rendering their good services to the country.[10] By renaming the geographical entities, the CUP wanted to foster unity of the "fatherland" and greatly authenticate the historical Turkish presence in these localities As Azaryahu and Golan argued in their work on renaming practices in Israel, 'the reference to places by particular names not only acknowledges these places as constituents of the physical world and social reality but also evinces nationalist assumptions and arguments.'[11]

During the First World War, the deportation of Anatolian Armenians, particularly to Syrian deserts, was meticulously planned in Istanbul. They were not alone however, and in fact nearly all of the ethnic, religious and linguistic minorities were similarly affected by these policies. Utilizing the sources Fuat Dündar unearthed in the Ottoman Archives in recent years, we can summarize the size and scope of demographic engineering implemented by the CUP between 1913 and 1918. Dündar reviews the population movements between 1922 and 1924 as follows:

Here is the estimated breakdown of the displaced population: nearly one million Balkan refugees, approximately 2 million Kurdish and Turcoman nomads, 5000 Arab families of Syria, nearly 1.5 million eastern refugees [from the Russian front] ... In other words, more than one-third of the Muslim population of Asia Minor was transferred to places far away from their habitat. If we add to this picture the departure and

---

[10] *Ibid*, 82
[11] M Azaryahu and A Golan, "(Re)Naming the Landscape: The Formation of the Hebrew Map of Israel 1949-1960," *Journal of Historical Geography*, 27 (2001): 181.

elimination of the non-Muslim population, i.e. nearly 1.2 million Greeks and more than 1.5 million Armenians, then we can conclude that half of the Anatolian population was affected by the Committee's policy.[12]

A statistical analysis of Ottoman Population Censuses yields similar results. According to the 1906 Ottoman Census, the population within the borders of present-day Turkey was nearly 15 million. However, the first Turkish Population Census, which was undertaken by the Turkish Republic in 1927, demonstrates a decrease to 13.6 million. Justin McCarthy calculates that nearly 18 per cent of the Muslims in Anatolia perished in the wars from 1912 to 1922.[13]

As the result of forced migration and massacre of Ottoman Armenians in 1915, and compulsory exchange of population between Greece and Turkey in 1923, the changes in the ethnic and religious composition of the population were also dramatic and succinctly summarized by Çağlar Keyder as follows: "Before the war, one out of every five persons [20 per cent] living in present-day Turkey was non- Muslim, after the war, only one out of forty persons [2.5 per cent] was non-Muslim."[14]

Therefore, within ten years the Anatolian population was Turkified, in the first instance at least, along religious lines. Sociologically, the departure of Greeks and Armenians from Turkey meant that the most productive elements of the population, and a good deal of the entrepreneurial know-how, left the country for good. Thus, according to Keyder, during the ten years of war, most of Turkey's commercial class was eradicated, and when the Republic was formed the founding fathers of the nation-state found themselves unobstructed.

In eliminating propertied classes on such a scale and in such a broad sweep, the Young Turks and Kemalists could be compared quite rightly to Bolsheviks who, after the October Revolution, expropriated the Russian bourgeoisie. The Young Turks and Kemalists either deported/massacred their commercial bourgeoisie or exchanged them. These drastic changes in the social fabric of the country enabled the Kemalists to implement Turkification policies in the early years of the Republic without much opposition.

It is also quite obvious that if the demographic engineering policies of the CUP had not been implemented between 1913 and 1918, the national resistance movement, started under the leadership of Mustafa Kemal Pasha (later Atatürk), against Greek occupation would not have been able

---

[12] Fuat Dündar, The Settlement Policy, 43.
[13] Justin McCarthy, *Muslims and Minorities: The Population of Ottoman Anatolia and the End of the Empire* (New York: New York University Press, 1983), 133.
[14] Çağlar Keyder, *State and Class in Turkey: A Study in Capitalist Development,* (London: Verso, 1987), 79.

to take root in Anatolia. In particular, if we think about the abandoned property left behind by the non-Muslim minorities in Anatolia, and the consequent pillage of these properties amongst Turkish Muslim local notables, only then can we understand the *raison d'être* of the material and manpower support granted to national resistance movements between 1919 and 1922.[15] In other words, the demographic engineering and homogenization of Anatolia on ethnic and religious lines not only secured the victory against Greek occupation forces, but it also paved the way for building the Turkish nation-state in 1923.

Turkey for the Turks! Creating a 'national bourgeoisie'

One of the most important features of the Turkification policies was an attempt to create a national bourgeoisie – a process that had already started under CUP rule between 1913 and 1918. The terrible experience of the Balkan Wars and the rising anti-minority sentiment among the urban masses helped the CUP to implement nationalist economic policies effectively. The CUP government did everything possible to invite the Turkish/Muslim element to act as entrepreneurs in a highly protected economic environment, and actually sponsored the formation of 'national companies', introduced protectionist customs duties and finally abolished most of the economic privileges granted to foreigners during the war.[16] The outbreak of war in Europe enabled the CUP government to abolish the trade privileges and capitulations previously granted to European powers. In this turbulent period of conflict a whole set of new laws and regulations were prepared and implemented hastily. For example, in May 1915, a so-called 'language reform' was put into effect banning the usage of French or English in commercial correspondence. This was one of the first attempts to increase the employment of the educated Turkish elite in private companies, and was also intended to eliminate the Levantine population who did not speak or write Turkish. The Ottomans' entrance into war, if acted upon appropriately, could yet create very favorable circumstances for the nurturing of an emergent Muslim commercial bourgeoisie. The CUP government supported this nascent bourgeoisie through nepotism and by the allocation of certain public facilities. For instance, due to the price differences for basic foodstuffs between big cities and the Anatolian countryside, anyone who could obtain special permission to transport goods to Istanbul via strictly controlled railways could and did become rich overnight. As a consequence of this type of

---

[15] Taner Akçam, *A Shameful Act: The Armenian Genocide and the Question of Turkish Responsibility*, (New York: Metropolitan Books, 2006), especially Chapter 8.
[16] See, Zafer Toprak, *Türkiye'de Ekonomi ve Toplum, 1908-1950: İttihat-Terakki ve Devletçilik*, (Istanbul: Tarih Vakfı Yurt Yayınları, 1995). And also, Zafer Toprak, *Milli İktisat, Milli Burjuvazi*, (Istanbul: Tarih Vakfı Yurt Yayınları, 1995).

support policies, the term "war profiteers" entered the daily vocabulary of the urban masses.

Furthermore, the CUP organized urban artisans and tradesmen into associations which, it was assumed, would control the market and regulate prices. However, just the opposite happened. Soon, most essential goods had disappeared from the open market, and prices had skyrocketed on the black market.[17] In the meantime, the so-called "work peace" had been secured and all strikes were banned. The Young Turks in government did everything possible to reorganize and reform the state apparatus of a collapsing empire: the transition from tax-farming to direct tax collection, the promotion of indigenous manufacturing industry by special legislation and the printing of paper money as the basis of a sound monetary policy.

In Anatolia, the "national" companies were formed along the same lines, encouraged by local governors, appointed by the CUP, which favoured such schemes. The partners of national companies formed during the war were not different from the local cadres of the CUP. They were also the ones supported and national liberation movement later.[18] However, these 'national companies' did not a substantive economic development in the provinces. Nonetheless, the political networks and loyalties structured during the war were extremely important. These networks not only enabled Kemalists to win the war against the Greek occupation forces but it also laid the stones of Turkish nation state in 1923.

On 30 August 1922, the Greek army was defeated at the battle near Afyon, and ten days later, on 9 September 1922, Turkish nationalist forces entered İzmir. This was the end of the Turkish War of Independence. Nearly a month later, on 11 October 1922, a ceasefire agreement was signed between the Allies and the Ankara government in Mudanya, which also brought the British and French occupation of Istanbul to an end a year later.

This was the beginning of a new era, and it was embarked upon with enthusiasm. Yet not surprisingly, this optimism was soon eclipsed by the sentiment of revenge. Summarizing the political developments of the period, the acting British Consul General, R. W. Urquhart, in İzmir wrote the following dispatch to London:

In September 1922 the Turkish people were filled with a spirit of

---

[17] Feroz Ahmad, "Vanguard of Nascent Bourgeoisie: The Social and Economic Policy of the Young Turks," in Osman Okyar, and Halil İnalcık, eds. *Türkiye'nin Sosyal ve Ekonomik Tarihi (1071-1920) - Papers Presented to the Conference on Social and Economic History of Turkey (1071-1920)* (Ankara: Hacettepe Üniversitesi, 1980), 339.

[18] Keyder, State and Class, 63.

Turkish nationality entirely new to them – a spirit of nationalism of the most primitive type, which expressed itself in insult to the non-Turk and glorification of the all-Turk. There was a riot of self- assertion … foreigners were denounced as the parasites who had impoverished the [country] politic[ally] and economic[ally] in the past, who were to be brushed away to permit of a glorious future for Turkey in purely Turkish hands.[19]

This ruthless attitude towards all foreign firms and establishments went hand in hand with *de facto* pressures exercised on foreign firms to employ more and more Turkish/Muslim citizens in their premises. In his dispatch to London, British ambassador Sir Ronald Lindsay complained about the news that "in the future only Turks would be allowed to act as chauffeurs."[20] Similar pressures were also exerted on foreign concessionaire companies, such as Izmir - Aydın railways, which had operated since 1860s. A representative of the company paid a visit to the British ambassador on 18 March 1926 and suggested that there was a strong feeling that the personnel of the railway should be entirely Turkish: "The railway company was willing to employ Turks as far as possible, but could not find any suitable for the task at hand!"[21] As the 1920s progressed, firms, shopkeepers, companies and even professionals such as doctors and lawyers were told to dismiss their non-Muslim employees and hire Muslim Turks instead. Most of these demands, perfect examples of the discrimination against non- Muslim minorities, did not have a legal basis or any constitutional justification. They were simply *de facto* pressures exerted by the Ankara government. Now Turkish-Muslim merchants receiving government support from Ankara identified themselves as "national merchants" (*milli tüccar*), thereby implying that the non-Muslim businessmen who remained in Istanbul were not national, and therefore were not to be trusted in their loyalty to the regime. It is clear that the main target of the Turkification schemes was not merely the creation of a nationalist bourgeoisie, but doing so at the expense of existing minorities and foreign-owned companies.

The Turkification policies continued unabated, and soon it was man-dated that foreign companies keep their books in the Turkish language, that the allocation of certain professions and state employees must be entirely to Muslim Turks, and that foreign-owned companies have Muslim Turks comprising at least 75 per cent of their total workforce in

---

[19] FO 424/258, From acting Consul General R. W. Urquhart in Smyrna to Foreign Secretary Lord Curzon in London: E 8317/199/44 dated 21 July 1923.
[20] Dispatch sent from Sir R. Lindsay in Istanbul to Sir Austen Chamberlain in London: FO 371: Foreign Office Correspondence / Document dated 3 March 1926 / E 1571/373/44
[21] Résume of the conversation between Sir R. Lindsay and Lord Howard of Glossop. FO 371: Document dated 18 March 1926 / E 1874/373/44

1920s.

So as to leave nothing to chance, and in order to make an accurate assessment of the number of non-Muslims and foreigners active in the different sectors of the economy, forms were prepared by various state institutions for the purpose of gathering statistical information. In these forms, there were questions about the number of Muslim Turks, Non-Muslim Turks and Foreigners working on the premises.[22] By law, every company had to answer these questionnaires and send them back to Ankara. Again in the 1920s special laws were passed regulating the practice of liberal professions such as lawyers, pharmacists, sea captains and medical doctors. All these laws mandated that the practitioners of liberal professions had to be 'Turkish'. Indeed being 'Turkish' was not interpreted merely as being a "citizen of the Turkish Republic." On the contrary, the Kemalist elite opted more and more for "ethnic" definition of the individuals' membership criterion within the national community. In practice, "Turkish" was understood as an ethnic-religious denomination, not necessarily bestowed automatically upon the citizens of the Turkish Republic. As a result, many pharmacists, for example, had to close down their premises, and of the 960 lawyers registered to the Istanbul Bar Association only 431 were permitted to practice their profession. The rest were either non-Muslims or the ones who had not provided their support to the Turkish War of Independence between 1919 and 1922. Naturally they had to close down their offices and look for employment somewhere else or migrate to Europe.[23]

In 1932 an interesting transformation in the treatment of minorities and foreigners took place. Until then, the pressures exerted were mostly at *de facto* level. However, since the beginning of the 1930s the Ankara government started to pass laws in the parliament in an absolutely anti-minority spirit. For instance, the law of 1932 entitled 'Restricting Certain Professions and Trades to Turkish Citizens Only' restricted the employment of aliens in certain strategic occupations in the country, all of which were carefully listed in detail. To name a few: street vendors, musicians, photographers, barbers, typographers, tourist guides, construction workers, drivers, waiters, watchmen, door- keepers in office buildings or apartments, male or female servants in hotels, offices or music halls, and singers in bars. The American Consul General in Istanbul, Charles N. Allen, wrote a "strictly confidential" dispatch to the US Secretary of Labor and explained the essence of the law as follows:

---

[22] Dispatch sent from Sir R. Lindsay in Istanbul to Sir Austen Chamberlain in London: FO 371/11541. Document dated 9 May 1926 / E 3016/373/44
[23] Rıfat Bali, *Cumhuriyet yıllarında Türk Yahudileri: Bir Türkleştirme Serüveni, 1923-1945* (İstanbul: İletişim yayınları, 1999), 225.

"As a matter of fact, there are reported to have been occasions on which the authorities attempted to obtain, not only dismissal of the aliens, but also the dismissal of non-Muslim Turkish nationals."[24]

Republic Day parade in the 1930s

A year later, the British ambassador Charles Morgan wrote a long report about this law and explained the fact that it had nothing to do with the economic conditions, i.e., Great Depression of 1929, although the officials in Ankara argued that economic necessity drove them as it did the other nations to restrict the employment of aliens. However, Ambassador Morgan argued the following:

> It is the culmination of years of steady work on a plan making Turkey a land fit for Turks only, and eliminating foreigners – save the temporary foreign specialist who will teach Turks better how to dispense with foreigners sooner. Beginning at Lausanne in 1923 with reservation of coastal shipping and maritime avocations to Turkish citizens, following this up by forbidding foreigners to inhabit the countryside, and driving them into towns by the Law on Villages, forcing concessionary and public utility companies, and large banking, industrial and commercial undertakings to employ only Muslims and dismiss the foreigner, the Turkish Government has steadily pursued its aim of weeding out the more highly paid foreign employee, and of replacing him – without

[24] From US Consul General Charles N. Allen in Istanbul to the Secretary of Labor in Washington, Records of the Department of State relating to the internal affairs of Turkey, 1930-1944. Document no. 867.504/5, dated 16 November 1932.

apparent loss of efficiency – by a Turkish citizen, and is now on the eve of driving out the foreign rank and file. The policy is clear, consistent, and unrelenting. The driving force of this xenophobia is partly fanaticism, inspired by the old rooted antagonism of Islam for Christianity, partly militarism which feels that the country is safer when foreigners are few and confined to the large cities, partly nationalism which is convinced that all activities in Turkey should be Turkish, and that Turks are as capable in any branch as foreigners, and partly greed, whetted already by the seizure of the proceeds of Greek and Armenian energy in Asia Minor, and ready now to step into the shoes of the foreigner, and enjoy what was his.[25]

As a result of the implementation of this law, nearly 9000 non-exchanged Greeks lost their jobs and soon thereafter migrated to Greece for good.[26] There can be no doubt that Turkification policies were directly responsible for the dwindling of the non-Muslim communities in Istanbul during the early years of the Republic.

From xenophobia to permanent paranoia

British diplomats serving in Turkey first categorized these pressures as "rampant xenophobia." However, they were also aware of the roots of this ideological movement. British High Commissioner Neville Henderson summarized the Turkish version of xenophobia as follows:

> Xenophobia is, of course, a phenomenon which ordinarily accompanies the rapid development of a strong national consciousness, and its violence is apt to be in direct proportion to the extent to which, previous to that development, the country concerned has been subject to foreign political and economic influence … It is natural that in Turkey, … it should be specially acute, owing to the fact that Turkey has in the past [been] peculiarly subject to such influence.[27]

In the same dispatch, Neville Henderson underlined the fact that in the long run xenophobia was to become an indispensable ingredient of

---

[25] Dispatch sent from James Morgan in Ankara to Sir John Simon in London: FO 371/16985: Foreign Office Correspondence / Document dated 15 April 1933 / E 2052/587/44.

[26] 'Établis Greeks' were the Istanbul Greeks who had obtained Greek citizenship in last years of the Ottoman rule. They were not exchanged in 1923 and later obtained a kind of "Green Card" type of work permit from Turkish administration. See, Ayhan Aktar, "Cumhuriyetin İlk Yıllarında Uygulanan 'Türkleştirme' Politikaları" [Turkification Policies Implemented during the Early years of the Turkish Republic] in Ayhan Aktar, *Varlık Vergisi ve Türkleştirme Politikaları*. (İstanbul: İletişim yayınları, 2000), 101 - 134.

[27] FO 424/260, From British High Commisioner Neville Henderson in Istanbul to British Foreign Secretary Lord Curzon in London. E 633/32/44 dated January 15, 1924.

Turkish nationalism. Utilizing an Orientalist and essentialist discourse in his dispatch, Henderson emphasized the sturdiness of xenophobia:

> Others again hope that the Turk will be forced, against his will, into a more reasonable frame of mind on seeing the damage to trade and to general well-being of the country entailed by his present attitude and the difficulty of getting foreigners to invest new capital in Turkey so long as he persists in it. Among these opinions I do not hazard a view of my own, except that the battle between acute xenophobia and common sense will be a long one, and, if the former dies a natural and enforced death, it will die hard.[28]

Neville Henderson's expectations were fulfilled in the coming years, not least after the devastating effects of the onset of the Great Depression from November 1929, when the founding fathers of the Turkish Republic lost much of their hope for a development strategy based upon the dynamism created by private entrepreneurship and liberal economy. In any case, the human capital that could have created this dynamism had either been deported or exchanged a long time ago.

In spite of all the efforts of the Ankara government to create an "indigenous Turkish-Muslim group of capitalists", the project failed. British diplomats posted in Turkey presented a grim picture of economic development, and this was typified when British Ambassador Sir George Clerk evaluated the performance of the newly formed, and heavily supported, Turkish firms as "incompetent" and then presented the following scornful assessment in November 1929:

> This incompetence is repeated in the numerous Turkish firms of smaller importance which have endeavored to replace the Greek and Armenian middlemen who were always the backbone of Turkish commerce. Almost invariably these new Turkish firms start business as commission agents, but they have neither the patience and the experience nor the temperament to build up their fortunes slowly in the same way as their Christian predecessors. In most cases they drift to Ankara, to the neglect of their agency commitments, and endeavor to get rich quickly by dabbling in large contracts. Further, commercial morality here has declined of late years.[29]

Ambassador Clerk's criticisms reveal that, at least in some cases, the continuing support from Ankara had not been sufficient to create the desired outcome. One could conjecture that if the members of the group

---

[28] Ibid.
[29] Dispatch sent from Sir George Clerk in Istanbul to Mr. A. Henderson in London: FO 371: Foreign Office Correspondence / Document dated 13 November 1929 / E 5984/89/44

replacing the minorities had received less protection and tutelage from Ankara, they might even have been forced to develop their entrepreneurial capacities much more effectively and successfully. Consequently, during the early years of the Republic, Kemalists adopted a social and economic development model based upon self- sufficiency and a high level of protectionism in their desire to create a command economy. State enterprises were established and industrialization programs were implemented, while étatiste measures further helped the Kemalist elite to develop firm fiscal foundations for the Republic. The founding fathers of the Turkish Republic went a step further in taking a more collectivist and authoritarian stance in identifying the actual properties of the Turkish nation-state. Xenophobia, once regarded as an infantile disorder of Turkish nationalism, now gained a special momentum and imposed its will on nearly every aspect of social and political life. Not only the existence of foreigners or non-Muslims in the economy, but anything that challenged the unconditional supremacy of Turkish ethnic identity in every aspect of social and political life triggered a sense of distress and concern among the ruling elite. Anything 'alien' or anything that had not been Turkified created a potential threat for the country and the wellbeing of the Turkish nation. Resultant laws and regulations then centralized xenophobia in such a way that the institutional and educational framework generated "paranoia" right down to an individual level for generations to come. Even today, whenever the officially disseminated feeling of "authenticity" is challenged publicly by remembering or using the original Greek, Armenian or Kurdish name of some location, the act of doing is regarded as a covert operation against the unity and integrity of the Turkish fatherland. Therefore, as journalist Yalçın Doğan argued in his column, the naming of animals like '*Vulpes Vulpes Kurdistanicum*' or '*Ovis Armeniana*' is indeed a sinister act. As British High Commissioner Neville Henderson anticipated in 1924, the battle between xenophobia and common sense would be a long one. Unfortunately, the legacy of institutionalized xenophobia that we have inherited from the founding fathers of the Turkish Republic does not die easily.

Bibliography

Archive documents

US National Archives

Records of the Department of State Relating to Internal Affairs of Turkey, 1930-1944 (Microfilm no: M1224).

British National Archives

FO 371, Foreign Office Correspondence.

Published Works

Ahmad, Feroz "Vanguard of Nascent Bourgeoisie: The Social and Economic Policy of the Young Turks," in Osman Okyar, and Halil İnalcık, eds. *Türkiye'nin Sosyal ve Ekonomik Tarihi (1071-1920) - Papers Presented to the Conference on Social and Economic History of Turkey (1071-1920)*. Ankara: Hacettepe Üniversitesi, 1980.

Akçam, Taner. A Shameful Act: The Armenian Genocide and the Question of Turkish Responsibility. New York: Metropolitan Books, 2006.

Aydın, Suavi "İsimler Milli Birliği nasıl bozar? Bak şu tilkinin ettiğine." *Toplumsal Tarih*, 143, (2005): 90-97.

Aktar, Ayhan "Cumhuriyetin İlk Yıllarında Uygulanan 'Türkleştirme' Politikaları." *Tarih ve Toplum* 156, (1996): 4-18.

———. Varlık Vergisi ve Türkleştirme Politikaları. İstanbul: İletişim yayınları, 2000.

Azaryahu, M, and A Golan. "(Re)Naming the Landscape: The Formation of the Hebrew Map of Israel 1949-1960." *Journal of Historical Geography*, 27 (2001): 178–95.

Bali, Rıfat Cumhuriyet yıllarında Türk Yahudileri: Bir Türkleştirme Serüveni, 1923-1945. İstanbul: İletişim yayınları, 1999.

Dündar, Fuat "The Settlement Policy of the Committee of the Union and Progress: 1913-18," in Kieser, Hans-Lukas. *Turkey beyond Nationalism: Towards Post-Nationalist Identities*. London: I.B. Tauris, 2006.

———. *İttihat ve Terakki'nin Müslümanları iskân politikası, 1913-1918*. İstanbul: İletişim Yayınları, 2011.

Keyder, Çağlar. State and Class in Turkey: A Study in Capitalist Development. London: Verso, 1987.

McCarthy, Justin. Muslims and Minorities: The Population of Ottoman Anatolia and the End of the Empire. New York: New York University Press, 1983.

Shaw, Stanford J, and Ezel Kural Shaw. History of the Ottoman Empire and Modern Turkey. Reform, Revolution, and Republic: The Rise of Modern Turkey, 1808-1975. Vol. 2. Cambridge: CUP, 1977.

Toprak, Zafer *Türkiye'de Ekonomi ve Toplum, 1908-1950: İttihat-Terakki ve Devletçilik*. İstanbul: Tarih Vakfı, 1995.

———. *Milli İktisat, Milli Burjuvazi*, İstanbul: Tarih Vakfı, 1995.

Toynbee, Arnold J. *The Western Question in Greece and Turkey*. Boston: Houghton Mifflin Company, 1922.

CHAPTER 5

"TURKIFICATION" POLICIES IN THE EARLY REPUBLICAN ERA*

In this article, we shall analyze some of the Turkification policies which were implemented during the early years of the Republic and which became crystallized only in the formation of the Turkish nation-state. In this context, by "Turkification" policies, I mean the way in which Turkish ethnic identity has been strictly imposed as a hegemonic identity in every sphere of social life, from the language spoken in public to the teaching of history in public schools; from education to industry; from commercial practices to public employment policies; from the civil code to the re-settlement of certain citizens in particular areas. The preconditions of the implementation of Turkification policies can be summarized as follows: the emergence of Turkish nationalism as a well-structured political ideology, the recognition of this ideology by the great majority of the political elite in power, and the existence of an international political conjuncture favorable to the implementation of these policies domestically.

In my article on anti-Jewish pogroms of 1934, it has been argued that the concept of "us" as in the dichotomy of "us" versus "others," which comprises the basic categories of all nationalist movements, defined by the Kemalists as "those who are part of the Turkish ethnic identity."[1] Previously, I described how the Kemalists claimed that all ethnic groups who had been living in Anatolia for centuries "were actually Turks." I also stressed the fact that with this method of inquiry an attempt was made to include all these different ethnic groups within the Turkish ethnic identity. In my article on anti-Jewish pogroms, I explained how the category of "us" was expanded during the single party period. However, the non-Muslim minorities who had been living in Anatolia for centuries under the protective umbrella of the Ottoman regime and keeping their own religious and ethnic identities intact were logically included in the category of "others." If examined carefully, it will be noticed that these two processes are two different sides of the same coin. Consequently, and according to the Kemalists' conception of nationalism, in order to extend the scope of

* This article was previously published in *Turkish Literature and Cultural Memory*. Edited by Catharina Duft. (Wiesbaden: Harrassowitz Verlag, 2009), 29–62. It's been translated into English by Adnan Tonguç, Tansel Demirel, and Amy Spangler.
[1] Ayhan Aktar, 'Trakya Yahudi Olaylarını Doğru Yorumlamak,' [Correctly Interpreting the 1934 Jewish Incidents in Thrace] *Tarih ve Toplum*, 155, (Kasım 1996): 55.

the category of "us," every person living in the country was declared to be a Turk! However, when this could not be implemented for structural reasons in the cases of non-Muslim minorities, the non-Muslim minorities in Turkey were in practice discriminated against and classified as "minorities" or "foreigners." Turkification policies implemented by the single party in power during the early years of the Republic (1925–1945) were thought to be "all-encompassing" for the Muslim population in the short term. Nevertheless, as far as the non- Muslim groups were concerned, these policies had "discriminatory/anti-minority" characteristics. If this is the case, then nearly all anti-minority policies implemented in Turkey cannot be described as being "antagonistic towards a particular ethnic or religious group," such as the Jews, the Greeks, or the Armenians. In other words, during the single party period, all social groups that could not be Turkified for structural reasons were discriminated against with- out exception.

Consequently, all the efforts to Turkify every sphere of social life during the establishment of the nation-state manifest themselves at once and inevitably as "anti-minority" policies. What comprises "us" versus the "others" in a nation- state, and the criteria on which these notions are based, give us clues about the dominant type of nationalism in a country. These notions also help us identify all the tensions that encompass the fault line between the dominant political class claiming to represent the so-called Turkish majority and the non- Muslim minorities.[2] At this point, we should turn our attention to the intellectual heritage that shaped the praxis of the Turkish political elite in relation to non-Muslim minorities.

I. A turning point in the intellectual heritage of the Kemalists: Ziya Gökalp

The Republic of Turkey, which was born from the ashes of the Ottoman Empire, had inherited a population comprised of many different religious and ethnic groups. Even though the overall population had decreased as a result of casual- ties incurred during the Balkan Wars, World War I, and the Turkish War of Independence, the share of the Muslim/Turkish population had increased in relative terms as a result of the Armenian deportation (1915 - 1917) and the Turkish- Greek Population Exchange (1922 - 1924). As Çağlar Keyder expresses it so succinctly: "… Before the war, one out of every five persons [20%] living in present- day Turkey was non-Moslem, after the war, only one out of forty persons [2.5%] was non-Moslem."[3] This radical change in the ethnic and religious composition of the population, combined with the political

---

[2] For the best study concerning the classification of different types of nationalism, see Liah Greenfeld, *Nationalism: Five Roads to Modernity* (Cambridge: Harvard University Press, 1995).
[3] Çağlar Keyder, *State and Class in Turkey: A Study in Capitalist Development.* (London: Verso, 1987), 67.

events of the period, resulted in the transformation of the conception of nationalism, from that developed by Ziya Gökalp before World War I, to that of Kemalist nationalism, which began to take shape in the 1920s. Even though these differences were not very obvious at the philosophical and ideological levels, they became utterly visible in the laws passed during the consolidation of the Republic.

Undertaking to formulate a nation-building project for a population comprised of widely diverse ethnic and religious groups, Ziya Gökalp designated culture (*hars*) as the defining criterion whereby an individual belonged to the national community. According to Gökalp:

> A nation is not a community bound by geographical, racial, political, or voluntary ties. A nation is a cultural class made up of individuals who share a common language, that is, who have been brought up in the same way. One prefers to live together with people who have had the same upbringing and who have the same mother tongue, rather than with people of the same blood, because our personality lies not in our bodies, but in our spirits. Even though our physical virtues derive from our race, our moral virtues derive from the society that has nurtured us.[4]

The concept of "culture," as so meticulously defined by Gökalp on the basis of sociological principles, placed individuals under the same, broad cultural umbrella, irrespective of their ethnic identities, so long as they shared the same mother tongue and socialization. According to Gökalp, Islam is one of the most important aspects of the process of "socialization," which he discusses as part of his conception of culture. In the same article, while underlining the importance of religion within the process of socialization, Gökalp also explains the social mechanisms that help people of the same religion but different ethnic identities accept the same national identity:

> We have many co-religionists, who even though they are not racially Turkish, have a Turkish spirit in terms of their upbringing and their culture, and who share our misfortunes as well as our joys... As a result of their upbringing, these people can live in no other nation but Turkish society, and can work for no ideal but the Turkish ideal.[5]

In this way, Gökalp points out the social function of religion, which must have been the most disturbing aspect of his teaching for Kemalists in later years. The new regime did not look very favorably upon

---

[4] Ziya Gökalp, 'Millet nedir?' In *Makaleler VII: Küçük Mecmua'daki Yazılar*, ed. by M. Abdülhalûk Çay. (Ankara: Ministry of Culture, 1982), 228.
[5] Gökalp, *ibid*, 229.

strengthening social solidarity via the ethical norms of Islam.[6]

Thus, we can clearly say that Gökalp's conception of "nation" is more encompassing than exclusionary. His approach was particularly suitable to the demo- graphic conditions in Anatolia at the time. This large umbrella would make it possible for those who felt themselves to be Albanian, Circassian, Bosnian, Kurdish, or Laz in terms of "ethnic identity" to nevertheless adopt a "Turkish national identity." As Taha Parla stresses in his groundbreaking study *The Social and Political Thought of Ziya Gökalp, 1876–1924*:

> In Gökalp's view, Turkish nationalism represented a cultural ideal, a philosophy of life which laid the basis of social solidarity. He believed that that applied to every [type of] nationalism. His was non-racist, non-expansionist pluralistic nationalism. Similarly, his unorthodox, Sufi brand of Islam with its emphasis on ethics rather than politics reinforced solidarity. Thus, Turkism became the cultural norm and Islam the moral norm in his societal model. Westernism or modernism, which Gökalp used interchangeably, meant the scientific, technological, industrial achievements of European capitalism, which were to form part of his program of national revival.[7]

True enough, in the years following 1908, when Gökalp's conception of nationalism was formulated, Jewish intellectuals like Moiz Kohen Tekinalp also contributed to the formulation of Turkish nationalism. Years later, Tekinalp would say the following about Gökalp:

> Gökalp's Turkism is not destructive, but rather constructive in the real sense of the word; it is not restrictive, but embracing... It has no aggressive tendencies or feelings towards any social institution that is not contrary to the good and well-being of the Turkish nation. In essence, he did not refrain from expressing his sentiments of love and respect towards non-Muslim Turkish citizens, or, as Ziya Gökalp himself expressed it, for his fellow members of the Turkish state (*Türk 'devletdaşları'*).[8]

This all-encompassing approach of Gökalp's when it came to inclusion in the national community changed somewhat, however, when the matter

---

[6] Uriel Heyd, who was the first to underline Gökalp's views about Islam, made the following comment: "But for the anti-Islamic attitude of Atatürk, Gökalp might have become the initiator of fully scientific investigation of Islam in Turkey and perhaps even the father of an interesting religious reform movement." See, Uriel Heyd, *Foundations of Turkish Nationalism; the Life and Teachings of Ziya Gökalp* (London: Luzac, 1950), 82.
[7] Taha Parla, *The Social and Political Thought of Ziya Gökalp, 1876-1924*, Social, Economic, and Political Studies of the Middle East ; v. 35 (Leiden: E. J. Brill, 1985), 26.
[8] Munis Tekinalp, *Türk ruhu* (İstanbul: Remzi Kitabevi, 1944) 218-219.

of non- Muslim minorities' dominant position in the economy came to the fore. The final stanza of the poem *"Vatan"* (Homeland) in Gökalp's book titled *Yeni Hayat* (The New Life), which was published in 1912, is in a way a manifesto of Turkish economic nationalism:

A country where all the capital in the markets,
Where science and technology guiding its crafts belongs to Turks.
Where its craftsmen are always in solidarity with each other;
Where the shipyards, factories, ships, and trains belong to Turks;
Oh, son of the Turk, that is your country! [9]

The wishes expressed here are on the one hand the abolition of the capitulations granted to foreign companies in fields like shipping lines, railroads, and port management, and on the other, the strengthening of social solidarity by means of the mutual help of professional organizations set up within a corporatist framework. The poem includes also a very clear message as far as the Turkification of capital is concerned. In his article "Yeni Hayat ve Yeni Kıymetler" (New Life, New Values, 1911), which he wrote around the same time, Gökalp describes the position of non-Muslim minorities from the cultural point of view as follows:

When our non-Muslim citizens decided to acquire a new life, they did not need to search for long. The urban lifestyle of European nations suited them like ready-made clothing purchased in a shop. The majority of Greeks, Armenians, and Bulgarians among us immediately adopted all the urban customs and social attitudes of Europeans. As for us Muslims, we could not imitate the ready-made rules and standard lifestyles of civilization, because of the particular characteristics of our lives. We needed lifestyles and rules tailored according to our own measurements, like a tailored suit, rather than a ready-made one.[10]

With these words, Gökalp seems at once to be making reference to a Latin American-style comprador bourgeoisie, as he also stresses the need to perceive the distinction between Muslims and non-Muslims at the level not just of religious but of cultural differences as well.

When analyzing the structure of late Ottoman society in light of the basic concepts of Durkheim's sociology, Gökalp states that the specialization and differentiation processes, which gave rise to a wide variety of professional groups as a consequence of the social division of

[9] Ziya Gökalp, *Yeni hayat ; Doğru yol*, ed. by Müjgan Cumbul (Ankara: Devlet Kitapları, 1976), 11.
[10] Ziya Gökalp, 'Yeni Hayat ve Yeni Kıymetler.' In *Makaleler II*, ed. by Süleyman Hayri Bolay. (Ankara: Ministry of Culture, 1982), 44-45.

labor, did not automatically serve to strengthen social solidarity:

> For example, in old Turkey, Turks and non-Muslims were living a common economic life. However, the social division of labor between them was not so much a genuine division of labor as it was a relationship of mutual parasitism, because these Turks and non-Turks shared no collective conscience. Turks were the political parasites of non-Muslims, and non-Muslims were the economic parasites of Turks. International economic relations are all of this kind. The second condition for the strengthening of this kind of [organic] solidarity is the creation of professional ethics in professional classes, following the organization of professional classes into national associations throughout the country.[11]

You will notice that Gökalp first underlines the differences between Turks and non-Muslims from the cultural point of view, and later states that these groups lived within the same society, as two culturally separate blocs, connected to each other by bonds of a parasitic nature. Gökalp argues that the society lacked a collective conscience, which is one of the most basic concepts of Durkheim's sociology, and adds that this could be established only within a corporatist state shaped according to the principle of "professional representation."

Here, Gökalp puts forward a radical critique of the social structure of the late Ottoman period. Non-Muslims had previously solved matters like taxation, education, and civil law within their own communities thanks to the *Millet* system, and later when this system was abolished, they managed to hang on to some of their privileges, while simultaneously benefiting from the egalitarian atmosphere brought about by the *Tanzimat* reforms. On the one hand, non-Muslims became relatively richer as a result of the development of commercial life once the Ottoman Empire had opened up to the world economy in the nineteenth century. On the other hand, they were placed under the protection of European states once the "minorities question" had come to the fore as an important axis of relations between the Ottoman State and the Great Powers. The complex web of relations in which Ottoman minorities found themselves in the late Ottoman period was strikingly described by Lewis and Braude as follows:

> One could not be a citizen of a sovereign nation, the protégée of a foreign power and the subject of a would be egalitarian empire at one and the same time. Neither physics nor politics allows such

---

[11] Ziya Gökalp, Yeni hayat ; Doğru yol, 87.

things to occur, at least not for long.[12]

After 1908, the administration of the Committee of Union and Progress (*İttihat ve Terakki*) was striving to both eliminate the capitulations and introduce egalitarian measures that would make all members of society equal under the law, such as centralizing the educational system, changing the conditions whereby non-Muslims were allowed to pay for exemption from military service, and overhauling other institutions that had been inherited from the Ottoman *ancien régime*. At the end of the Balkan Wars and World War I, the above-mentioned demographic changes occurred, the conflict between different nationalisms ended in disaster for some, and, finally, the Ottoman Empire collapsed.

The "problem of minorities" in the negotiations for the Lausanne Peace Treaty and the Civil Code

The "problem of minorities" came to the fore once again in 1923, when the vic- torious commanders of Ankara were laying the foundation of the new Turkish state in Lausanne. Undoubtedly, the most difficult negotiations were those that concerned the capitulations of a judiciary nature rather than the financial capitulations. İsmet İnönü summarized the situation in his memoirs as follows:

> Since the very first day, the Allies had accepted the need to abolish the financial requisites of capitulations, but they did not accept the outright abolition of the capitulations in the judicial field, and at the very least, they insisted on a five-year transition period.[13]

The problem of judicial capitulations and privileges consisted of deciding which courts would have jurisdiction to handle cases or conflicts between members of different communities. In a way, judicial capitulations meant the existence of more than one judicial system within the same country. Keeping in mind that the Civil Code was enacted in 1926, or three years after the Lausanne Treaty, it is clear that the foreigners/minorities who did not want to be tried in courts subject to the Muslim canonical law were asking the new regime to provide them with guarantees on this matter. It is for this reason that all the institutions that had been inherited from the Ottoman *ancientt régime*, like pious foundations, schools, church courts, etc., were scrutinized during diplomatic negotiations in Lausanne.

As negotiations were going on in Lausanne, Hasan Saka, who was a member of the Turkish delegation, came back to Ankara and informed

---

[12] Bernard Lewis and Benjamin Braude, *Christians and Jews in the Ottoman Empire: The Functioning of a Plural Society*, vol. 1, (New York: Holmes & Meier Publishers, 1982), 33.
[13] İsmet İnönü, *Hatıralar*, vol. 2 (Ankara: Bilgi Yayınevi, 1989), 88.

the Turkish Parliament about how things were progressing. During closed sessions held in the Turkish Parliament, which had assembled on January 1, 1923, the following juridical principles were established: All Turkish citizens, whether Muslim or non-Muslim, were to be placed under the same juridical system. And for non-Muslim citizens, all procedures having to do with private law, like marriage, divorce, legal origin of children, alimony, etc., were to be taken away from the churches and placed under the jurisdiction of the Turkish administrative system, thus making them subject to Turkish courts rather than community courts. However, this could be possible only if the newly founded nation- state were to renounce canonical law completely and enact a new Civil Code regulating relations between all Turkish citizens.[14]

Hasan Saka's speech in the Turkish Parliament is of particular significance, because it shows that at Lausanne, the Turkish Delegation promised the Allies that a new Civil Code would be enacted within three years' time. Hasan Saka spoke as follows:

> Once the privileges of the religious communities have been abolished, the minorities' legal issues with regard to religious affairs, marriages, parentage, and alimony will remain, and these issues should be resolved by subordinating them to the Civil Code. We now have the obligation of reforming, completing, and enacting the laws related to family affairs within the Civil Code in a way that is in accordance with the requisites of the religions and denominations of all minorities, and since the need has arisen to register all marriages and divorces, including those of minorities, in our official records, through our official courts, we are also obligated to enact our laws accordingly.[15]

By enacting the Civil Code around three years later, the Ankara government eliminated the most significant problem of the community-based social system of the preceding Ottoman *ancien régime*. In this way, it both broke the traditional resistance of non-Muslim communities by making them subject to a secular system that was under its complete control, thus turning non-Muslim minorities into Turks from a legal point view, while also adopting the role of protector of non-Muslims, consequently annulling the influence of the Great Powers, which had been meddling in Turkey's affairs. Thanks to the enactment of the Turkish Civil Code, the newly established nation-state had finally acquired the power

---

[14] For the most comprehensive work on the Turkish legal transformations during the process of modernization, see Gülnihâl Bozkurt, *Batı hukukunun Türkiye'de benimsenmesi: Osmanlı Devleti'nden Türkiye Cumhuriyeti'ne resepsiyon süreci, 1839-1939*, (Ankara: Türk Tarih Kurumu Basımevi, 1996).

[15] *TBMM - Gizli Celse Zabıtları* [Turkish Grand National Assembly - Minutes of the closed sessions], vol. 3, (Ankara: İş Bankası Yayınları, 1985), 1173.

to regulate through the juridical system the private lives, too, of all its citizens. From the point of view of the Kemalists, this law was not just a reformist legislation that had "raised juridical relations between individuals to the level of contemporary civilization," but also the most important step taken by the nation-state on the road leading to its complete monopoly of power over its citizens' legal affairs.[16] It is for these reasons that the enactment of the Civil Code cannot be considered as just "a step leading to the level of contemporary civilization," since this law provided the Kemalists also with the magic key that let them not just be in power, but also made them capable of exerting unlimited power over the citizens of the Turkish State.[17]

To get back to Lausanne, Dr. Rıza Nur represented the Ankara government in the sub-commission for minorities at the Lausanne conference. Şükrü Kaya, the Minister of the Interior, who would also happen to be responsible for the Exodus of Jews from Thrace in 1934, was an active member of this commission.[18] In these negotiations, during which all institutions of the Ottoman State were discussed, the question of minorities played a key role.

We can state that the negotiations about minorities during the Lausanne Conference in 1923 broadened the horizons of Turkification both emotionally and intellectually for the founders of the new Turkey, and that they led to what we might term the "groundwork" for what would later become the Settlement Law, and to 1934 pogroms in Thrace. Within this context, I think the following passage from the memoirs of Dr. Rıza Nur is particularly significant:

> According to the Europeans, we have three different types of minorities: racial minorities, linguistic minorities, and religious minorities. This is a very serious situation as far as we are concerned; a great danger! It is remarkable how well and how profoundly these men think, when they are contemplating against

---

[16] Niyazi Berkes occupies a prominent place among the scholars who have written about Turkish reforms; however, it is interesting to note that even though Berkes took up this matter in detail, he did not approach it from the point of view of the "struggle for power." See, Niyazi Berkes, *Türkiye'de çağdaşlaşma*, (Ankara: Bilgi Yayınevi, 1973), 470-471.

[17] The matter of state power was expressed in the following terms in the justifications for the enactment of the Civil Code: "To ensure that laws should be applicable to all of society in those states whose subjects are members of various religions, these laws should be severed completely from religion; this is a requirement of national sovereignty as well, because if laws are based on religion, a state that accepts freedom of conscience will have to enact different laws for different groups of subjects, and such a state of affairs is completely discordant with the political, social, and national unity required by contemporary states." Quoted in Bozkurt, *Batı hukukunun Türkiye'de benimsenmesi, 193.*

[18] For the activities of this commission, see *Lozan Barış Konferansı; Tutanaklar, Belgeler* [Lausanne. Conference on Near Eastern Affairs], Edited and translated by Seha Meray, vol. 1, part 2, (Ankara: Ankara Üniversitesi Basımevi, 1969), 151-288.

our interests... From a racial point of view, they will place the Circassians, the Abkhazians, the Bosnians, the Kurds, etc. together with the Greeks and the Armenians. From the linguistic point of view, they will make a minority of those who are Muslim but who speak other languages. From the religious point of view, they will make a minority of the two million Kızılbaş (Alevites), who are pure Turks. In other words, they intend to divide us into bits and pieces. I shuddered when I heard this project.... With all my strength, I sought to eliminate this terminology. I fought very hard to do so. Albeit with great difficulty, I succeeded. *The moral of the story*: The basic, most just, and most vital matter for us, is to ensure that no people of another race, language, or religion should remain in our country. It is for this reason that a long time ago I turned from Turkism to extreme Turkish Nationalism... It is for this reason that first priority should be given to disperse the Circassian, Albanian, etc. villages and to settle them together with Turks.[19]

Observations and generalizations of the sort seen in the quotation above, which are reminiscent of the "stream of consciousness" literary technique of Western literature, are not frequently encountered in the memoirs of the Kemalist elite. Due to his incurably fanatic character, Dr. Rıza Nur's memoirs are full of accusations against national heroes that could be defined at the very least as "unstable." Despite his tendency to exaggerate, we can safely claim that Dr. Rıza Nur's sentiments about minorities are sincere, especially once you read the memoirs' sections referring to Lausanne together with the official minutes of the conference.

Non-Muslim communities renounce the rights they gained at Lausanne

Turkish Civil Code (*Türk Medeni Kanunu*), which is actually a translation of the Swiss Civil Code, was approved by the Turkish Parliament in February 1926 and, following a transition period, came into force in October of the same year, together with the new Turkish Penal Code, which was adopted from Fascist Italy. However, other steps that paved the way towards the implementation of the Civil Code were finalized in the summer months of 1925, when the Civil Code was still being prepared.[20] Just before the Civil Code went into effect, the minority representatives—who thought that, thanks to Article 42 of the Lausanne Treaty, their rights had been guaranteed—were pressured by the

---

[19] Rıza Nur, *Hayat ve hatıratım*, vol. 3, (İstanbul: Altındağ Yayinevi, 1967), 83. Emphasis is mine A.A.
[20] Dispatch sent from Mr. R. H. Hoare in Istanbul to Sir Austen Chamberlain in London: FO 371: Foreign Office Correspondence / Document dated 9 August 1926, E 4663/35/44.

government and, as a result of said pressure, assembled their Community Councils and declared that they renounced all the rights bestowed upon them at Lausanne.[21]

The three commissions that had to be established, in accordance with Article 42 of the Lausanne Treaty, were formed in May 1925. The members of these Greek, Armenian, and Jewish commissions were appointed by the government. Following long discussions and intense pressure from government circles, the commission, which included Jewish members, announced on 10 September 1925 its decision to renounce all the rights given to the Jewish community in accordance with Article 42 of the Lausanne Treaty.[22] This was followed by a similar decision on the part of the Armenian community. The Greek community resisted for a while, but sub-committees that were supposed to "generate recommendations" were continuously being formed. At times, some members of the sub-committees were removed and replaced with more "moderate" members. Finally, the day before the sub-committee was going to vote, the members most adamantly opposed to renouncing the rights granted by Article 42 were arrested by the police. As a result of all this, on November 27, 1925, 55 of the 72 members of the sub-committee voted in favor of signing the document, whereby the Greeks, too, then renounced their minority rights. The main committee approved this decision.[23] Thus was the last vestige of Ottoman *ancient regime* abolished, and so, having been deprived of all the privileges they had derived from being part of minority religious and ethnic communities and which had been guaranteed by international treaties, non-Muslim citizens became Turks from a "legal standpoint."

The Turkification of capital and of the labor market

Another policy that began during the first decade of the Republic and

---

[21] Official English translation of Article 42 of Lausanne Treaty is as follows: "The Turkish Government undertakes to take, as regards non-Moslem minorities, in so far as concerns their family law or personal status, measures permitting the settlement of these questions in accordance with the customs of those minorities. These measures will be elaborated by special Commissions composed of representatives of the Turkish Government and of representatives of each of the minorities concerned in equal number. In case of divergence, the Turkish Government and the Council of the League of Nations will appoint in agreement an umpire chosen from amongst European lawyers. The Turkish Government undertakes to grant full protection to the churches, synagogues, cemeteries, and other religious establishments of the above-mentioned minorities. All facilities and authorization will be granted to the pious foundations, and to the religious and charitable institutions of the said minorities at present existing in Turkey, and the Turkish Government will not refuse, for the formation of new religious and charitable institutions, any of the necessary facilities which are guaranteed to other private institutions of that nature."

[22] For the text of the decision, whereby the Jewish community renounced the rights granted to it by Article 42 of the Treaty of Lausanne, see Abraham Galanté, *Türkler ve Yahudiler: tarihi, siyasi araştırma* (İstanbul: Gözlem Gazetecilik Basın ve Yayın, 1995), 70-74. Also, see Alexis Alexandris, *The Greek Minority of Istanbul and Greek-Turkish Relations, 1918-1974* (Athens: Center for Asia Minor Studies, 1983), 135-138.

[23] Alexandris, *The Greek Minority of Istanbul and Greek-Turkish Relations, 1918-1974, 138.*

that con- tinued during the following years was the policy of Turkification of capital and of the labor market, which we might term "economic nationalism," and which was carried out according to the principles laid out by Gökalp in his poem "*Vatan*," published in 1912. The main targets of this policy were foreign companies operating in Turkey, and the foreign or non-Muslim personnel employed in these companies.

The reports and letters written to their headquarters by representatives of the Great Powers, whose interests in Turkey had been damaged by this policy of Turkification, are full of details concerning the practical implementation of said policy. For example, in his report to the British Foreign Secretary Sir A. Chamberlain, the British Ambassador in Istanbul Sir R. Lindsay first presented a general assessment of the situation, and then stated: "Turkish nationalism does not differ in essentials from other forms of European nationalism." In this report, the British Ambassador explained the wave of nationalism in Turkey by saying: "It is, however, aggravated by isolation of Turkey in her distant capital at Ankara and by the novelty of the disease which runs a high fever in its early stages."

In this fascinating report, it is stated that "numerous orders and decisions by the police of municipal authorities, which are never put in writing, are being produced to force foreign firms of all kinds, whether shops, banks etc. to employ at least 75 per cent Moslem Turks on their staff." In the last part of the report, it is underlined that "when the port services were nationalized, foreigners and non-Moslem Turkish subjects were prevented from carrying on professions such as pilotage, diving and ship-chandling."

The following is another point that did not escape the attention of the British Ambassador:

> The Municipal authorities are trying to reserve all kinds of callings for Turks. For example, on the plea of revising chauffeurs' licences, they are holding back all licenses belonging to foreign and non-Muslim Turkish chauffeurs. Also foreign masters and engineers employed on vessels flying the Turkish flag have been notified that these callings are reserved for Moslem Turks.[24]

At the end of his report, the ambassador states that, as a result of the intense lack of trust towards non-Turkish groups, the Republican administration wanted to establish a state that was surrounded by some kind of a Chinese wall and belonged to them alone. The British Ambassador added that this lack of trust derived from the Great Powers'

---

[24] Dispatch sent from Sir R. C. Lindsay in Istanbul to Sir Austen Chaberlain in London: Document dated February 8, 1926, E1072/373/44.

policies towards Turkey during the previous century, and stressed the fact that the Republican administration had the intention of insulating themselves completely against eventual pressures from foreigners.[25]

In those same days, J. E. Kingsbury, who was the representative in London of the Istanbul Telephone Company founded with British capital, wrote a letter to the Foreign Office, in which he quoted from a letter written by the general manager of the company in Istanbul in which the latter complained about the policy of Turkification. This is what the general manager in Istanbul wrote:

> I'll have to sack Nicos, my chauffeur who has been with me since 1912. The Prefecture won't license him to work as a chauffeur. They are driving out all non-Muslims from being waiters, including dozens of Russian refugee girls who, at present, are earning an honest living.[26]

Kingsbury states that there had not been as yet any pressure concerning the few British specialists working in the company, but that they were facing great difficulties finding qualified personnel to employ in place of the non-Muslims who had been dismissed.

Similar complaints came also from the company running the Izmir-Aydın railway. Mr. Shewan, the general manager in Izmir, said that "there is a very strong feeling [in Ankara] that all the railways ought to be in the hands of the state," a view reinforced by the example of the Turkish-run Anatolian Railways. He added that "the successful management of the Anatolian Railway is popularly quoted in proof of the ability of the Turks to hold their own against foreigners in all railway affairs, not knowing or ignoring the fact that it has been worked at a loss, the state paying the deficit."[27] One of the subjects discussed during the meeting about the Izmir-Aydın Railway Company on March 18, 1926, is particularly interesting. In the minutes summarizing the complaints made by company managers to the Foreign Office, it was stated that following the nationalization of the Izmir Port Authority, the railway company was denied the right to use the jetty, wharf, and cranes that it owned, because its workers in the port were foreign, and thus considered to be potential spies, and that for this reason alone, the authorities were demanding that they be dismissed.[28]

A questionnaire sent by the Statistics Department of the Turkish

---

[25] Ibid.
[26] From J. E. Kingsbury in Istanbul to the Under Secretary of State in London, dated February 18, 1926, E1186/373/44.
[27] Letter from General Manager T. M. Shewan in Smyrna to the London Manager and Sectary of the Ottoman Railway from Smyrna to Aidin, dated March 2, 1926, FO 371:E1470/373/44.
[28] Ibid.

Ministry of Commerce to the representatives of all insurance companies around two months later contained detailed questions concerning the companies' capital structure, the foreign countries in which their headquarters were located, and the share- holding structures of the companies that they represented or were a subsidiary of. However, the second part of the questionnaire aimed to collect information that would be especially valuable for the purposes of Turkification policies. In this part, the companies were asked to provide not only detailed lists of the salary levels of their employees, but also the distribution of the employees with- in each group in terms of the categories "Muslim Turk," "non-Muslim Turk," and "Foreigner." In his report to London, the British Ambassador Lindsay said that "the document is interesting as a proof of the distinction drawn by the Turkish Government between Moslem and non-Moslem Turkish subjects: a distinction which the Government has always maintained does not exist."[29]

When the Wealth Tax (*Varlık Vergisi*), which was an "anti-minority" tax, was introduced during World War II, about seventeen years later, similar categories were used to classify taxpayers. In the summer of 1942, Faik Ökte, the head of Financial Revenue Office in Istanbul, received a secret order from Ankara, recommending him to begin preparations for the collection of a once-for-all tax. Mr. Ökte decided to put together names of the businessmen accumulating extraordinary profits due to war conditions by classifying them according to ethnic and religious background.[30]

Another law enacted on April 10, 1926, by the Turkish Parliament made it obligatory for all companies to "use Turkish in all operations, contracts, correspondence, accounts, and book-keeping conducted within Turkey."[31] As for foreign companies, they were obliged to use Turkish in their contacts with Turkish citizens and in their official books. Actually, this law was the re-make of a very similar law passed by the Union and Progress government during World War I.[32] However, contrary to the previous law, which could not really be enforced during wartime and the armistice, its Republican version was implemented with utmost strictness. The true aim of both laws was not to ensure that foreigners working in Turkey should learn Turkish, but to pressure foreign countries into

---

[29] Dispatch sent from Sir R. C. Lindsay in Istanbul to Sir Austen Chamberlain in London: FO 371: Document dated March 3, 1926, E2778/373/44.

[30] In his memoirs, Faik Ökte explains the process as follows: "Lists were firs divided into M and G. The group M represented Muslim tax payers and G represented non-Muslim minorities. Later the D added to these for Crypto-Jews [migrated from Salonica] and E added for foreigners." See, Faik Ökte, *Varlık vergisi faciası*, (İstanbul: Nebioğlu Yayınevi, 1951), 48.

[31] Law No. 805 on the "Obligatory Utilization of Turkish Language in all Economic Enterprises," dated April 22, 1926. For the text, see *Düstur* - III. Tertip, vol. 7, 219.

[32] Zafer Toprak, *Milli iktisat, milli burjuvazi*, (İstanbul: Tarih Vakfı Yurt Yayınları, 1995), 60.

employing Muslim Turks.

These attitudes, which were the tangible manifestation of economic nationalism aimed specifically at the markets themselves, might at first glance be regarded as a "left-leaning, anti-imperialist reaction." If, in the early Republican era, steps had been taken to nationalize the companies owned by foreigners, by altering their ownership structures, then it might have been possible to perceive the entirety of events that we have been summarizing as the implementation of an anti-imperialist economic policy in favor of national independence. However, the Turkification policies that were implemented in the 1920s were directed not only against foreign capital, but against foreign or non-Muslim employees as well. Consequently, the matter went beyond the ownership structure of the companies. What the Republican/Kemalist elite sought was the elimination of "those who are not one of us"—even if the person in question was a simple worker! It is for these reasons that Turkification policies manifested themselves as a set of discriminatory policies.

Employment in the public sector: the last Ottomans and the single party regime

Beginning from the second half of the nineteenth century, the Ottoman bureaucracy underwent a great transformation with regard to the ethnic and religious characteristics of its employees. At that time, non-Muslims educated in modern schools established throughout the empire began to find more and more employment opportunities in the Ottoman bureaucracy, both central and provincial. For example, if we look at the numbers provided by Carter Findley on the basis of the employment records for the Ottoman Foreign Ministry for the years 1850–1908, we see that in that period, minorities comprised around one third (29%) of all career officials.[33] Despite the unfavorable effects of the nationalist and secessionist movements amongst the minorities in the late Ottoman Empire, it is quite clear that equal opportunity in terms of state employment was achieved within the Ottoman Foreign Ministry.

Likewise, even during the 33-year reign (1876–1909) of Sultan Abdülhamid II, who skillfully employed Islamic and Turkish symbols as part of his project to promote "Imperial Ottoman Nationalism," the Sultan in no way took measures to keep minorities from being employed or subsequently rising within the ranks of the Ottoman bureaucracy.[34] In his study on the employment of non-Muslims in the Ottoman bureaucracy

---

[33] Carter Findley, 'The acid test of Ottomanism: The Acceptance of Non-Muslims in the late Ottoman Bureaucracy' in Bernard Lewis and Benjamin Braude, *Christians and Jews in the Ottoman Empire*, vol. 1, 343,
[34] Selim Deringil, *Simgeden millete: II. Abdülhamid'den Mustafa Kemal'e devlet ve millet*, (İstanbul: İletişim, 2007), 53-93.

during the reign of Sultan Abdülhamid II, İlber Ortaylı states that the fact that non-Muslims were being appointed to and employed in the Ottoman bureaucracy "could not really be ascribed to the pressure exerted by foreign Christian states." Ortaylı also adds:

> [T]he state had begun to become more cosmopolitan from the eighteenth century onwards, and young non-Muslim men, especially those educated in the secular schools of the nineteenth century, entered state service and were appointed to various positions just like their Muslim counterparts. Thanks to this new development, an old standard of the traditional bureaucracy was done away with in the period of the *Tanzimat* reforms."[35]

As for the single party period (1923–1946), the employment of non-Muslims in public service was first stopped *de facto*, and then *de jure* by means of the enactment of a specific law. In Article 4 of the Law on State Employees, dated March 18, 1926, (Law No. 788), it was stated: "The following requirements are necessary to become a state employee." The first requirement in clause "a" was that one "must be a Turk."[36] This law, which spelled out the requirements for becoming a state employee by making direct reference to Turkish ethnic identity, rather than simply stating that one "must be a citizen of the Republic of Turkey," remained in force until 1965.[37] The Law on State Employees during the single party period gave only ethnic Turks or Laz, Bosnian, Circassian, Kurdish, etc. citizens who could be Turkified (i.e., ethnically non-Turkish Muslims) the right to work in the public service, thus simultaneously encouraging a significant portion of the population to become Turks, and constituting a typical example of the "discriminatory" policies against non-Muslims. This law thus barred non-Muslim citizens of Turkey - i.e., those who, because of their ethnic identities, could in no way be considered or "become ethnic Turks" - from state employment, regardless of their education or qualifications.[38]

---

[35] İlber Ortaylı, 'II. Abdülhamit Devrinde Taşra Bürokrasisinde Gayrimüslimler' *Sultan II. Abdülhamid ve Devri Semineri: 27-29 Mayıs 1992 : Bildiriler* (İstanbul: Edebiyat Fakültesi Basımevi, 1994), 168.

[36] For the complete text of the Law on State Employees, see *Düstur - III. Tertip*, Vol. 7, 667.

[37] Article 48 of the Law on State Employees number 657, which was enacted on July 14, 1965, and is still in force, has finally been amended, so that the requisite for being a state employee has been changed to that of "being a Turkish citizen." See *Düstur - V. Tertip*. Vol. 4, Book 3, 3053.

[38] During a public debate believed to have been held in the 1980s, Dr. Hagop Sivaslıyan, a journalist of Armenian origin, responded to a university teacher who had told him, "Armenians are not second class citizens, there is no distinction between Turks and Armenians. Armenians are free to work in any kind of business environment, and non-Muslims benefit from all rights enjoyed by Turks," as follows: "The fact that during Ottoman times Armenians could become pashas or administrators is frequently mentioned. Okay, so the Armenians of Ottoman times were very bright and capable, but what about the Armenians of Republican times? Are they all stupid? Why isn't the same still happening? ... I am ... a journalist, I have studied medicine, but I have never practiced this profession, I am nevertheless employed... I don't want anything to do with commerce. I want to be a *Nahiye Müdürü* (appointed governor of a small county).

"Certain professions" are reserved for Turkish citizens

Another law of particular importance for the Turkification process is the "Law Reserving Certain Professions, Trades, and Services to Turkish Citizens." Enacted by Turkish Parliament on 4 June 1932 (Law No. 2007), this law banned non- Muslims from practicing certain professions outside the public sector. In his speech during the presentation to parliament of this law (the full text of which is provided in the appendix), Interior Minister Şükrü Kaya had the following to say:

> This law, or in other words, the law that prohibits foreigners from practicing certain crafts, is a law that all independent nations have been implementing for a long time. In international law, this is called *régime d'étrangers*, that is, the procedures and rules that apply to foreigners. It has long been our wish to pass this law; however, the capitulations, which have always hindered the development and future of our country, made us incapable of realizing this wish, until now. When the capitulations were unilaterally abolished during World War I, some crafts were reserved exclusively for Turks. We gained the greatest of such rights at Lausanne. At Lausanne, we reserved the practice of certain crafts and professions for the citizens. However, there were still a few steps that needed to be taken, and now, we have perfected and completed those last few steps with this law. The following are the principles upon which this law is based. Professions related to public security, professions related to public service, and some economic and social statuses and conditions... Some professions related to public security had already been reserved for the citizens by means of laws regulating professional classes, like the Law on Practicing Medicine and the Law on Practicing Pharmaceutical Professions, while some were regulated by means of the Law on Maritime Shipping (*Kabotaj*). Now all that remains are professional classes like chauffeurs and janitors. We are filling in this gap now by means of this law, where- by we reserve these professions for the citizens.

> Secondly, there are those jobs related to public service, such as that performed by porters. We are reserving those, too, for the citizens. I mean jobs like street vendors (*ayak satıcılığı ve bohçacılık*).

> Thirdly are the social and economic positions, and these, too, we have reserved for the citizens. This also is an economic necessity.

That's my hobby! And I believe that I would be the best governor in Turkey, no matter how many governors of small counties there are in Turkey. But I am not allowed to become a governor. And if I am not allowed to become a governor, it means there is a problem." See, Şengün Kılıç, *Biz ve onlar: Türkiye'de etnik ayrımcılık : araştırma-röportaj*, (İstanbul: Metis Yayınları, 1992), 65.

These are arts, crafts, and professions that require limited capital and limited skill. Being a street vendor is the best example of this. Whenever a citizen is in need, he should be able to take his handkerchief out of his pocket and sell it in the market in order to put food on his table at home. If he has to compete with people from other nations, our citizen would be deprived of this right.[39]

The Interior Minister's speech clearly demonstrates the *raison d'être* of many laws, insofar as they serve to further the policy of Turkification, enacted during the second half of the 1920s, not all of which we have been able to analyze in this article. In particular, the fact that even chauffeurs and janitors were considered important for public security is very enlightening in that it shows the extremely broad definition of public security adopted by legislators.

Children's Day celebrations in the 1930s

It is not difficult to imagine who Minister Şükrü Kaya was referring to in the last paragraph of his speech, when he mentioned the categories of "foreigners" and "people from other nations." Before the signing of the Lausanne Treaty, the "Treaty Concerning the Exchange of Greek and Turkish People" was signed on January 30, 1923, according to which the Greeks of Istanbul were exempted from the population exchange and given the right to live and work in Istanbul without becoming Turkish citizens, on the basis of the status of *établis* [settled]. According to the 1927 population census, there were 26,431 Greek citizens in Istanbul.

---

[39] *TBMM - Zabıt Ceridesi,* [Turkish Grand National Assembly - Record of Minutes]. Devre 4, cilt 9. (Ankara: TBMM Matbaası), 65.

Consequently, the targets of Law No. 2007 were first of all the Greek citizens in Istanbul, but also minorities like the White Russians, who had refugee status.

According to Article 5 of this law, "foreigners must resign from their jobs within six months following the publication of this law in the Official Gazette." Later this transition period was extended to a year and then, with a final amendment on May 31, 1933, to two years, but the decision concerning "which of the jobs indicated in this law would be forbidden at what date" was left to the cabinet Let us see what happened in the summer of 1934, when the transition period established by this law ended.

The Istanbul Greeks who lost their jobs migrated to Athens

A few days before the 1934 pogrom concerning the Jews of Thrace, or to be more exact, on June 28, 1934, the US Ambassador Robert P. Skinner invited the Greek Consul in Istanbul to lunch. During lunch, the Greek Consul mentioned the fact that, because of the end of the transition of the above-mentioned law, around 15,000 Istanbul Greeks would lose their jobs. As a result of the decisions made by the cabinet in May 1934, this minority group, comprised primarily of professionals, small merchants, and craftsmen, found itself unemployed and was therefore getting ready to migrate to Greece.[40]

In the summer months of 1934, around 2,000 Istanbul Greeks with Greek passports began to emigrate from Istanbul. According to the 1935 census, the number of Greek citizens living in Istanbul had decreased to 17,642. This meant that, in comparison to the 1927 census, the number of Istanbul Greeks with Greek passports had decreased by around 9,000.[41] As for the White Russians, who at the time numbered around 2,000, they were able to hold on to their jobs thanks to the fact that the US Ambassador made a special plea to Foreign Minister Tevfik Rüştü Aras, and requested also for the intervention of the League of Nations in Geneva.[42]

Faced with this situation, the Greek government was at a loss as to what to do. It was useless to give land to the Istanbul Greeks, who were immigrating to Greece, and to ask them to become farmers, because these people did not have a rural background. As for the bigger cities of Greece, they were already full of urban Greeks who had arrived from Anatolia

[40] Dispatch sent from Robert P. Skinner in Istanbul to the Secretary of State in Washington, dated June 30, 1934, 867. 504/11. The Records of the Department of State relating to Internal Affairs of Turkey, 1930–1944.
[41] Alexandrēs, *The Greek Minority of Istanbul and Greek-Turkish Relations, 1918-1974*, 185.
[42] From Chargé d'Affaires G. Howland Shaw in Istanbul to the Secretary of State in Washington, dated September 18, 1934, 867. 504/19.

about ten years earlier, as part of the population exchange. On July 24, 1934, the US Ambassador in Athens notified Washington of the Greek press's highly critical coverage of the Turkish government's expulsion of Greek natives of Istanbul, stating: "Greek friendship must mean something, after all, to a nation like Turkey which stands such a fear of the growth of Italian power in the Aegean."[43] Despite the rapprochement between Turkey and Greece in those days, the Turkish administration did not budge; the Turkification policy was continuing.

"Citizen, speak Turkish!" – The situation in 1937 from the point of view of the minorities

Lastly, we shall analyze a debate that began with the "Citizen, speak Turkish!" campaigns, which comprise the most important aspect of the Turkification policies.[44] Following the "prohibition of speaking in languages other than Turkish within city limits" implemented by certain municipalities in 1937, the Chief Editor of *Tan* newspaper, Ahmet Emin Yalman, wrote an article on this subject, and Marsel Franko, President of the Lay Council of the Chief Rabbinate and of the Jewish Community, responded with an open letter; you can find both articles in the appendices. This debate gives insight into the conditions in which non-Muslims, who were perceived as "others" within the Kemalists' conception of nationalism, found themselves in 1937, and the sensitivities of their community leaders.

Since the "Citizen, speak Turkish!" campaigns of the single party period could be the subject of a separate article, I do not want to analyze them in detail here. As you can see from Yalman's article, the people to whom this campaign was addressed were not just the non-Muslim minorities. Yalman advises also the Muslim migrants from Balkan countries settled in Turkey that it would be best to drop their habit of speaking other languages in public "for the sake of the political and social union and harmony" of the country. Yalman also states that not too much pressure should be put on non-Muslim minorities who insists on speaking in their

---

[43] From Ambassador Lincoln Mac Veagh in Athens to the Secretary of State in Washington, dated July 24, 1934, 867. 504/13.

[44] These campaigns began during the single party period, and were repeated on various occasions up through the mid-1960s. As a result of government pressure, minorities strove to adapt and formulated a theoretical framework for the campaigns that they carried out to this end. For example, in his work titled *Türkleştirme* (Turkification), originally published in 1928, Moiz Kohen Tekinalp, a Jewish intellectual who had worked closely with Ziya Gökalp, summarized in "ten commandments" what the Jews had to do to ensure that the Jews of Turkey should be included in the "collective conscience" that was the basis of Turkish national union: "1. Use Turkish names; 2. Speak Turkish; 3. Say at least some of their prayers in the synagogues in Turkish; 4. Turkify their schools; 5. Send their children to national schools; 6. Get involved in the affairs of Turkey; 7. Establish close contacts with Turks; 8. Eradicate community spirit; 9. Do their duty in the field of national economics; 10. Know their rights." See, Jacob M. Landau, *Tekinalp, Turkish Patriot, 1883-1961*, ([Leiden]: Nederlands Historisch-Archaeologisch Instituut te İstanbul, 1984), 289.

own mother tongues, and that the best approach to such people is simply to tell them, "as you please," and show them to the door. Although it may appear as if the subject of Yalman's article is the use of Turkish in public places, what was actually being debated was the problem of the integration of non-Muslim minorities, and in particular the Jews, into Turkish society.

As for Marsel Franko's open letter, it addresses the problem directly and dis- cusses the ways by which the 80,000 Jews of Turkey might adapt to Turkish culture. After stating that many Jews considered it degrading to even discuss their loyalty to the nation, Franko, head of the Jewish community, stresses the fact that it is the right of these people to expect "to be promoted from part- time citizenship, visitor status, and mere Civil Code Turkishness, to full moral citizenship, as a normal result of the [Republican] regime." In addition to this, Franko writes that Jewish youth were not being admitted to national youth organizations, and goes on to list the Jewish community's expectations of the state, and remind the readers that they wished for the "discriminatory" policies to come to an end and expected "clear signs and guidance" from statesmen on the subject of integration.[45] Reading between the lines, we can discern that Franko meant to say that Jews were ready to join the Turkish national community, but at the same time, he had complaints regarding discriminatory policies, which he referred to as relegating minority populations to "part-time citizenship, visitor status, and mere Civil Code Turkishness."

In lieu of a conclusion

I stated at the beginning of this article that Turkification policies were at the same time a set of discriminatory, "anti-minority" policies. The Kemalist conception of nationalism that defined the criteria of membership in the Turkish national community or in the Turkish nation as "being part of the Turkish ethnic group" was very different both from the "Ottoman Nationalism" of the reign of Sultan Abdülhamid II, and from the conception of "cultural nationalism" formulated by Ziya Gökalp. These differences become blatantly obvious in expressions of Kemalist nationalism, particularly in official publications and in the Kemalists' speeches and statements. In his pioneering study on the official ide- ology of the single party period, Taha Parla reveals the two faces of Kemalist

---

[45] Turkification policies were also valid for youth organizations. Article 1 of the "Law Concerning Turkey's Youth Organizations Being Exclusive to Turkish Citizens" (Law No. 1246, enacted on May 12, 1928) imposed a limitation by stating that "the right to establish youth organizations as rangers, explorers, boy scouts, or with any other name or title, within the borders of the Republic of Turkey, in schools or outside schools, is exclusive to Turkish citizens." Law No: 1246, adopted on May 12, 1928 by the Turkish Parliament.

nationalism. The first is a defensive, egalitarian, ethnically pluralistic, and cultural conception of nationalism. The other is a conception of nationalism that is implemented especially against non-Muslim minorities, foregrounding the Turks as an "ethnically dominant-monopolistic-exclusionary" majority. Parla argues that minorities became the target of the second conception of nationalism and "in the Republic of Turkey, they have been perceived as people with 'condition- al citizenship' and 'limited rights,' who have been 'relegated to the fringes of society' as people who 'do not belong to us after all'"[46] You will notice that the situation described by Parla as "being relegated to the fringes of society" was described by Marsel Franko as "part-time citizenship, visitor status, and mere Civil Code Turkishness." Franko's wish was for this situation to be remedied by means of positive steps to be taken by the central authorities. As far as we know, such steps were never taken. Quite to the contrary, by means of laws like the Wealth Tax Law, which was passed during World War II, the position of non-Muslim minorities as "part-time citizenship, visitor status, and mere Civil Code Turkishness" has been further reinforced.[47]

In this article, I preferred not to enter into a detailed analysis of Turkish nationalist ideology and its transformation, as I have done elsewhere. Instead, I tried to elaborate actual practices in the early years of the Republic, especially by describing discriminatory policies directed towards non-Muslim minorities.[48] Considered within this framework, what I have done here is analyze the 1934 pogrom against the Jews of

---

[46] Parla, *The Social and Political Thought of Ziya Gökalp, 1876-1924,* 209.

[47] An interview in *The London Times* with then - Prime Minister Şükrü Saracoğlu, dated January 16, 1943, at a time when the collection of the Wealth Tax was still ongoing, is particularly enlightening in this respect. As he explains the reasons for the Wealth Tax, Saracoğlu provides clues about his own perception of minorities: Many things have been said about the Wealth Tax that has been introduced by the Turkish government in order to satisfy urgent financial and economic needs. This law is not just legitimate and appropriate, but it is nearly certain that other countries, too, will introduce a similar tax before the end of the war. Turkish peasants have had to bear the burden all by themselves for centuries. The Turkish nation in its entirety has responded gallantly and willingly to the measures requiring sacrifices that the government has introduced to be able to face the exceptional circumstances caused by the war. Only some people and merchants have shut their ears to the pleas of the government, and have abused the freedom and trust afforded them by the new government when it was formed last year. It was as a result of this that the need to introduce this law appeared. It has to be admitted that certain aspects of this law are onerous. However, those who prove their good faith and they are good citizens will be facilitated, and material mistakes will be corrected. This law will be applied with all its force against those who, *even though they got rich thanks to the hospitality shown them by this country* have refrained from carrying out their duty towards it in this precarious moment. For the Turkish version of this interview, see *Ayın Tarihi,* no. 110, (March, 1943): 38. (Emphasis is mine!).

[48] At this point, I would like to underline Taha Parla's method of analysis in order to understand corporatism in general. Parla argues the following: "Corporatism as a model and philosophy of society, then, may be expressed in the form of a well-formulated, programmatic political ideology, or it may remain as a loose worldview. At another level, or dimension, corporatism is a system of actual practices and policies that are the result of, or in conformity with, such a world- view or ideology. At a third level or dimension, corporatism, beyond the *de facto* manifestations of the second level, unfolds in *de jure* manner as tangible political institutions and legal structures." Parla, *The Social and Political Thought of Ziya Gökalp, 1876-1924,* 46.

Thrace, which was the subject of my previous article, as well as some discriminatory practices and their ideological reflections. However, in this article, as I was examining Turkification policies, I furthermore tried to analyze both some actual circumstances and the process by which those circumstances were transformed into legislation, by focusing on some key laws of the period. In this way, I traced the process whereby what was *de facto* later became *de jure*, and thus gave rise to tangible political institutions. It seemed to me that the most effective way of understanding the creation of a national state, the resulting power structure, and the dominant conception of nationalism, was to follow the shadow of the state over the minorities. In a way, what I did was try to understand some structural characteristics of the main formation by subjecting that shadow to a detailed analysis.

Appendix I:

Law No. 2007 on "Restricting Certain Professions and Trades to Turkish Citizens Only"[49]

Article 1 – Within the borders of the Republic of Turkey, the following crafts and services are to be carried out exclusively by Turkish citizens. Non-Turkish citizens are forbidden from carrying out these crafts and services.

A. Street vendors; musicians; photographers; barbers; typographers; dealers [middlemen]; clothing, cap, and shoe manufacturers; brokers in stock markets; sellers of state monopoly goods; interpreters and guides for tourists and travelers; construction workers, and iron and wood industry workers, permanent or temporary workers in public transport or utilities like water, electricity, heating, and communication; loading and unloading of land transport vehicles; chauffeurs and their assistants; all kinds of manual workers; concierge, janitors, and porters in all kinds of institutions like merchant houses, apartment buildings, offices, hotels and companies; female or male servants, waiters, and waitresses in hotels, offices, public baths, coffeehouses, night-clubs, dance halls, and bars; bar entertainers and singers.

B. Veterinary doctors and chemists.

Article 2 – Unless authorized with a special license by the Council of Ministers, the following professions cannot be carried out by foreigners:

A. Aircraft machinists and pilots.

B. Institutions owned by the state or by provincial governments, or municipalities and facilities owned by municipalities.

Article 3 – If the need arises, the Council of Ministers may prohibit foreign citizens from performing crafts and services that have not been reserved for Turkish citizens by this law.

Article 4 – The janitors and doorkeepers of the embassies and consulates of foreign countries in the Republic of Turkey, and the workers who are citizens of their own or of another foreign country and who drive the vehicles under their orders.

Article 5 – Foreigners, who on the date of publication of this law are carrying out crafts and services that have been reserved for Turkish citizens, are obliged to leave their jobs within *one year* after the date of

---

[49] Law No. 2007, dated June 11, 1932. For the full text of the law, see *Düstur - III. Tertip*, Vol. 13, 519–, March 4, 1937.

publication of this law.

Article 6 – Foreigners who continue to carry out crafts and services that

have been reserved for Turkish citizens after the end of the term indicated in Article 5, will be prevented from carrying out these crafts and services by the orders of the highest local authority, and together with an official record indicating this breach of the law, they will appear before a court of first instance, where they will be condemned to pay a penal fine ranging from ten to five hundred liras.

Article 7 – The citizens of countries that impose administrative or legal limits upon Turkish citizens may be prohibited from carrying out the crafts and services that previously permitted to them in Turkey, by a decision issued by the Council of Ministers.

Article 8 – Foreigners are forbidden from opening shops in the villages.

Article 9 – This law will be valid from the moment of publication.

Article 10 – The Council of Ministers is responsible for the implementation of the requisites of this law.

Appendix II:

Turkish in Public [50]

Ahmet Emin Yalman

Municipalities in various parts of the country have prohibited the public usage of languages other than Turkish. There have been rumors in newspapers to the effect that this measure would be taken in Istanbul as well; however, this has not turned out to be the case.

We have to admit that the situation in Istanbul is unlike that of any other place in Turkey. Even though ensuring that no other language but Turkish be spoken in public is not the job of municipalities, in various parts of the country municipalities have taken this matter upon themselves in response to general public sentiment. However, the situation in Istanbul is a matter of state policy, and cannot be achieved by the municipality alone.

Voices across the country object to the fact that citizens who have immigrated from abroad continue to speak languages such as Greek,

---

[50] *Tan*, daily 4 March 1937.

Bosnian, Albanian, and Circassian, as was their habit in their former countries. For the sake of the political and social union and harmony of the nation, it is absolutely necessary that we should engage in a determined struggle to combat these habits. An ugly mosaic-like situation is encountered in many parts of the country. We find that in the villages of people who have immigrated to Turkey half a century ago, a language other than Turkish continues to function as the mother tongue. Rather than being the result of a lack of national sentiments among the people concerned, this is due to the neglect and lack of interest of the former government and of society. In revolutionary Turkey, which adheres to a coherent national policy in every sphere, it is imperative that this mosaic-like situation be eliminated as soon as possible.

The unique status of Istanbul

As for Istanbul, here conditions are not suitable for such a prohibition. One must consider all facets of the issue and seek out solutions for all the different manifestations of the problem at hand.

A certain degree of homogeneity throughout the country has been achieved by means of the population exchange. Only Istanbul was exempt from this practice. Istanbul is at the same time a major economic center. In such a major business hub, there should be no excess or any factors that might disturb or upset the general atmosphere.

In Istanbul there are citizens whose mother tongue is not Turkish. The younger generations of these citizens are learning Turkish at school. Among the older generations, there are not a few who do not know Turkish, or who know only very little. What will happen if such people speak a language other than Turkish, as they inevitably will? Most certainly, some citizens will caution them not to do so. When people feel justified in taking the enforcement of law and order into their own hands, some are certain to act in excess. In our country, this has never happened, for positive and comprehensive measures have always been taken to solve problems.

White and black sheep

Being a Turkish citizen is the greatest attribute in the world. We do not need people who do not appreciate the privilege of being part of this nation while enjoying the status of Turkish citizenship and who do not strive to make amends for the unforgotten events of the armistice period and regain the genuine trust of the Turkish nation. Why should we encourage the hypocrisy of those who are not compelled by their own desire, love, and interests to follow this path? There are those who make their lack of appreciation for their Turkish citizenship blatantly clear by means of their language and actions, and who have no desire to adapt to the public life of the country; let those people reveal themselves for what they are and expel themselves from the system as alien bodies. We need to find a way to distinguish the black sheep from the white. If the aim is to homogenize those groups who do not meet national standards, then pressure and excess are the worst, least productive means to this end. The best thing to do is to keep the door open and to declare: "as you please..." However, this should be done on condition of not placing those individual citizens who show that they really consider themselves Turkish and part of Turkish life, and who prove that they are trying to be useful to their nation, in the position of black sheep. As individuals, we know such Jewish, Greek, and Armenian citizens, who really consider themselves Turkish, but who, despite this, suffer because their nation does not fully accept them.

The condition of the Jews

The language problem is different for different groups. Jews are in the most precarious state of all. There is no country in the world in which the Jews who have settled there have failed to adopt that country's language as their mother tongue. Strangely enough, Turkey is the sole exception to this rule: Turkey, which for centuries has treated the Jews warmly as friends, and which has always acted to thwart potential extremist actions against them... In this case, the fact that the Jews should consider Spanish [Ladino] or French their mother tongue, and that they should use these languages in public, is nothing but a blatant declaration of the alienation that they have forced upon themselves. Plenty of Jewish citizens have genuinely comprehended this and struggle to correct this unfortunate state of affairs. Jews who prefer to speak Spanish or French in public, even though they speak perfect Turkish, should not be surprised that this attitude is perceived as contempt towards others and that it should elicit a feeling of bitterness.

Armenians and Greeks

For the Armenians, it is a matter of deciding on an individual basis whether or not they wish to fully adopt Turkish citizenship in accordance with their own wishes and interests. There is absolutely no need to encourage hypocrisy by introducing a prohibition upon the language.

For the Greeks, however, the situation is different. The exemption of the Greeks in Istanbul and of the Turks in Western Thrace from the population exchange was a reciprocal act. The new close friendship between Turkey and Greece has further increased the significance of this exemption. The friendship between the two countries should be treasured, and everybody should avoid extreme acts that might threaten it.

It is not just that the Turks speak Turkish in Western Thrace. On my way back from Athens, I met a railroad inspector on the train. He spoke perfect Turkish. I thought that he must have migrated to Greece as part of the popu- lation exchange, and so I asked him where he was from. He said something that sounded like Sivas; thereupon I started talking about Sivas. The poor man laughed and corrected my mistake:

- No, I was born in the old Greece. I have been here for three years. The people speak Turkish. So I thought that it would be a good idea to learn the language of the people. Learning a new language is not a loss but it is a gain. Especially now that we are talking about a Turco-Greek union...

Responding in kind to the friendly and magnanimous attitude displayed by Greece would be a just and natural act.

Cosmopolitan Turks

As we see it, those who deserve the greatest censure as far as the question of language is concerned are those Turks who speak a language other than their own just to show off. Any Turk who, rather than rebuffing the salesperson in a Beyoğlu shop for addressing him in a language other than Turkish, answers in the same language, should be held responsible for committing a crime against Turkishness. The same is true for any Turk who, when a foreigner addresses him in fluent or broken Turkish, tries to respond in the foreigner's own tongue rather than replying in Turkish. Nowadays, all foreigners who live in our country would like to learn Turkish. They complain that by talking to them in a foreign language Turks deny them this opportunity.

Three reasonable measures

1. In conclusion, we are of the opinion that it would be appropriate to take the following three steps to solve Istanbul's language problem:

2. Increase the number of free Turkish language courses.

3. Encourage and congratulate members of non-Turkish communities who have learned and are speaking Turkish; emphasize the fact that those who do not do so will be looked down upon; however, avoid prohibitions that might lead to extreme acts or individual interventions in public places.

4. Be generous in helping those immigrant Turks who consider a language other than Turkish to be their mother tongue, and be very strict towards those people with a cosmopolitan spirit who belittle and neglect their own language...

Appendix III

Open Letter from Marsel [Franko][51]

[Following our lead editorial about the language issue the day before yester- day, we have received a very clear, well-written, and important letter signed "Marsel [Franko], President of the Lay Council of the Chief Rabbinate and of the Jewish Community." You shall read in these columns this letter in its entirety, a significant document in and of itself.]

Sir, yesterday, in your article, you subjected the matter of generalizing Turkish culture to such a sophisticated and realistic analysis that there is neither a single word to be added to what you wrote, nor the faintest light to be added to the light you emanated. I thank you in the name of common sense.

However, now that the illness has been so masterfully diagnosed, it falls upon every literate citizen to seek out a cure to the problem you have identified.

The fact that the language issue is one facet of the problem of integration is a reality accepted by all who examine the Jewish matter closely and objectively. What really matters is not just speaking Turkish, but thinking and feeling like a Turk. Though aware of the public reaction that this might elicit, I would like with your permission to pose a few questions and attempt to provide answers regarding this issue of primary importance for our community. In these questions and answers, I address the matter of the time, the means, and the conditions required for the integration into Turkish culture of the 80,000 Jews in Turkey.

Is integration possible?

It is. It would be ridiculous to seek obstacles. Some Jews who had migrated to Turkey later settled in England and Holland. These have integrated so well with the local populations that they can no longer be distinguished from the natives. There are a handful of Jews who have lived amongst the Turks in our eastern provinces for centuries, and whose faces even have become indistinguishable from those of the Turks. These Jews have solved the problem of integration in practice.

---

[51] *Tan*, daily 6 March 1937.

Actually, Jews are creatures who possess the capacity to adapt to their respective environments.

There are no spiritual or moral obstacles to integration either. Jews have always lived comfortably in this country. Not only have they been permitted to live comfortably, they have never asked for political privileges or sought to set themselves apart. There are no painful or blood-soaked memories of ancient political feuds inherited from history that could inhibit relations between the Jewish community and the main group of this country. The path to integration is smooth and clear; there are no obstacles in sight.

Is integration desirable?

The leaders of this country have made clear by means of their actions that there is no place for "state anti-Semitism" among the principles of the regime, and that all those who adopt Turkish culture can become members of the Turkish community. These are the words of our statesmen, who have conquered the hearts of world public opinion with their dignity, sincerity, and earnestness, and have rendered baseless even the slightest of doubts. Clearly, integration befits the doctrines and policies of this state.

Need I show that integration also serves the nation's best interests? Clearly, this lack of harmony undermines national unity and must be eliminated.

It is both logical and natural that 80,000 Turks, who have been living in this country for centuries, should be integrated into the national community.

Is integration desirable for the Jews?

Some people claim that the Jews' desire for integration is actually driven by ulterior motives. However, those familiar with history will know that the Jew is a creature who lives and is willing to die for what we call faith and ideals.

There are more of us than you can imagine who find it demeaning to have their loyalty to the nation made a matter of debate and who are deeply hurt by claims of disloyalty. These citizens, who silently suffer from a feeling of spiritual and emotional exile, are justified in their wish to be promoted from part- time citizenship, visitor status, and mere Civil Code Turkishness, to full moral citizenship, as a normal result of the regime.

Has the time for integration come?

It has come, and it is about to pass, for various reasons. One of these reasons is absolute: It is the mingling of youth, in schools, in barracks, and in sports. The generation that would take over the administration of the government in the future is being brought up and educated in isolation from the Jewish citizens. In other words, it is probable and natural that tomorrow, this generation will treat the Jewish citizens not as brothers and friends, but as foreigners.

Ensuring substantial and continuous contact amongst the youth is an urgent duty. This is the second reason: Spirit and nature cannot bear voids. *L'âme a horreur du vide.* [The soul despises voids.] Denied the right to embrace the national ideal, the Jewish Turk is left with no other choice but to seek artificial ideals.

There is no need to elaborate upon the disastrous effects of this tendency with respect to national unity.

This is the third reason: Today, the organization or lack of organization of the Jewish community is headed by a few intellectuals who have a program to finalize the integration process, and who are prepared to help facilitate the relevant measures that will inevitably be taken by our leaders.

The aforementioned intellectuals have been preparing the Jewish public for integration in a methodical way for the last three years now. With the authority vested in me as the leader of this movement towards integration, I can assure you that the conditions have matured!

What are the requirements for realizing integration?

First of all, let me make clear that when I say requirements, I mean natural requirements, not the conditions of a negotiation... Having made this clear, let me now list the requirements one by one:

1. The first condition is that we not underestimate the challenges of the mission at hand. Most Jewish Turks live in Galata and Beyoğlu. The atmosphere in that area is well known. In those quarters, you can meet true Turks of the kind who think it appropriate to answer in French even when you speak to them in Turkish.

In addition to this, there are Jews of foreign nationality who are connected to Turkish Jews by bonds of friendship and affinity, and trying to get them to accept local culture would be a waste of our efforts.

2. The second condition is that this issue be considered a state

affair. Everything that has happened in this country from the creation of the new regime onwards—all reforms, both major and minor, from industry to clothing and from the alphabet to railroads—have all been realized thanks to the earnest and systematic intervention of the state.

3. So long as the state fails to explicitly declare its interest in the issue of integration and to prove that its concern is genuine by means of its acts and practices, failure is inevitable. What is more, at a time when there are so many cowards who consider engaging in politics a sin rather than a duty, it would be utterly unrealistic to expect a weak community to overcome its timidity (that naturally derives from its weakness) and to launch a system- atic effort to tackle such a precarious issue.

4. The third condition is that the integration of Jewish Turks should not be subordinated to the integration of other minorities. Politics is built on realities, not on dreams... It would be wrong to ignore the particular characteristics of each minority. This point is both an important and a delicate one.

This is what we are expecting from the state:

A. The state should treat those individuals who have integrated as true Turks, so that the doubters will see that the road to salvation, the true path, is the one that leads to Turkishness.

B. There should be an end to the "save the day" regime (*idare-i maslahat*) that governs the so-called communities (*cemaat*), which are legal freaks based upon obsolete regulations and decaying traditions. A new legal regulation in keeping with the secular principles of our Republic is needed. This regulation should confine community (*cemaat*) activities to the spheres of religion and charity and ensure with objective disinterest that all such activities are regulated, facilitated, and overseen in a proper manner.

C. The problem of [minority] schools should be solved in a reasonable and radical way. With regard to this matter, the state can trust in the good faith of those governing the community, of this I am certain.

D. The state should keep the doors of its youth organizations open to Jewish children.

This is an outline of our main views, which should be taken up as a whole. However, we, who are determined to turn these ideas into reality, are equally devoted to national discipline.

We know that our leaders, who have successfully transformed Europe's sick man into Europe's only healthy man, have drawn up a comprehensive program whereby each task is to be performed when the time has come.

We think it meaningless to undertake any action whatsoever until we have received clear signs and guidance from them. We believe that in making the public opinion aware of this issue by presenting it in a clear, honest, and sincere way, and by bringing this issue to the attention of our superiors, we have performed an essential duty to our nation and completed the requirements of our moral responsibility. Now it is up to the state.

Bibliography

US National Archives

The Records of the Department of State relating to Internal Affairs of Turkey, 1930–1944 (Microfilm no. M1224).

British National Archives (Kew, London)

FO 371: Foreign Office Correspondence.

Official Publications

Düstur – III ve V. Tertip.
TBMM - Zabıt Ceridesi, [Turkish Grand National Assembly - Record of Minutes]. Devre 4, Ankara: TBMM Matbaası, 1975
TBMM - Gizli Celse Zabıtları [Turkish Grand National Assembly - Minutes of the closed sessions], 4 vols. Ankara: İş Bankası Yayınları, 1985.

Other Academic Works and Memoirs

Alexandris, Alexis. The Greek Minority of Istanbul and Greek-Turkish Relations, 1918-1974. Athens: Center for Asia Minor Studies, 1983.
Aktar, Ayhan 'Trakya Yahudi Olaylarını Doğru Yorumlamak,' [Correctly Interpreting the 1934 Jewish Incidents in Thrace] *Tarih ve Toplum*, 155, Kasım 1996.
Berkes, Niyazi. *Türkiye'de çağdaşlaşma*. Ankara: Bilgi Yayınevi, 1973.
Bozkurt, Gülnihâl. Batı hukukunun Türkiye'de benimsenmesi: Osmanlı Devleti'nden Türkiye Cumhuriyeti'ne resepsiyon süreci, 1839-1939. Ankara: Türk Tarih Kurumu Basımevi, 1996.
Deringil, Selim. Simgeden millete: II. Abdülhamid'den Mustafa Kemal'e devlet ve millet. İstanbul: İletişim, 2007.
Findley, Carter. 'The acid test of Ottomanism: The Acceptance of Non-Muslims in the late Ottoman Bureaucracy' in Vol. 1. New York: Holmes & Meier Publishers, 1982.
Galanté, Abraham. *Türkler ve Yahudiler: tarihi, siyasi araştırma*. İstanbul: Gözlem Gazetecilik Basın ve Yayın, 1995.
Gökalp, Ziya 'Millet nedir?' In *Makaleler VII: Küçük Mecmua'daki Yazılar*, ed. by M.

Abdülhalûk Çay. Ankara: Ministry of Culture, 1982.

Gökalp, Ziya. *Yeni hayat; Doğru yol.* Ankara: Devlet Kitapları, 1976.

Ziya Gökalp, 'Yeni Hayat ve Yeni Kıymetler.' In *Makaleler II*, ed. by Süleyman Hayri Bolay. Ankara: Ministry of Culture, 1982.

Greenfeld, Liah. *Nationalism: Five Roads to Modernity.* Cambridge: Harvard University Press, 1995.

Heyd, Uriel. Foundations of Turkish Nationalism; the Life and Teachings of Ziya Gökalp. [London]: Luzac, 1950.

İnönü, İsmet. *Hatıralar.* Ankara: Bilgi Yayınevi, 1985.

Kılıç, Şengün. *Biz ve onlar: Türkiye'de etnik ayrımcılık.* İstanbul: Metis Yayınları, 1992.

Landau, Jacob M. *Tekinalp, Turkish Patriot, 1883-1961.* [Leiden]: Nederlands Historisch-Archaeologisch Instituut te İstanbul, 1984.

Lozan Barış Konferansı; Tutanaklar, Belgeler. Edited and translated by Seha Meray. [Lausanne Conference on Near Eastern Affairs] Ankara: Siyasal Bilgiler Fakültesi Yayını, 1969.

Lewis, Bernard, and Benjamin Braude. *Christians and Jews in the Ottoman Empire: The Functioning of a Plural Society.* Vol. 1. New York: Holmes & Meier Publishers, 1982.

Ökte, Faik. *Varlık vergisi faciası.* İstanbul: Nebioğlu Yayınevi, 1951.

Parla, Taha. *The Social and Political Thought of Ziya Gökalp, 1876-1924.* Leiden: E. J. Brill, 1985.

Rıza Nur *Hayat ve hatiratim.* İstanbul: Altindağ Yayinevi, 1967.

Ortaylı, İlber. 'II. Abdülhamit Devrinde Taşra Bürokrasisinde Gayrimüslimler' in *Sultan II. Abdülhamid ve Devri Semineri: Bildiriler.* İstanbul: Edebiyat Fakültesi Basımevi, 1994.

Tekinalp, Munis [Moiz Kohen]. *Türk ruhu.* İstanbul: Remzi Kitabevi, 1944.

Toprak, Zafer. *Milli iktisat, milli burjuvazi.* İstanbul: Tarih Vakfı Yurt Yayınları, 1995.

CHAPTER 6

"TAX ME TO THE END OF MY LIFE!" ANATOMY OF ANTI-MINORITY TAX LEGISLATION, (1942 - 3)*

Grant them removed, and grant that this your noise
Had chid down all the majesty of England:
Imagine that you see the wretched strangers,
Their babies at their backs and their poor luggage,
Plodding to the ports and coasts for transportation,
And that you sit as kings in your desires,
Authority quite silenced by your brawl,
And you in ruff of your opinions clothed:
What had you got? I'll tell you, You had thout
How insolence and strong hand should prevail,
How order should be quelled: and by this pattern
Not one of you should live an aged man,
For other ruffians as their fancies wrought
With self same hand, self reasons, and self right,
Would shark on you, and men like ravenous fishes,
Would feed one on another.

Shakespeare, *Sir Thomas More.*[1]

Approved by the Turkish parliament during World War II, the Wealth Tax was clearly an important measure, not only from an economic, but also from a political and cultural point of view. The introduction of this Wealth Tax essentially involved a number of component processes, such as: drawing up the law, its ratification by the Turkish parliament, the support given by the press, the procedures whereby the commissions would determine who was to pay how much tax, the announcing of taxpayers' names and amounts of tax payable, the period in which payment was to be made, which in no case exceeded one month, the levying of distress over and subsequent compulsory sale of the property. Those who failed to meet their tax liabilities within this period were dispatched to labor camps so that they might "work off their debts with

---

* This article was previously published in Benjamin C. Fortna et al., *State-Nationalisms in the Ottoman Empire, Greece and Turkey: Orthodox and Muslims, 1830-1945*, (New York: Routledge, 2013), 188-220.
[1] The play *Sir Thomas More*, one of whose authors was Shakespeare, is about a rebellion that broke out in London in 1517. London's tradesmen and artisans staged a rebellion in support of their demand for the deportation of Protestant German artisans in London. Shakespeare penned the section devoted to the role played by Sir Thomas Moore, the author of *Utopia*, in calming the rebellion.

physical labor." In the work camps in Aşkale and later Sivrihisar twenty-one taxpayers, all of them non-Muslims, died due to several illnesses and callous working conditions.

When all these stages are examined in combination, the Wealth Tax Law serves as a perfect example of the "anti-minority" policies of the single-party period in Turkey (1925–45). Istanbul provided the backdrop for all these relations. Istanbul, in which the commercial bourgeoisie was most strongly represented, was at the same time the city in which social differentiation was most pronounced, where conditions most favored displays of conspicuous consumption and extravagance, and which had a large concentration of minorities coming from different walks of life and lifestyles. Examining the introduction of the Wealth Tax from the standpoint of the economic center of Turkey, which was Istanbul in those days, it helps to shed light on relations between the non-Muslim minority and the Turkish nation state with its dominant form of nationalism.

The context

With the outbreak of war in Europe, the government in Ankara was becoming paralyzed in terms of its economic policies. At first, in 1940, nearly one million men were mobilized and drafted to the Army.[2] Once again, as in the good old days, the Turkish peasant was called for duty. The general mobilization had created a deadly effect on the well being of the economy. In an economy based upon agriculture, where nearly 90 percent of the population lived in the countryside, and with a total population of less then twenty million, this military mobilization meant a significant withdrawal of laboring men from the production process. Naturally agricultural production decreased. However, this decrease was not recognized or felt until 1941. Between 1938 and 1945 Turkey experienced the most destructive inflation of its recent history. Prices increased from a base of 100 in 1938 to 126.6 in 1940, to 175.3 in 1941 and finally to 339.6 in 1942.[3] Furthermore, increasing defense expenditures were met by printing more bank notes since. Increasing the money supply was perceived as the remedy to all economic problems. Thus money in circulation increased from 193 million in 1938 to 733 million in 1942. In other words, while money in circulation increased 3.7 times in four years, the general prices increased 3.4 times. Price controls and the usual administrative measures did not work. Even the most basic consumption goods disappeared from the market. Stockpiling, speculation and hoarding

---

[2] Cemil Koçak, *Türkiye'de Millî Şef dönemi: 1938-1945 : Dönemin iç ve dış politikası üzerine bir araştırma*, (İstanbul: İletişim, 1996), 229-341.
[3] Faik Ökte, *Varlık vergisi faciası*, (İstanbul: Nebioğlu Yayınevi, 1951). For the English edition of this rare memoir, see Faik Ökte, *The Tragedy of the Capital Tax* (London: Croom Helm, 1987).

practices were considered to be an inevitable mode of existence in an inflationary economy.

The administration of a war economy in a country that declared itself "neutral" created further ideological difficulties for the Kemalists. Starting from the world economic crisis of 1929, the Ankara government had implemented several *étatist* measures to control the economic fabric of the society. State economic enterprises were formed and "self-sufficiency at all costs" became the main motto of the Kemalist regime. Strict currency regulations, high taxation and tightly designed trade monopolies were the main tenets of Ankara regime.[4]

Since the beginnings of the 1930s the Kemalists had developed a harsh critique of liberal economic principles. For them, the destructive and cruel nature of the free market economy was not something to be simulated at home. Thus they opted for a more controlled "command economy" of the rising authoritarian/totalitarian "New Order" of inter-war years. Liberal economic principles and the possessive individualism of so called "corrupt" Western democracies were evils to be avoided in the formation of the young Turkish Republic. Ultimately they were able to form a highly centralized authoritarian party-state that promoted the rule of a single party (the Republican People's Party, hereafter RPP), a parliament composed of appointed members, and a state ideology that denied the existence of any social or economic cleavages in society. This solidaristic/corporatist and to a certain extent ethnically pure model of society was designed to create a new type of Turkish citizen without any social and economic "rights," but only "duties" prescribed by the Turkish state.

In this system of conduct, there was a limited place for trade and commercial activity in general. Merchants had to be controlled by the central authority in Ankara. In this respect, the existence of a commercial bourgeoisie in Istanbul was perceived as a type of "social malady", which was symptomatic of differentiation in society, promoted a cosmopolitan way of life, and made conspicuous consumption seductive for the rest of Turkish society. Furthermore, commercial activities and especially foreign trade had traditionally been the retreat of non-Muslim minorities in Turkish society. Excluded from the Army and public service in Ottoman times, non-Muslim minorities had always been active in local and international trade. Their cosmopolitan manners, Levantine ways of life (such as summer residences in the Prince's Islands or on the Bosphorus), and their command of foreign languages intensified the fear and xenophobia in the minds of the Turkish bureaucrats. Moreover, the

---

[4] Çağlar Keyder, *State and Class in Turkey: A Study in Capitalist Development* (London : Verso, 1987), 91-115.

collective consciousness of the Turkish Republican elite was full of reminiscences of the Great Powers' interventions in the domestic matters of the Ottoman state on behalf of non-Muslim minorities. Each intervention had brought up a new form of capitulation or trade concessions. Finally, direct European financial control and the threat of colonization impaired the Ottoman state. Besides, hadn't the Greeks, Armenians and Jews collaborated with the Great Powers to ruin the late Ottoman economy and enrich themselves at the expense of the poor, toiling Anatolian peasant? Plagued by such concerns, the Turkish Republican elite visualized the minorities as a kind of a fifth column provoked and supported by the foreign powers.

In the first section of this chapter, an attempt will be made to present an annotated chronology of the various stages involved in the introduction of the Wealth Tax; the second section is devoted to the assessment process in which it was determined who was to pay how much tax; and the third section contains an examination of the process by means of which the tax was collected in Istanbul. In the fourth section, information obtained through studying the archives of the Istanbul Beyoğlu-Şişli, Eminönü, Fatih, Kadıköy and Adalar Land Registry Offices will be presented in the form of tables.

Istanbul as the center of all evils!

The Wealth Tax, when it was introduced, made a disproportionate impact on Istanbul. Istanbul's special position in this regard becomes evident from a careful study of Table 1. The extent to which this tax was concentrated on Istanbul, which had the greatest number of Wealth Tax taxpayers with 54 percent of the total, becomes more evident when it is considered that 68% of the total amount of tax assessed and 70 percent of the final amount paid was recorded here.

Official declarations claimed that the Wealth Tax Law was introduced with the aim of taxing extraordinary profits made under the special conditions prevailing during World War II, and reducing the amount of money in circulation.

Istanbul certainly had a special status in that it was the city where the commercial bourgeoisie was most strongly represented. But the extent to which the Wealth Tax was concentrated on Istanbul cannot be accounted for solely in economic terms. The plurality evident in the city's ethnic and religious structure, a legacy of the Ottoman period, and pressures exerted ever since the initial years of Republican government on non-Muslim minorities in other regions of the country to migrate to Istanbul made the city particularly vulnerable to policies directed against minorities. The special focus on Istanbul when the Wealth Tax was introduced had as much to do with the city's social, cultural and demographic features as with its economy.

Table 1. Wealth tax assessment and payment

	Istanbul	Turkey
A. Total number of taxpayers	62,57	114,368
	54%	100%
B. Wealth Tax Assessed (TL)	317,275,642	465,384,820
	68%	100%
C. Wealth Tax Paid(TL)	221,307,508	314,920,940
	70%	100%
D. Proportion of assessed tax to paid (C/B)	69.7%	74.3%

Source: Faik Ökte

Basic chronology of the Wealth Tax

Before embarking on a detailed examination of the processes by means of which the Wealth Tax was assessed and collected, let us present the various stages involved in the introduction of the Wealth Tax in chronological manner.

The Ankara government, which had responded to the outbreak of war in 1939 by mobilizing around one million men and was attempting to meet rising defense expenditure by printing money, began in the spring and summer of 1942 to seek ways of taxing extraordinary profits. A commission set up by Minister of Finance, Fuat Ağralı, was in the process of drafting a new law. At that time, certain newspaper columnists, noting that in particular non-Muslim merchants were benefiting from shortages of goods that were caused by high inflation and reduced imports, were calling for a commission to be established that would tax the speculative profits which these non-Muslim elements were making.[5]

On July 7, 1942, the sudden death of Prime Minister Refik Saydam led to the appointment of Foreign Minister Şükrü Saracoğlu to this post. Through- out the summer of 1942, prominence was given in the Istanbul press to news that tended to associate non-Muslims with acts of theft,

---

[5] Ahmet Emin Yalman in his leading column in 29 May 1942 in *Vatan* daily newspaper, having established that, "there is in general terms certainly a lower degree of attachment to the motherland among minorities," sketched the first outlines of the Wealth Tax Law: "If it were up to me, especially in the large cities, extraordinary committees should be established with the aim of imposing this tax on a one-off basis and leading bankers, leading members of chambers of commerce and honest people capable of representing every sphere of commerce should serve the motherland on these committees. They should be guided in their work, along with ledgers and so forth, by certain comparisons and conjectures, and they should create the circumstances under which the real profiteers are forced to pay their debt to the motherland. In any case, since the real profiteers number in hundreds, solutions can be found."

black marketing, extortion, profiteering and speculation.[6] Comics appearing in that period mainly used caricatures of Jews in anti-minority cartoons. According to Laurent Mallet's analysis, the Jewish cartoons published in the *Karikatür* comic made fun not only of Jews, however by association all non-Muslims.[7]

Faik Ökte, on the day on which he first reported for duty at the Istanbul Financial Office (September 12, 1942), was shown an official letter that had been sent to him from Ankara fifteen days earlier. This letter contained the request:

> After it was stated that our laws failed to tax extraordinary profits made as a result of war and profiteering, and that consequently minorities in particular had amassed vast wealth, that by means of making an urgent investigation into the market it be determined who had made extraordinary profits in this manner and *that minorities be shown in a separate table.*[8]

Ökte, who was working on this matter, based on information originating from various tax offices in Istanbul, listed taxpayers who were believed to have made extraordinary profits, classifying them according to their religious and ethnic origins.[9]

The ground was laid for the Wealth Tax, then, by disseminating the appropriate propaganda, after which technical preparations were made. The law already existed in the minds, all that remained was for it to be drawn up on paper and voted on in the parliament. Ökte argues that the text of the law was dictated as a note from Prime Minister Saracoğlu to the Minister of Finance. Undersecretary to the Finance Ministry Esat Tekeli then converted these notes into the articles of the law.[10]

Rumors reached Istanbul that the government was drawing up a law aiming specifically at taxing non-Muslims. A group of non-Muslim community representatives visited Prime Minister Saracoğlu in Ankara. The non-Muslim minority representatives, stating that they had heard

---

[6] Some examples of headlines accompanying such news: "Two Jewish Children Stole Rosette Money Collected for the Air Foundation," *Cumhuriyet* (August 31, 1942). "A Jewish Contractor cheated the Turkish Treasury Thousands of Lira," *Tasvir-i Efkar* (September 1, 1942) and "Two Jewish Hoarders Apprehended," *Tasvir-i Efkar* (September 9, 1942).
[7] According to Mallet, who has analyzed the content of cartoons involving Jews appearing in the *Karikatür* comic between 1936 and 1948 and the frequency with which they appeared, the number of such cartoons published in this comic in the months of April - September 1942 represented the highest levels reached during the period 1936 - 48. See L. Mallet, "Karikatür dergisinde yahudilerle ilgili karikatürler, 1936–1948," *Toplumsal Tarih* 34 (1996): 30.
[8] Ökte, *Varlık vergisi faciası*, 47.
[9] Faik Ökte described the classification of taxpayers in his memoirs as follows: "The tables were divided into two with the labels M and G. M was the Muslim group, and G represented the non-Muslim minorities. To these letters were later added D for converts and E for foreigners" (Ökte, *ibid*, 48).
[10] Ökte, *Varlık vergisi faciası*, 50.

about preparations for the Wealth Tax, made a proposal to the Prime Minister:

> Minority representatives - "Sir, how much are you thinking of raising through the tax? ... Do you want to raise 300 million, [or] do you want to raise 200 million? You leave this to us; let us raise this [among ourselves and] give it to the government!"

> Prime-Minister Saracoğlu - "How can we accept this offer? We are [a modern] state!"[11]

Saracoğlu thus rejected this proposal, reminiscent as it was of the workings of the Ottoman *millet* system.

Two days later, President İnönü, when he officially opened the parliament on November 1, spoke in similar terms: "Old-school crooked landowners who consider these turbulent times to be a unique opportunity, and voracious, profiteering merchants who would turn the very air we breath into a tradable commodity if they could, and a number of politicians who think that all of these hardships are a great opportunity for realizing their political ambitions and with respect to whom it is hard to determine which foreign nation they are working for are brazenly seeking to sabotage the entire life of a great nation."[12] In a lengthy speech to the parliament in the morning of November 11, in which he addressed the economic situation in detail, Prime Minister Saracoğlu revealed a package of economic measures that also contained the Wealth Tax Law. Prime Minister Saracoğlu explained the aim of the Wealth Tax to the parliament in the following terms:

> The aim that we are pursuing with this law is to reduce the amount of money in circulation and create reserves to meet our national requirements. Along with this, the existence of secondary benefits that will result from the implementation of this law such as a strengthening of Turkish currency, the dispelling of popular bitterness felt towards profiteers, and the moderating effect on prices that will be exerted as property is of necessity put up for sale to pay the taxes, cannot be discounted.[13]

However, at the RPP group meeting which was closed to the press, Prime Minister Şükrü Saracoğlu presented the same law to the RPP group

---

[11] An interview conducted on April 17, 1992 with late Ambassador, Fuat Bayramoğlu, who served as Prime Minister Saracoğlu's Private Secretary 1943-5. The actual research on Turkish Wealth Tax was conducted 1991 - 95. In this manner, many of the retired tax inspectors and statesmen were interviewed. The first article on this topic was published in 1996. See, Ayhan Aktar, "Varlık Vergisi ve İstanbul," *Toplum ve Bilim,* 71 (Kış, 1996): 97-149.

[12] *Ayın Tarihi* 108 (Kasım 1942): 23.

[13] *Ayın Tarihi* 108 (Kasım 1942): 41.

in the parliament as follows:

> This law is at the same time a revolutionary law. We are presented
> with an opportunity to obtain our economic independence. The
> foreigners who dominate our market will thus be eliminated and
> we will place the Turkish market in the hands of Turks.[14]

The bill was not much discussed in the CHP group and a decision was
taken to pass it as law. The Wealth Tax Law was approved with very trivial
debates at the parliament's afternoon session on November 11, 1942. The
law was promulgated in the *Official Gazette* the following day and took
effect.[15]

Peculiarities of the Wealth Tax Law

Article 7 of the Wealth Tax Law provided for the formation "of a
commission, or more than one if necessary, in the center of every province
and sub-province for the purpose of establishing the degrees of liability
of persons possessing wealth and income, to be headed by the most senior
civil service administrator in that place, and comprising most senior
financial officer along with two members, each of chambers of commerce
and municipalities, to be elected from among their own members."
Article 11 of the same law made the amounts of tax determined by the
commission unalterable with the provision: "The commission's decisions
are of a final and binding nature and a suit may not be filed to contest
them with district administrative and judicial authorities."

As soon as the law took effect, three separate commissions were
established in the Istanbul province. These commissions, along with the
Ministry of Finance bureaucracy that supplied them with information,
completed their business, which we will describe in greater detail later,
within one month (November 12 - December 17, 1942). After the
commissions had determined who was to pay how much tax (assessment
procedure), the lists showing the amounts of tax were displayed on notice
boards at tax offices in Istanbul on December 18, 1942.

Article 12 of the Wealth Tax Law provided for payment of the tax
within fifteen days. This period ended with the close of business on
January 4, 1943. Moreover, pursuant to the same Article, interest on
arrears at the rate of 1 percent for one week and 2 percent for two weeks
was to be applied in the case of taxpayers who failed to pay their taxes
within given period. Since a number of public holidays intervened, these
periods were slightly extended and came to an end on January 20, 1943.

---

[14] Faik Ahmet Barutçu, *Siyasî anılar*, (İstanbul: Milliyet Yayınları, 1977), 263.
[15] *Resmi Gazete*, no. 5255, 12 Teşrinisani [November] 1942.

HALKIN SIRTINDAN GEÇİNENLER:
Vurguncu — Haydi, uzun etme, ikimiz
de yükümüzü tuttuk!..

Anti-semitic cartoon. 8 October 1942 *Karikatür.*

Defaulters and labor camps in eastern Turkey

On January 21, 1943, visits were made to the homes and businesses of those taxpayers who failed to pay their tax within the above-mentioned periods and, initially, distress was levied over their property, and later tax began to be collected by means of the sale of such property and furniture. Those taxpayers who were unable to pay their tax within one month began to be sent to work camps with the aim of performing physical labor and working off their taxes. The first party of thirty-two persons, consisting entirely of Istanbul non-Muslims, set off for Aşkale, Erzurum on January 27, 1943.

Between February and September 1943, a total of 2,057 people were collected from their homes by the police and brought to the detention centers at Sirkeci/Istanbul, Izmir/Tepecik. Of these taxpayers, 1,400 people were sent, initially to Aşkale, to work. The remaining 657 people, on the other hand, paid their tax debt while waiting at detention centers or after having been sent to their work location. At the work location of Aşkale itself, 21 people died "in debt." Since the obligation to work was only imposed on non-Muslims, all of those who died were non-Muslims and all of them had been sent to Aşkale from Istanbul. The process of collecting Wealth Tax by means of levying distress over and selling taxpayers' property continued throughout the summer of 1943. Meanwhile, on August 8, 1943 approximately 900 defaulters working at Aşkale were sent to Eskişehir/Sivrihisar.

New York Times coverage and the absolution of the Wealth Tax

The journalist and proprietor of the *New York Times*, Cyrus L. Sulzberger, who visited Turkey that summer, wrote a series of articles about the Wealth Tax which were published in the *New York Times* between 9 - 13 September 1943. Sulzberger noted in his articles that certain observers to whom he spoke on his journey said that an attempt was being made by means of the Wealth Tax to eliminate the minorities, who occupied an important place in Turkey's commercial life. Sulzberger included extracts from the *Cumhuriyet* newspaper in his articles, and spoke of the "sensitivity" of the press toward this matter and the support given to the government.[16] Thus, detailed press coverage of the implementation

---

[16] Sulzberger's article dated September 12, 1943 refers to the unsigned leading article in the *Cumhuriyet* daily dated January 22, 1943. The latter contains excerpts of an interview given by Prime Minister Şükrü Saracoğlu that was printed in *The Times* (London) on 16 January 1942. The Prime Minister said the following: "Various things have been said about the Wealth Tax which has been introduced by the Turkish government to meet urgent financial and economic needs [.] Under these circumstances, it has proved necessary to introduce this law. It is necessary to accept that certain aspects of this law are harsh. At the same time, leniency will be exercised towards those who demonstrate their good faith and civic virtue, and material errors will be corrected. In the case of people who have shirked their duties at this critical hour even though they *have become rich on the back of the hospitality* shown by this country, this law will be applied with all its force. Certain people have apparently still inadequately comprehended the enormous changes that have occurred in Turkey and the world in the past twenty-five years. However, let me state that the majority of these are not persons of foreign nationality, but *certain individuals who are nominally Turkish and whom we have inherited from the Ottoman Empire and have as yet been unable to eliminate.*" After broad coverage of this interview had been given in the leading article of the *Cumhuriyet* daily, the following comment was made: "There remain two things to be done with those who refrain from spending a portion of the wealth they have earned in Turkey in the interests of defending the Turkish homeland: [if they are] our subjects they will roll up their sleeves and wield a pickaxe, *if they are foreign they will depart from this land.*" [Emphasis is mine].

of the Wealth Tax was provided for the first time in the West. We estimate that Sulzberger's articles had a considerable effect on the Ankara government. Precisely four days after the articles were published in the *New York Times*, the parliament, convening on September 17, 1943, authorized the Ministry of Finance, in respect of Wealth Tax taxpayers, "to absolve those who are [1] employees or [2] persons subject to income tax on gross daily income, and who have proved incapable of paying their tax, of their outstanding debts." In Istanbul alone, the total number of Wealth Tax taxpayers falling under these two categories amounted to 26,404 people (see Table 2).

On October 6, 1943, the Foreign Minister in Ankara, Numan Menemencioğlu, spoke with the Undersecretary Robert F. Kelley, who was representing the US Ambassador Steinhardt. Since Steinhardt had been summoned to Washington at that time, Robert F. Kelley was deputizing for him. Menemencioğlu complained, with reference to Sulzberger's articles, about so-called "anti-Turkish" articles in the US press. He expressed a fear that similarly anti-American articles would appear in the Turkish press. Undersecretary Kelley immediately informed Ambassador Steinhardt of this situation. Steinhardt, in the telegram he sent by way of reply on October 8, 1943, stated that he had discussed this matter with the proprietor of the *New York Times*, Arthur Sulzberger, and had received assurances that no further articles concerning the Wealth Tax would appear in this newspaper.[17]

In the wake of these developments, a process aimed at eliminating the notorious Wealth Tax was initiated. In the first week of December, the taxpayers who had been freed from Eskişehir - Sivrihisar were finally returned to Istanbul.[18] The final stage in removing the Wealth Tax from the statute book took the form of a law that was passed on March 15, 1944. The state renounced all claims that had remained outstanding until that date in respect of this tax.[19]

Having presented a brief history of the sixteen-month period in which the Wealth Tax was implemented, we can turn to the tax assessment process.

The process of tax assessment in Istanbul

Tax assessment process is important because it demonstrates how loopholes in the law gave rise to arbitrary practices, how all the weaknesses

---

[17] US National Archives, Records of the Department of State relating to the Internal Affairs of Turkey, 1930 - 44, From Wallace Murray in Washington to US Embassy Undersecretary Robert F. Kelley in Ankara, dated October 8, 1943, 867.512/245.

[18] *Tan,* 7 December 1943.

[19] *Resmi Gazete*, No. 5657, 17 March 1944.

of the Republican bureaucracy were exposed and finally how conspicuous consumption in Istanbul was penalized to the maximum possible extent. This section draws heavily on the memoirs of Director of Financial Administration, Faik Ökte, who was in charge of implementation in Istanbul. The distribution of Wealth Tax tax- payers in Istanbul by groups is shown in Table.2.

Table 2. Groups for assessment in Istanbul

	Religious Origin	Number of Taxpayers	%	Amount of Wealth Tax Assessed TL	%
Extraordinary Taxpayers / Muslim	M	460	1%	17,294,549.-	5%
Extraordinary Taxpayers / Non-Muslim	N	2,563	4%	189,969,980.-	54%
Declarant Taxpayers / Muslim	M	924	1%	3,128,310.-	1%
Declarant Taxpayers / Non-Muslim	N	1,259	2%	10,364,466.-	3%
Tradesmen and Merchants etc. paying Income Tax on Assessed Rental Income	M	2,589	4%	4,055,100.-	1%
Tradesmen and Merchants etc. paying Income Tax on Assessed Rental Income	N	24,151	39%	72,811,850.-	21%
Itinerant/domestic workers having daily gross earnings	N	15,413	25%	9,629,450.-	3%
Employee Worker – State Employee / Non Muslim	N	10,991	18%	6,880,500.-	2%
Joint-Stock Companies	N-M-F	159	0	7,490,910.-	2%
Large Farms	M	222	0	1,122,450.-	0
Contractors	N-M	376	1%	6,546,372.-	2%
Real Property Owners	N-M	2,258	4%	16,525,045.-	5%
Total of the districts outside the Istanbul city boundaries	N-M	1,210	2%	3,664,437	1%
TOTAL		**62,575**	**100**	**349,483,419.-**	**100**

Source: Ökte, Varlık Vergisi

In Table 2, "non-Muslim" taxpayers make up 87 percent of the total number of taxpayers. "Muslim" taxpayers constitute a mere 7 percent of the total number of taxpayers. The remaining 6 percent was a mixed group, but is estimated to include principally non-Muslim and foreign taxpayers.

Careful examination of Table 2 with reference to ethnic and religious origin reveals that the "extraordinary class of non-Muslim taxpayers" was required to pay 54 percent of the total amount of tax assessed in Istanbul. The average amount of per-capita assessed Wealth Tax amounts to TL 74,120. If we add the E[xtraordinary] M[uslim] and Declarant category (DM + DN) to this group, we see the first four groups were expected to pay 63 percent of the amount of tax paid by all of the taxpayers. The persons assigned when the Wealth Tax was implemented to the categories of "Extraordinary and Declarant class of Taxpayer" were those people reputed to be the wealthiest in Istanbul in 1942–3.

Here, wealth was not defined in terms purely of the monetary value of all their possessions. In this respect, the nature of the consumption patterns exhibited by that person and the extent to which such patterns brought them to prominence in public space, were significant. For example, if one of two people engaged in the same line of profession lived in a select neighborhood of Istanbul, spent his summer holidays on Prince's Islands and participated in the posh "Republic Day Balls," while the other, although earning the same income, had a more modest and introverted lifestyle, most probably the amount of tax paid by the first would be greater than that paid by the second.

The following interview provides us with a useful insight into this process:

> My father [Lawyer Jak Hatem] was a person who was held in high esteem by those around him and, in terms of his social life, was a member of clubs to which the elite of the period belonged. He would go to Yalova for certain months of the year and take a cure at the Termal Hotel. His partner, Bensiyon Garin, on the other hand, led a more family oriented, modest life. He was on very good terms with the famous penal lawyer of the day, Sadi Riza Dağ, who operated his legal practice on the same floor as himself. In fact, at the time when I was graduating from the Law Faculty, I served as an internee with Mr. Dağ When the Wealth Tax lists were displayed, we saw that the amount of tax imposed on my father, Jak Hatem, was 140,000 liras and the amount of tax imposed on his partner, Bensiyon Garin, was TL 90,000 liras. By contrast, the amount of tax imposed on Lawyer Sadi Riza Dağ, who was engaged in the same profession on the same floor, was

6,000 liras only! [20]

A brief comparison of the amount of tax imposed on two people who, if nothing else, they were included in the same professional category shows that the Wealth Tax was implemented in an extremely unjust and disproportionate manner to the detriment of the minorities.

Not only does the above example show that discrimination was practiced between Muslim Turks and non-Muslims operating in the same professional group, but it also demonstrates that discrimination was practiced between non-Muslims based on certain tacit criteria. The point here is that two Jewish lawyers, who shared the same office as partners, were taxed in an extremely different manner due to the different "lifestyles" that they had adopted and the different "consumption patterns" that they displayed. This example is quite illuminating because it offers an insight into the mindset of the Ankara government in the single-party period. In the above example, Lawyer Jak Hatem and his partner, Bensiyon Garin, were obliged to pay different amounts of tax based not on their wealth, but on their different individual lifestyles in terms of the degree to which they made this wealth displayed through conspicuous consumption.

This critical stance adopted toward conspicuous consumption and extravagance in relation to social status in fact accorded with a solidaristic/corporatist mindset which aimed at progressing through an *étatist* model of development, which accepted the existence of social classes, but was extremely uneasy about class struggle and perceived the society as an organic whole.[21] The notion that that conspicuous consumption is a form of behavior which breaks down social harmony can be traced back to the days of the "National Economy" policies practiced by the Committee of Union and Progress. However, within an imperial setting and under the conditions imposed by World War I, the Committee of Union and Progress was only able to implement these policies to a limited extent. Protectionist economic policies were only implemented on a wide scale following the founding of a nation state in Turkey in 1923 and after the 1929 world economic crisis.

Financial bureaucracy in assessment process

Information provided by the Turkish commercial banks, which the estimators wanted to use in the course of collating information about taxpayers' wealth, was extremely limited. Apart from that, information

---

[20] Interview conducted with Mr. Izzet Hatem on 23 August 1991.
[21] For a detailed analysis of Turkish corporatism, see Taha Parla, *The Social and Political Thought of Ziya Gökalp, 1876-1924*, (Leiden: Brill, 1985).

reached the estimators from the Turkish Intelligence Service of the period through the state channels and from the governing Republican People's Party through the party inspector Suat Hayri Ürgüplü. Ökte described in his memoirs that such information was extremely exaggerated and continued as follows:

> All of those who cooperated with us on the supposition that they would guide us in the right direction, rather than pulling us in the direction of the truth and moderation, pushed us, and the tax, in an extreme and disastrous direction ... Those who guided us tended to lead us up the wrong path, and on the day on which assessment ended they would wash their hands of the matter and wriggle off the hook, leaving our weak shoulders to bear this strange coffin![22]

The estimators working under these conditions spoke to the staff at tax office branches and sneakily walked past the fronts of shops owned by people who were supposed to be taxed, and reference was made to exceptionally inconsistent income tax statements, but the final decision was made with reference to "the estimators' own powers of imagination, the only resource that was available in abundance." Faik Ökte stated that conversations of the following kind were frequently encountered among estimators in the commissions:

— What's he worth?

— 500,000.

— One million.

— What do you know?

— What do *you* know?

— Let's split the difference.[23]

The famous film-theatre owner Cemil Filmer, when speaking in his memoirs of events that negatively affected his company, mentions the Wealth Tax: "The third heaviest blow [dealt to me], however, was the Wealth Tax. They put me down for 125,000 liras in tax just because I used to dine at the Abdullah Efendi Restaurant.[24] However hard I tried, I could not stop this and I had no choice but to pay up and like it."[25] The mentality that we have described above clearly dictated that a businessman who operated the most luxurious cinemas of the day would be included

---

[22] Ökte, *Varlık vergisi faciası*, 74.

[23] Ökte, 75.

[24] 'Abdullah Efendi Lokantası' used to be the finest restaurant in Istanbul until 1960s.

[25] Cemil Filmer, *Hatıralar: Türk sinemasında 65 yıl* (İstanbul: Emek Matbaacılık ve İlâncılık, 1984), 169.

in the most heavily taxed. At the same time, the cinema patrons of the day were described in Filmer's memoirs in the following terms: "Not only were the cinemas high-class places in those days, they also attracted rich clientele. The mink fur shone on the backs of the women alighting from cars."[26] If the proprietor of places at which such splendor and luxurious consumption were displayed also dined at one of Istanbul's most luxurious restaurants, it comes as no surprise to learn that he was dealt with in such a punitive manner by the mentality that imposed the Wealth Tax.

In this regard, the Wealth Tax did not indiscriminately target those segments that in economic and social terms boasted a high income and were wealthy, but more specifically those who displayed their wealth through consumption. Consequently, it cannot be claimed that an anti-capitalist mindset lay behind the Wealth Tax. For the taxation process was not rooted in production and property; quite the reverse, it revolved around consumption and property. The aim of the solidarist/corporatist model of state and society to create an illusion of classless society by means of erasing social differences found its first concrete expression in an attempt to blunt the social differentiation that appeared in the sphere of consumption.

Peddlers, white collars and workers are also taxed

Prime Minister Saracoğlu instructed the finance officers to impose the Wealth Tax on specific professions such as drivers, greengrocers, petit commission agents, middlemen and fruit and vegetable wholesalers operating on an "itinerant" basis and having no fixed premises, along with "employees" such as white-collar staff, secretaries and janitors employed in the private companies. Thus the "itinerant" group that was consisting up 25 percent of the total number of taxpayers in Istanbul (15,413 people) was brought within the scope of the tax. The average per capita amount of Wealth Tax imposed on this group amounted to TL 624.

The average per capita amount of Wealth Tax imposed on the "employees" group that was engaged on a salaried basis in various workplaces and which was similarly brought within the scope of the tax was 626 liras. The "employees" group consisted of 10,991 people, and this group made up 18 percent of the total number of taxpayers. The instruction to apply the Wealth Tax, which until that time had been perceived of as a kind of "capital tax," to persons working within the private sector or on their own account was the final straw that broke the camel's back. This measure was an enormously unjust act against this

---

[26] Filmer, 162.

group that had already been crushed by the burden of wartime inflation. It should also be noted that only non-Muslims in these groups were taxed, Turkish Muslims in these jobs were not taxed at all.

The Turkish bureaucracy of the single-party period and the Wealth Tax

One of the most interesting conclusions that can be drawn from a study of the implementation of the Wealth Tax is that the Turkish civil service at the time of World War II lacked adequate concrete information about society. Following the founding of a national state in 1923, this feature of the Ottoman administrative structure did not change greatly, in spite of all the Kemalist regime's reform initiatives that targeted individuals' daily lives. As Metin Heper has aptly observed, the Kemalist elite attempted to reorganize the bureaucracy with the sole aim of achieving more narrowly focused goals that could be described as "creating a new society." Adopting the principle of secularism and attempts to achieve total Westernization can be considered to have, "opened the way for the bureaucracy to acquire legal - rational [in the sense used by Max Weber] attributes." But as Heper has noted, "the fact that bureaucracy ... was considered to be the vehicle for implementing Kemalism led to the 'bureaucratic' dimension taking precedence over the 'rational' dimension."[27] Moreover, at the dawn of the Republic, the bureaucrats inherited from the Ottoman Empire underwent a kind of "quality control" in which they were questioned as to their support for the national struggle, with those failing to demonstrate the necessary conviction and zeal being purged.[28]

By the time World War II had arrived, efforts to bring Kemalist reforms into being had left a legacy of "militancy and tiredness" in the Turkish civil service. The most important reason for the politicization of the civil service was the considerable influence that was exerted over bureaucrats' professional life by a system of professional evaluation which attached as much importance to the factor of allegiance to Kemalist reforms, a criterion which was of equal importance as merit in the appointing and promoting of civil servants as such widely accepted criteria for assessing civil servants as professional education, knowledge

[27] Heper.
[28] Drawing on sacked diplomat Galip Kemal Söylemezoğlu's memoirs, Metin Heper describes this process as follows: "In the first years of the Republic, an attempt was made to purge the lower levels of the bureaucracy based on political criteria. A law was issued on 1 October 1922. This law eliminated the administrative staff in its entirety and authorized each ministry to create a new bureaucratic staff from among the redundant civil servants. Various purge commissions appeared in the wake of this law" See, Heper, 104. A purge took place using similar methods between 1932 and 1934 in the course of transforming the "Darülfünun" - the only existing university inherited from the Ottoman regime - into Istanbul University, as a result of which 157 of 240 academic staff members had lost their positions.

and skills. When appointment and promotion were based on the criterion of "political loyalty" rather than "professional competence," it comes as no surprise to learn that the civil service of the Republican period was characterized by nepotism and low levels of motivation.

As capitalist relations become more widespread in a country, a need develops for a "new kind of bureaucracy" that is capable of exercising initiative and taking clear and speedy decisions, is well informed about the cases it handles, operates in a spirit of institutional continuity and performs its tasks with the aid of laws dominated by rationality. As Max Weber cogently states, the "bureaucracy develops more perfectly, the more it is 'dehumanized,' the more completely it succeeds in eliminating from official business love, hatred, and all purely personal, irrational, and emotional elements which escape calculation."[29] The civil service administration in the Republican period, on the one hand, reinforced the extremely centralized administrative structure that it had inherited from the Ottoman period, and on the other, became excessively politicized as a result of efforts to bring about Kemalist reforms. Alongside all of this, as a consequence of the lack in the single-party period of any opposition parties that might audit the bureaucracy, the Republican bureaucracy was not even remotely subjected to any kind of "technical/professional" control apart from "ideological monitoring."

> In a report with racist undertones written during World War II by the British Military Attaché to Ankara, Brigadier General A. C. Arnold, on March 12, 1942 to the British War Ministry, the Turkish bureaucracy, and in particular military bureaucracy, is described as follows:

The weaknesses are not only inherent to the race, but are initiated and encouraged from the very top, that is, by the President of the Republic and the "gang" of "Heroes of the War of Independence" who surround him ... The main weaknesses which are apparent are:

    a)   Over-centralization to a quite fantastic degree.

    b)   Secrecy mania resulting in insufficient preparation amongst their armed forces and inadequate information being given to their allies.

    c)   A conceit in their own ability, a product of extreme nationalism ...

    d)   A natural lack of any mechanical understanding or ability. This

---

[29] Max Weber, *Economy and Society: An Outline of Interpretative Sociology*, vol. 2, (Berkeley: University of California Press, 1978), 975.

results in gross negligence and mechanical inefficiency which is not punished ...

e) Concealment of inefficiency and ineptitude is generally encouraged, since inefficiency ultimately reflects on senior officials who must be exposed to criticism lest the "old gang" or the Party become involved.

f) A return of the time-honoured system of graft.[30]

In the report, it was also noted that, in common with all of the civil service, the decision taking mechanism in the military bureaucracy was exceptionally centralized, and there was a tendency even for military commanders to sit and await the arrival of orders from Ankara.

The evaluation entitled "Turkey Twelve Years On" by K. Helm, who served between 1921 and 1930 in Istanbul as a translator and embassy clerk, and was again appointed British Embassy as Under Secretary in Ankara on 30 June 1942, is very interesting. Helm stressed in his report that the bureaucracy had lost its room for man oeuvre and underlined the fact that, along with corruption, extreme centralization had contributed to a worsening of the bureaucracy. Helm, who stated that the administrative structure had grown visibly worse when he compared 1930 - the time he last served in Ankara - to 1942, provides the following interesting example of extreme centralization. The wife of the British Ambassador at that time, Lady Knatchbull-Hugessen, wished to make use of the Turkish postal services which by virtue of Turkey's remaining neutral in the war continued to operate with Germany and send used tennis balls to British prisoners of war in Germany. In order for these used tennis balls to pass through Turkish customs, the signatures of all the members of the Cabinet were required![31]

Things were not very different at the Ministry of Finance. The Ministry of Finance inspectors involved in implementing the Wealth Tax, when confronted by the question of who was to pay how much tax, had access to an extremely limited amount of information about taxpayers. In those days the income tax was assessed based on the property tax value of the taxpayers' premises. For example, a taxpayer might simultaneously obtain income from renting his apartment building, profit from his own business and dividends from companies in which he was a shareholder. It was impossible for the Finance Ministry bureaucracy to monitor these revenues collected from different sources given the information gathering

---

[30] British National Archives, Foreign Office Correspondence, FO 371/33375, Letter from Military Attaché in Ankara to War Office in London, dated March 12, 1942. R 2467/1941/G.
[31] FO 371/33375, From British Ambassador Sir H. Knatchbull-Hugessen in Ankara to Mr. A. Eden, Foreign Secretary in London, dated August 14, 1942. R 5552/810/44

mechanisms at its disposal. The following interview sheds light on the attempts made by a Finance Ministry inspector to gather information as part of the process of implementing the Wealth Tax:

> In the course of administering the Wealth Tax, I initially began to investigate the tax to be imposed on real estate. The title deed records for the properties were in a real mess. There was no chance of gleaning anything from these. Because of this, we worked by visiting places in the field. [In other words, we asked] who does this building belong to? How many buildings are there in this road? [We looked at things] according to their importance. [Say] there was a three-storey building with one room on each floor, adjoining the one next to it. We paid no attention to this kind of building! However, if we notice a villa with a garden of four acres or six acres - or even a house in an eight acres garden— well, these were the ones we recorded. We generally recorded business premises that took the form of office blocks. I travelled from Karaköy to Bebek, after Bebek as far as Emirgan, and after Emirgan right along the European shore of Bosphorus ... There was no road and I had to go on foot. We arrived in Emirgan, and at this time they provided me with a high-ranking Municipal clerk to accompany me... Of course, there is no way I can know this neighborhood. I went on foot together with him. As we walked along, I gathered information like, "Whose residence is this? What does the owner do?" Later we collated all of this. We took notes all the time. Then we made them up into lists... The value of the buildings emerged, as did that of their owners. We thus passed them on to the commission that was to impose Wealth Tax on real property... In fact, rather than true value, we evaluated people according to their external appearance. In our country, you can never tell who's got the money, or who's really pious! [In the course of administering the Wealth Tax], it was only possible to impose the tax based on a person's status. [Say] a man has a loan
>
> with the Ottoman Bank. [Similarly,] he has a loan with the İş Bankası. Statements made about him that, "He is an open-handed man, he is generous" or considerations such as, "He helps the poor" came into play. For instance, if it was said about somebody that, "He helps the poor", we got an idea about the man's wealth in this way... Apart from this, no information was available to us. There was no inventory, either.[32]

As this interview makes clear, the Finance Ministry bureaucracy in

---

[32] Interview conducted with Ministry of Finance Inspector, the late Mr. Barık Ulugön July 16, 1993.

those days was only capable of taxing individuals based on extremely rudimentary considerations such as whether they made displays of wealth or had prestige. Those who concealed their wealth or led modest lifestyles were the fortunate ones in the assessment process. Due to the primitive nature of the mechanisms available to the civil service for gathering information about society, the machinery for assessing the amount of Wealth Tax to be paid was based on "subjective" criteria.

In fact, the imposition of an "anti-minority" policy such as the Wealth Tax in a country such as Turkey in which an outdated bureaucracy held sway meant that Finance Ministry staff would base their decisions, as Max Weber was quoted saying above, on irrational feelings of love and hate, and would thus err in their calculations when taking bureaucratic decisions. It is not very easy to put "anti-minority," or at a higher level "racist," policies into practice. For in implementing such policies, the state structure must be very sound in technical terms, and a legal–rational bureaucracy, in the sense given to this by Max Weber, must be equipped with extremely detailed information about society.

The natural consequence of taxing conspicuous consumption: arbitrariness

The tax assessment process involved incredible degrees of arbitrariness, in spite of all the attempts to systematize it. The law itself was the source of arbitrariness at the first instance. The Wealth Tax law left the final decision as to who was to pay how much tax to the commissions. Moreover, the tax rate was not specified and recourse was denied at the outset to objections against decisions taken by the commissions.

As has been shown above, preparations were being made whereby people of different religious and ethnic origins would be taxed differently. This was the "unwritten" principle behind the law. This arbitrariness then took firm root as the bureaucracy, which had no information about society, attempted, as we have shown above, to gather information through individual efforts. Finally, basing taxation not on concrete wealth, but on conspicuous consumption and prestige, forced the door to arbitrariness wide open and an "anti-minority" measure was turned into a tragic-comic state policy. At this point all those affective and human frailties (love, hate, jealousy, revenge, comparing old records, etc.) that should have no place in the decision-making processes of modern bureaucracy as defined by Max Weber came into play. The following interview is a good example of the way a certain kind of lifestyle was punished with the imposing of a high level of Wealth Tax:

In the period in which the Wealth Tax was passed I was a young timber merchant who was only 31. The amount of tax imposed on me was 150,000 liras. Consider that a lorry load of timber in those days cost 25 liras only, and even if I sold all of my assets I was not in a position to pay this amount... However, from what I learnt from a friend of mine who was on the assessment commission, the amount of tax imposed on me was actually twice this amount, and had been reduced thanks to my friend's efforts. In other words, I had as many enemies as friends. For example, I was having an affair with Miss Cahide Sonku [a famous film star]... I know that those who were jealous of me because of this relationship used the Wealth Tax as an opportunity to get their own back. However, I had plenty of romantic adventures of this kind. I had relations with Benli Belkıs and her sister, but I am still unable to comprehend why it was Cahide Sonku that brought me to such prominence.[33]

Here a young, handsome Armenian Parseh Gevrekyan, who had an affair with the famous film star, Cahide Sonku, was penalized on two levels: On the one hand, he was heavily penalized as a result of a mentality which deemed his extravagant and decadent lifestyle, conspicuous consumption and extravagance to be forbidden. On the other hand, it was as though the handsome Armenian who had "overstepped the mark" was being "pulled into line" with these actions.

A further dimension of arbitrariness that appeared as the Wealth Tax was implemented was political. Most of the members of "Commission No: 1" previously belonged to the Committee of Union and Progress (CUP) who ruled the country between 1908 and 1918. The CUP was also responsible for the deportation and massacre of the Anatolian Armenians.[34] Some of them were quite experienced in "anti-minority" policies ever since this period and their appointment to the commission was no coincidence. If we read between the lines, Faik Ökte makes reference to this state of affairs in his memoirs: "The former unionists quadrupled the tax on Mr. Asador [Güdükian] of Kadıköy to 400,000 liras on the grounds that he was the leader of the *Dashnakzutiun* (Armenian Revolutionary Federation, ARF)."[35]

The form of arbitrariness that we most frequently encounter in the process of assessing the Wealth Tax involves that ubiquitous feature of

---

[33] An interview conducted by Rıdvan Akar with the late Parseh Gevrekyan. See, Rıdvan Akar, *Varlık vergisi kanunu: tek parti rejiminde azınlık karşıtı politika örneği*, (İstanbul: Belge Yayınları, 1992), 106-107.
[34] Taner Akçam, *A Shameful Act: The Armenian Genocide and the Question of Turkish Responsibility*, (New York: Metropolitan Books, 2006).
[35] Ökte, *Varlık vergisi faciası*, 99.

bureaucratic life, cronyism. For instance, Governor Lütfi Kırdar's tailor, Izzet Ünver, had his tax reduced. These examples are related in detail in that definitive account of events, Faik Ökte's memoirs.

The conclusion that emerges from all of these examples is that the appearance, due to certain structural reasons which we have summarized above, of practices which we have referred to as "arbitrary" when the Wealth Tax was assessed, is hardly coincidental. Such arbitrary practices were molded in a sphere which was the product of certain social and political sensitivities, or else were determined by such phenomena. Let us now turn to the process by means of which the tax was collected in Istanbul.

The tax collection process in Istanbul

The functions assigned to the Istanbul press during the tax collection were not limited to "ideological affirmation" and "strengthening legitimacy." It undertook the task of providing information about the amounts of Wealth Tax deposited each day, making known which taxpayers had avoided paying the tax, and showcasing the positive effects of the tax, and systematically devoted leading articles and published news of this kind:

> Only three or four days after the Wealth Tax was displayed in Istanbul, the price of a kilo of rice, which was previously sold at 200 kuruş, has fallen to 100 kuruş. The price of seedless grapes, which a week ago fetched a retail price of 100 kuruş, has fallen to 80 kuruş. The price of gold has fallen by two-thirds in two weeks. To see the beneficial effects of the Wealth Tax, it is sufficient to take account of the way the prices of goods, which were rising at a frenzied rate, have turned back in this way. This trend towards lower prices will not halt, it will continue from now on. Those who previously invested their money in goods and hid them in secret warehouses are, one by one, being brought into the open and forced to sell.[36]

One or two weeks after the Wealth Tax lists were displayed, the attitude of the press began to harden further. The "anti-minority" attitude of the news reporting and leading articles that appeared to the press became more pronounced. In particular, during the process of levying distress and sending taxpayers to Aşkale, anti-minority sentiment reached its zenith. At the same time, a further dimension involving criticism of conspicuous consumption and extravagance began to show more clearly. In this respect, the column of Peyami Safa entitled "Turkey: Paradise for

---

[36] Asım Us's column, *Vakit,* 23 December 1942.

Minorities" tells a lot:

> The life of Turkish minorities living in countries outside Turkey is hell; the life of minorities living in Turkey is heaven... For twenty years, the Republican government has made no distinction between minorities and the pure Turkish element. If there is a difference, it is in your favor: if you earn more, you live more comfortably. Minorities live in the best parts of Istanbul. The Anatolian shore of the Bosphorus is in ruins accommodating the pure Turkish element, but the European shore is well kept and full of minorities. The Yachting Club and all the hotels on Prince's Islands, the Thermal Waters Resort in Yalova, the beach and club in Suadiye and the most luxurious quarters and apartment buildings in Istanbul are eighty percent occupied by minorities. You cannot see such levels of wealth and happiness in any other city in the world... It is once again you who create the difference between yourselves and us. In Turkey minorities differentiate themselves from us with their accents. For they did not wish to learn Turkish until they had to. Although there are Turkish lessons in minority schools, are there not still those who insist on not learning Turkish and in particular on not speaking Turkish in public places? [37]

This is precisely what the Ankara government wished for. Once the final payment date for the Wealth Tax had passed, and the process of assembling the As, kale convoys and collecting payment by means of levying distress had begun, the press began to play a much more discernable role. The Istanbul dailies provided coverage in full detail of the levying of distress and sales. Certain newspapers published lists of the items on sale at auction rooms "for the benefit of their readers."

In the first days, the Istanbul press provided coverage down to the last striking detail of the distress levied and sales conducted at the homes of extraordinary taxpayers who, in one sense by way of protest against the wealth tax, had made very minimal amounts of payment. The reporting of heartbreaking instances of sale was presented as a "stern warning" for all other taxpayers who had delayed meeting their liabilities:

> The sale commenced in the flat at 10.30... The flat was packed with people. The rooms were small. At least 100-150 people had squeezed into this dollhouse. Nobody could see further than the back of the man or woman standing in front of them; it was as though the auctioneers voice was emanating from a distant, invisible place as though it was coming from the pit of Hell.

---

[37] *Tasvir-i Efkar,* 29 December 1942.

Climbing with their muddy shoes onto soft armchairs and sofas, *Maroccain* leather chairs and lacquered tables, clambering onto one another's shoulders in an effort to see the goods on sale were people gripped with a frenzy to get something at a knock-down price... Among the goods for sale were a complete dining room, a bedroom, two living rooms, a library and rest room and all of the furniture in these rooms. Family albums passed from hand to hand, pictures were examined in detail, valuable and stylish items were examined individually, and antiques, *objets d'art* and oil paintings were admired.[38]

Later, as it became apparent that there was a large amount of property to be sold, in addition to the auction hall in the Covered Bazaar run by the municipality, temporary auction rooms were put into service in three different neighborhoods of Istanbul. Since initially office and domestic furnishings of the "taxpayers with evil intent," to use the terminology of the day, were put up for sale, there were very few buyers. It emerged that this property, which only possessed value under the logic of conspicuous consumption, did not particularly strike a chord with the Istanbul middle class, and those trades- men who were engaged in supplying them. The class of people who would potentially have shown an interest in such goods was in any case trying to find a way to pay their Wealth Tax. On the other hand, those who thronged into Istanbul from Anatolia in the hope of getting goods at knocked-down prices were left wondering how they would transport the goods they had hoped to purchase on the State Railway.

Speeding up collection with the "Aşkale threat"

One of the most interesting features of the collection of the Wealth Tax was the way that, especially in the case of extraordinary taxpayers, the threat of "being sent to Aşkale" was constantly held up in front of them. In a by-law that was promulgated on January 12, 1943, before the statutory deadline for paying the Wealth Tax had expired, the principles concerning the "Labor Taxpayers" were laid down in the Official Gazette.[39] Accordingly, taxpayers would be sent to work locations in the following order:

1. First and foremost, those who had failed to make any payment whatsoever in respect of their Wealth Tax liabilities.

---

[38] *Tan,* 5 February 1943.
[39] "Regulations concerning the application of Articles 12 and 13 of the Wealth Tax Law number 4305 containing provisions with reference to the requirement to work." See, *Resmi Gazete*, no. 5302, 12 January 1943.

2. Later, those who, having paid a portion of their tax, had concealed property over which distress might be levied.

3. Then, those who had not concealed property and had displayed good faith in the matter of meeting their liabilities.

The aim behind the by-law was essentially to force taxpayers into displaying good will in the matter of payment and to reduce the number of protestors.

Once the deadline for paying the Wealth Tax expired on the evening of January 20, 1943, the time had come to round up those taxpayers who were to be sent to the Aşkale Labor Camp. This process was operated as follows: Initially the Directorate of Finance provided the Governor's Office with lists of taxpayers who required to be sent to Aşkale, following which the Istanbul Governor used the police to collect taxpayers from their homes and take them to the warehouse in the district known as Demirkapı that in those days adjoined Sirkeci Railway Station, where they were to await their transfer date.

When we consider that those who were to be sent to Aşkale were transported "in third class carriages attached to the Erzurum train," which departed from Haydarpaşa Station, the Istanbul press at the time had great difficulty in comprehending why those taxpayers who were classified as having "evil intent" were held at Sirkeci, the station from which trains to Europe such as the *Orient Express* departed. In principle, it would have made more sense to hold them on the Asian shore. In fact, the first thirty-two extraordinary taxpayers who were in the initial convoy that went to Aşkale on January 27, 1943 were taken from their homes on January 23, 1943 and accommodated for five days in a guest - house on the Asian side. Certain taxpayers met their liabilities while awaiting transportation and thus avoided going to Aşkale. Meanwhile, critical articles began to appear in the press with headlines of the kind: "Why are they being treated so well?" The administration, allegedly in response to this reaction on the part of public opinion, abandoned the policy of using relatively comfortable guest - houses as detention centers, and instead acquired the ex-warehouse building in Sirkeci / Demirkapı which it used to hold those awaiting transportation.[40]

---

[40] The logic behind this objection is explained in *Tasvir-i Efkar* on 27 January 1943 as follows: "A few days ago, we complained about the comforts provided at the *Moda Palace* and *Apergis* guest houses and the extreme politeness displayed towards those embracing of evil intent who have failed to pay the Wealth Tax. Having witnessed the way some of them conjure up large sums of money within an hour and thus avoid transportation, we once again pointed out that there is no point in behaving politely towards such holders of ill intent. Just as our soldiers who are summoned to the defense of the motherland are not assembled in guest houses and hotels, are not transported first class, we should similarly arrange for the transport of Wealth Tax taxpayers, whom we have summoned to perform a compulsory service in the interests of

Going to work in Labour Camp, Askale. 11 February 1943, *Tasvir-i Efkar,* daily.

On February 12, 1943, the date on which the second thirty-eight-person convoy set out for Aşkale, Colonel Binns of the British Embassy went to Sirkeci- Demirkapı to visit the British Embassy's lawyer Eskinazi, and conveyed his impressions in a report to the British Ambassador Sir H. Knatchbull-Hugessen. Colonel Binns's report is important in that it furnishes us with a description of the detention center at Sirkeci-Demirkapı:

> This morning I visited the barn at Demirkapı where some 40 merchants, lawyers and others have been imprisoned for the last 10 days and are being dispatched this evening to Aşkale and join the 32 already there. The room in which they are imprisoned, guarded by the police, is some 15 yards length by yards in width. Some 6 feet above the floor and running round two sides of the barn there is a platform some 6 feet in width. The deportees had laid out the bedding etc. brought by themselves (no mattresses) the whole length of this platform as well as round the two sides of the room below the platform. There is not a stick of furniture of any kind with the exception of one stove. The room was full of weeping men, women and children who had come to say goodbye and to bring the deportees odd parcels of food and clothing. A most depressing and wretched picture... I had gone to see our lawyer, Mr. Eskinazi, aged about 55. He told me that when arrested he had 11 liras with him. 10 liras taken by the police and he left with one lira.[41]

---

constructing the country, in tent camps in the courtyards of mosques and standard carriages. If nothing else, it is right that the holder of ill intent atones for the inequality in terms of the good things in life that he acquires for himself by sharing equally in any discomfort that is to be borne."

[41] Colonel Binns's report submitted as an attachment to the British Ambassador's correspondence, BNA,

The sole aim behind holding debtors who were awaiting transportation to Aşkale under harsh conditions was to speed up collection. For, in having defaulters removed from their homes by the police and taken to Sirkeci, the Ministry of Finance bureaucracy drove home to taxpayers that this was a serious business.

In those days Sirkeci was at the very heart of Istanbul's commercial center. The friends of the indebted taxpayers were most probably the owners of shops and workplaces that were within ten or fifteen minutes walking distance from Sirkeci. They could visit their friends during the lunch breaks. The indebted taxpayers were thus placed in the Demirkapı warehouse, not solely with the aim of scaring them into parting with their last hidden cache of money, but simultaneously to speed up collection more generally by providing those other debtors who had not yet been placed in the camp with a "stern warning." The Istanbul press provided detailed coverage of the names, amounts of unpaid tax and the amounts paid up until that date of those taxpayers who were held at Sirkeci and, if necessary, sent to Aşkale.

Sales of real property in connection with the Wealth Tax

In order to meet their Wealth Tax liabilities, taxpayers, initially made recourse to liquid funds at their disposal, and then sold the moveable property in their homes and businesses so as to convert these into cash. As of 21 January 1943, the date on which house sales and transportation to Așkale commenced, we have observed through an examination of the daily entry ledgers in which day-to-day transactions were recorded in that period at the Beyoğlu-Şişli, Eminönü, Fatih, Kadıköy and Adalar Land Registry Offices that sales of real property increased throughout Istanbul, and particularly there was an increase in the number of sales of homes, businesses, apartment buildings, plots and office blocks owned by non-Muslims.[42]

The information that we will present in this section were collected by the writer and involved recording *all sales of real property* conducted at the Beyoğlu- Şişli, Eminönü, Fatih, Kadıköy and Adalar Land Registry Offices

---

FO 371, 37402, no. R2416/7/44 sent by the British Ambassador to Ankara Sir Knatchbull-Hugessen to the British Foreign Minister Anthony Eden (March 5, 1943). Although Colonel Binns's report is undated, it was most probably written on February 12, 1943, the date on which the second convoy departed.

[42] This archive research was possible with a special permission granted to the scholar. In obtaining this permission, late Ömer Faruk Batırel, a professor of finance who was the Rector of Marmara University in early 1990s did his best to solve bureaucratic difficulties. I would like to express my gratitude to him. Interestingly, ten years later, a young MA student from Mersin University applied to the authorities replicate the similar research in Mersin. His application was refused without even consideration. I believe my publications on the Wealth Tax in 1996 must have created an unpleasant attitude among certain circles. This feeling must have led them to stop all further applications in relation to academic research by utilizing the Turkish Land Registry Archives.

between December 28, 1942 and June 30, 1943, and then processing these into tables with the aid of a computer. Sales of real property in those months, in which collection continued at full speed, will shed light on the nature of the transfer of wealth that took place through the implementation of the Wealth Tax.

Home auctions, Istanbul

A consideration that facilitated the conducting of this study, in that it enabled us to determine which particular sales were directly related to the

Wealth Tax, was the existence of a restriction that was put in place by Article 14 of the Wealth Tax Law. The final paragraph of Article 14 of the law reads as follows: "In the case of real property sales, land registry offices shall not perform registration unless certification is made by the relevant tax revenue office that it has no connection with Wealth Tax liabilities. Such registration as may be performed shall be null and void." We have stated at the beginning of this chapter, when describing the assessment process, that the Finance Ministry bureaucracy had access to little information about taxpayers' wealth and that certain Finance Ministry inspectors took it upon themselves to roam the streets in an effort to impose tax on the owners of real property. The lawmakers, aware of this situation, provided for the voiding of all transactions that might be conducted unless those wishing to sell their real property obtained a "clean bill of health" from a branch of the Ministry of Finance. This condition thus applied to all sales and title deed registration transactions that were conducted in this period.

Those property sales that were conducted with the aim of meeting Wealth Tax liabilities took place under the supervision of the Directorate of Finance. In such cases, the buyer and seller, accompanied by the Director of Land Registry or an officer whom he had appointed for this purpose, conducted the sales transaction at the relevant Finance Office branch, and consequently the proceeds of the sale were "instantly seized" and used to meet tax liabilities. In certain cases, the buyer initially went and paid the Wealth Tax of the person from whom he was going to buy the property and presented the tax receipt to the seller in place of cash and had the real property registered to his name.[43] All of this information is to be found in the individual real property files at Land Registry Offices.

In the first six months of 1943, 2742 sales transactions were conducted in the six boroughs of Istanbul. A mere 16 percent of these were sales that were directly connected with the Wealth Tax. However, if we look at the amount of the real property stock that was sold in connection with the Wealth Tax, this proportion rises to 48.5 percent. Thus the real property that was disposed of in order to pay the Wealth Tax was of greater value than the remaining property. Indeed, as Table 3 makes clear, while the average amount of sales transactions conducted in direct connection with the Wealth Tax was 25,177 liras, the average price of real property which changed hands in other sales was 5,101 lira. Moreover, it is stated in Director of Finance Faik Ökte's memoirs that in the course of

[43] For example, the sale conducted at Eminönü Land Registry Office on June 25, 1943 and recorded in the Daily Entry Ledger under number 2578: "Illias [Elias] sold a ¼ share in the real property to Mehmet Nuri Topbaş son of Ahmet, and the amount of the purchase was deposited against receipt number ... dated 25/6/1943 with Hocapaşa Payment branch to be set off against Wealth Tax."

collecting the tax in Istanbul 883 units of real property were put up for sale by auction, netting a total of TL 2,695,999.[44] The average proceeds from forced sales conducted by means of auction by the Finance Ministry bureaucracy was TL 3,053. It will be noted that the amount obtained in sales by auction of distrained property by the Finance Ministry bureaucracy was extremely low: the real property thus sold for the most part went at "bargain basin" prices.

We have stated above that, in the course of our investigations conducted in the Land Registry Office Archives, we recorded all sales that were conducted between December 28, 1942 and June 30, 1943. Similarly, to the extent that this was possible, we assigned the forenames and surnames of the parties who sold real property to pay the Wealth Tax to groups. We assigned those non- Muslims whose religious and ethnic origins could not be determined from their names and those groups which had little significance in numerical terms to the category of "other." Since it was impossible to identify members of the convert group from their names, we can only assume that such persons are included along with the "Muslims."

Table 3. Sales in connection with wealth tax in six sub-provinces of Istanbul

	Number of sales transactions conducted	Proportion of total sales	Total amount of real property sold (TL)	% of property sold	Average amount of real property sold (TL)
Sales directly connected to the Wealth Tax	440	16%	11,077,949	48.5%	25,177
Other sales	2302	84%	11,744,632	51.5%	5,101
TOTAL	2742	10%	22,822,581	100%	8,323

Source: Beyoğlu-Şişli, Eminönü, Fatih, Kadıköy and Adalar Land Registry Office Archives

The distribution by group of persons selling real property with the aim of paying Wealth Tax is shown in Table 4.

An examination in terms of groups of persons selling real property to pay Wealth Tax reveals that the most valuable real estates was sold by the Jewish community. This was followed by the Armenians and Greeks. Moreover, we were unable adequately to calculate the average value in this table with respect to minority companies. This is because one particular

---

[44] Ökte, *Varlık vergisi faciası*, 233.

sale comprised a complex containing buildings which occupied an important place on Istanbul's cultural and social map and that are still to be found in Beyoğlu today such as the Emek, Rüya and İpek movie theatres, the *Cercle D'Orient* and *Baylan Patisserie* which changed hands as a single item in order to pay Wealth Tax. We should state that, similarly, certain items of real property such as large office blocks, stores and apartment buildings located in Istanbul's central business district (Eminönü, Sirkeci, Karaköy, Beyoğlu) were disposed of in order to pay the tax.

Table 4. Persons selling real property to pay wealth tax

	Total amount of real property sold (TL)	Proportion of total sales	Number of units of real property sold	Average amount per unit of real property
Jews	4,404,820	39%	151	29,170
Armenians	3,275,747	28%	211	15,523
Greeks	1,370,440	12%	124	11,051
Minority Companies	1,110,375	10%	4	
Foreigners	605,700	5%	27	22,433
N and M partnerships	189,500	2%	2	94,750
Other minorities – Bulgarian, Russian etc.	37,700	0.3%	7	5,385
Muslims	92,642	0.8%	10	9,264
Companies with Muslim partners	1,025	0.1%	1	1,025
TOTAL	11,077,949	100%	543	20,401

Source: Beyoğlu-Şişli, Eminönü, Fatih, Kadıköy and Adalar Land Registry Office Archives

Table 5 shows the identity of the buyers of the 543 items of real property that changed hands in 440 sales transactions whose sellers are shown in Table 4. As is evident from the Table 5, 67.7 percent of those items of real property that were sold to pay Wealth Tax were bought by the Muslim-Turkish group. We can say that this property, whose average value was 16,521 liras, constituted the most valuable real estates in Istanbul in those days. A small portion of the real estate that was sold – only 2.3 percent in terms of value - were bought by minority groups. For the most part, these were people who, having sold an expensive building and paid their tax, bought a new property with any remaining funds they may have had.

The most striking conclusion that can be made from Table 5 is that official and semi-official entities such as public economic enterprises (*Sümerbank*, Agricultural Products Office, Turkish Sugar Factories), national banks (*İş Bankası*), national insurance companies (*Umum Sigorta, Milli Reasürans*), Istanbul Municipality and the General Directorate of Pious Foundations (*Vakıflar Genel Müdürlüğü*) purchased the most valuable real estates that were put up for sale due to the Wealth Tax.

Table 5. Groups buying real property

	Total amount of real property bought (TL)	Proportion of total purchases	Number of units of real property bought	Average amount per unit of real property
Groups buying real property:				
Muslim Turks	7,434,593	67,1%	450	16,521
Muslim Turks' companies	65,500	0,6%	2	32,750
Intermediate Total		67,7%		
Public Economic	1,693,584	15,3%	23	73,634
Enterprises, National Banks and National Insurance Companies Istanbul Municipality and	1,624,530	14,7%	11	147,684
The General Directorate of Foundations Intermediate Total		30%		
Armenians	109,867	1%	24	4,577
Greeks	82,900	0.7%	20	4,145
Jews and other Non-Muslims	66,975	0,6%	13	5,151
Total	11,077,949	100%	543	20,401

Source: Beyoğlu-Şişli, Eminönü, Fatih, Kadıköy and Adalar Land Registry Office Archives

The acquisition of 30 percent, in terms of value, of this property by state-controlled bodies is a further important dimension to the transfer of wealth that took place under the Wealth Tax. Most of the buildings purchased were buildings that as architectural vehicles for the outward expression of splendor were predecessors to today's skyscrapers/plazas. The way in which these sales were reported in the Istanbul press was also very interesting in that it reflected the ethnic nationalistic ethos of the day. For instance, an Armenian businessman, Vahram Gesaryan's prestigious building was bought over by Sümerbank. Mr. Geseryan was the owner of a number of concerns, most notably the His Master's Voice record company, and acted as the representative of certain foreign companies such as AEG. This event was reported in the *Cumhuriyet* newspaper as follows:

We were happy to announce that the "His Master's Voice" (HMV)

building in Beyoğlu was bought by *Sümerbank* and placed at the disposal of the Beyoğlu branch of the Local Goods Markets. In this way, a further fine building has been *nationalized* (!).[45]

Clearly, the term "nationalize" is not used here in its conventional sense. Even within the context of this brief news report, the most critical aspect of the Kemalist nationalist mindset comes to the fore. What is meant by the word "nationalization" which is emphasized in the report is the "Turkification" of the building in that ownership has passed to one of "us." As we have briefly stated at the beginning of this chapter, the acquisition by "state institutions" of buildings owned by minorities, who by definition were excluded from the category deemed to be the essential constituent of the country and perceived to be "non-national elements," was conveyed to readers in a vengeful manner. This sensitivity, which made itself manifested in the case of a single building involved in the Wealth Tax, went as far as fuelling a proposal for the total "Turkification" of Beyoğlu, which had a large concentration of minority and foreign residents and was an area in which displays of conspicuous consumption and extravagance took place.[46]

In lieu of a conclusion

At the beginning of this article we stated that we would consider the implementation of the Wealth Tax to be an example of the axis of tension that existed between the national state and non-Muslim minorities during the single-party period, and to attempt to throw light on certain less well-known dimensions of Kemalist nationalism. Within the process that began with the "Turkification" policies practiced in the first years of the Republic, the application of the Wealth Tax constitutes a veritable "breaking point."

In the first place, I wish to consider this "breaking point" in terms of the emotional impact it had on those involved. In the course of this study I conducted face-to-face interviews with persons who were either taxpayers when the Wealth Tax was introduced or their first-degree relatives. If never expressly couched in these terms, the implementing of the Wealth Tax had a negative impact on the process of integrating

---

[45] *Cumhuriyet* 23 February 1943.
[46] The series entitled "How the Beyoğlu gang strangles Turkish entrepreneurs" by Feridun Kandemir, which was published in *Tasvir-i Efkar* dated March 8, 1943, describes the struggle between the "oppressed Muslim entrepreneur," without whom there can be no "Turkification" policies, and the "minority merchant who stands by those of his own kind." The article goes as follows: "[Try to] picture Beyoğlu before the Republic. Were you able to encounter even a single pure Turkish establishment, store or shop? In this street which every other day was turned into a street in a foreign country as, to mark some festival or feast of those other than us, it was decked out from top to bottom in a riot of alien flags, for example a famous Turk of many years standing such as Hacı Bekir [famous Turkish delight producer], even should he wish and attempt to do so, could find no place, and would not be permitted to do so."

members of non-Muslim minorities into society. The advent of the Wealth Tax finally shattered the conviction of those who thought that those anti-minority policies (appointments to the civil service, etc.) that had come into effect would sooner or later be lifted.

Those members of non-Muslim minorities who consented to this state of affairs continued to live in Turkey, while those who were unhappy migrated to European countries, Israel or America. In particular, following the founding of the State of Israel, about 30,000 members of the Jewish community migrated to Israel within the space of two years (1948–9). Most of those emigrating were poor workers and craftsmen.

It is necessary to note at this point that it was not only Jews who emigrated from Turkey. If we compare the data concerning religious affiliation from censuses conducted between 1927 and 1965, we are struck by the significant degree of erosion among all non-Muslim minorities.

The downward trend that is evident in Table 6 between 1927 and 1965 continued in the following years, and as a consequence of the September 6–7, 1955 pogroms against non-Muslim minorities and the deportation of Istanbul Greeks in 1964 in relation to the Cyprus crisis, Turkey finally attained the status of a country whose population is, as we have of late so often been told, "99 percent Muslim and Turkish." As a consequence of these changes to the religious make-up of society, which, while possibly minor in numerical terms, were very important from a cultural point of view, the "non-Muslim" minorities, which the Republican administration had inherited from the Ottoman Empire and who had indirectly left their mark on a number of decisions taken by the central authority in the first years of the Republic, had effectively been eliminated.

The atmosphere of "uncertainty" created by the introduction of the Wealth Tax had an impact on decisions to migrate. It constituted one of the main factors behind what, on a personal level, was an extremely radical decision by members of minorities to migrate to another country. If we consider that forms of behavior such as tolerance, peaceful coexistence and accepting difference, which are currently the subject of much debate in Turkey, and are mainly acquired through the socialization process, can only be learnt by co-existing with minorities, it is possible to reach the conclusion that the Wealth Tax was "unfortunate" in that it led to the elimination of minorities. Particularly when we examine this question from the angle of Istanbul, the introduction of the Wealth Tax more than anything else contributed to the disappearance of the city's "multi-religious and multi-cultural" texture.

Second, I briefly wish to dwell on the point often suggested in connection with the introduction of the Wealth Tax; that is the entry of Muslim - Turkish entrepreneurs to the market. It can be no exaggeration to say that the Wealth Tax significantly weeded out the number of non-Muslims from among the ranks of the Istanbul bourgeoisie, which they had dominated, and those who managed to retain a foothold in the market in spite of this decimation were no longer able to flourish as before. There were no longer any large businessmen with roots in ethnic minorities in the single-party period. In fact, the large non-Muslim businesses currently in existence were rather companies that were set up and grown by young people who entered the markets after 1950. The Wealth Tax destroyed the chain of continuity.

Table 6. Distribution of the non-Muslim population of Turkey

Religious groups	1927	1935	1945	1955	1965
Muslims	13,269,936	15,838,763	18,497,801	22,804,048	31,129,854
Catholics	39,511	32,155	21,950	21,784	25,833
Orthodox	109,905	61,046	103,839	86,655	73,725
Protestants	6,658	8,486	5,213	8,952	22,983
Armenians	77,433	45,765	60,260	60,071	69,526
Jews	81,672	78,730	76,965	45,995	38,267
Other Christians	24,307	4,725	10,782	31,405	14,758
Total non-Muslims	339,486	309,140	279,009	254,862	245,092
% of non-Muslims	2,50	1,43	1,48	1,06	1,02

Source: State Statistical Institute, Statistical Yearbooks

Research conducted by Edward C. Clark among industrialists in the textile sector demonstrates that tension created by the Wealth Tax lay behind the reluctance shown by non-Muslim merchants after 1950 to move from commerce to manufacturing.[47] Some of the people we spoke to have stated that in the wake of the Wealth Tax they became reluctant even to entertain the idea of home ownership, preferring to live in rented accommodation, to say nothing of taking major decisions such as investing in manufacturing industry.

The retired finance inspectors whom I interviewed in the course of this study generally referred to the positive effects of the tax, and stated that it was only after 1943 and thanks to the Wealth Tax that Muslim entrepreneurs started to appear on the market. However, when I asked them to give me examples by stating the names of a few such people, they were unable to give more than one or two examples. In fact, these Finance

[47] Edward C. Clark, "The Turkish Varlik Vergisi Reconsidered," *Middle Eastern Studies Middle Eastern Studies* 8, no. 2 (1972): 205–16.

Ministry officials remained in their posts after the tax had been implemented and, if only at the level of inspection, stayed in touch with developments in the business world. Surely if the claims advanced by those who drew up and presented the Wealth Tax and those who mobilized the Finance Ministry bureaucracy to this end had been realized, these retired Finance Ministry officials should have been able to quote quite a few names.

The arrival in Istanbul of large and medium-sized landowners, who had become rich as a result of the shortages created by the war economy, is the topic for a separate piece of research. If nothing else, we can observe a change in the group whose proclivity toward conspicuous consumption was made the target of satire in comics, with minorities cast in this role until 1943, after which their place was taken "in purely visual terms" by *nouveau riche* "village pumpkins," whose bad manners and habit of being duped by alluring Istanbul women were made the butt of jokes.[48] To claim that the Wealth Tax first began to bear fruit after the influx into Istanbul of people from Anatolia with entrepreneurial know-how who took the place that had been relinquished by the minorities is tantamount to equating the social category we refer to as "entrepreneurs" with people who possess ready cash only. An entrepreneur is not merely somebody who has cash in his or her pocket; he or she is at the same time a person possessing knowledge and skills. It is thus wrong to imagine that the vacuum created by the introduction of the Wealth Tax could have been filled immediately.

Finally, I wish to state that for the researcher, to concern himself with a topic such as the Wealth Tax that carries such a "heavy emotional load" for those who experienced it made this task twice as difficult. In the case of both taxpayers and Finance Ministry officials, I was questioning them about a period of their life that they would prefer not to remember. Of all the interviews I conducted, one of them in particular moved me a great deal. An anecdote related by Finance Inspector, Mr. Burhan Ulutan, who was involved in implementing the Wealth Tax, in my opinion, very nicely sums up what the Wealth Tax was about. I wish to conclude this article with Mr. Ulutan's recollection:

At the time of the Wealth Tax I used to live in Osmanbey,

---

[48] The famous cartoonist Ramiz Gökçe had the following to say in the preface to his collection of cartoons named the *Nouveau Riche Bumpkin Album* which appeared in June 1946: "Dear Reader, the *nouveau riche* country bumpkins, who resembled astonished quails which had been blown into our city by powerful storms, rather than gold- finches, storks and swallows which arrive in flocks and, having multiplied, return to their own habitats, became the prey above all of we cartoonists. But we, unlike restaurants, bars and nightclubs, did not fleece them, nor did we place them in cages like the opportunists. Our sole transgression was, in the manner of natural historians, to observe and report the lifestyles of these inexperienced tourists. See, Ramiz Gökçe, *Hacı Ağalar Albümü* (Istanbul: Pulhan Matbaası, 1946).

Istanbul. And I used to go home for lunch. There was a tram stop at the place where there is now an entrance to Gülhane Park [Imperial Gardens of Topkapı Palace]. I used to get on the tram there. One day, on the way home, a hand tapped at my shoulder. And I just turned and saw that it was our Professor of Finance, Ibrahim Fazıl Pelin [from Istanbul University]. He leaned over and said:

- "So much for all my efforts!"

And I said, "I beg your pardon, sir." He continued:

- "Come now, you have forgotten everything I taught you [in the university]. Your dull wits were unable to absorb it. Have you forgotten those four rules of Adam Smith on taxation?"

- "Yes, sir. You taught them all to us. I know them and repeat them. But, sir, you taught us something else. I will also remind you of it."

When I said this, he stopped. [I continued]:

- "You also taught us about the capitulations. You taught us how the capitulations crushed the Turkish people. You also taught us the trickery that was employed." Having said this, I asked, "Is that not so?" And I went on:

- "Very well, we have now got rid of the capitulations [in 1923]. All fine and well, but [imagine that] there are two contestants. One of them has all resources at his disposal and dominates all of the country's economic life. And the Turks are still in a wretched [position]. In any case, they were [previously] villagers; they are weak and poor. They are still poor, still downtrodden, and it is still they [in other words, the minorities] who are ahead. Isn't it necessary to correct this? In other words, isn't it necessary to eliminate the harm done by the capitulations and the results of the wrongs that they have caused? In the interests of making up for lost ground and putting them on the same level."

- "Yes", he said.

Then we spoke about this matter. He was unable to provide me with many answers on this matter. He was a very good, a very honorable person. But he said the following to me:

"You speak very fine words, you are right and correct, but... you know, there is a saying. You know, one of those very fine Ottoman sayings: *It goes 'You cannot achieve perfection with evil instruments!'* That's another consideration. What about that?" [49]

Bibliography

Turkish Archives

Beyoğlu-Şişli, Eminönü, Fatih, Kadıköy ve Adalar Tapu Müdürlükleri Arşivleri, İstanbul. (Land Registry Directorates' Archives of the Boroughs of Beyoğlu-Şişli, Eminönü, Fatih, Kadıköy and Adalar / Istanbul)

US National Archives

The Records of the Department of State relating to Internal Affairs of Turkey, 1930–1944 (Microfilm no. M1224).

British National Archives

(Kew, London)
Foreign Office Correspondence, FO 371

Official Publications

Ayın Tarihi, years: 1942-1944.
Resmi Gazete, years: 1942-1944.

Daily Newspapers

Cumhuriyet, Tan, Tasvir-i Efkâr, Vakit. Years: 1942-1944.

Other Academic Works and Memoirs

Akar, Rıdvan. Varlık vergisi kanunu: tek parti rejiminde azınlık karşıtı politika örneği. İstanbul: Belge Yayınları, 1992.
Akçam, Taner. A Shameful Act: The Armenian Genocide and the Question of Turkish Responsibility. New York: Metropolitan Books, 2006.
Barutçu, Faik Ahmet. *Siyasî anılar*. İstanbul: Milliyet Yayınları, 1977.
Clark, Edward C. "The Turkish Varlik Vergisi Reconsidered." *Middle Eastern Studies Middle Eastern Studies* 8, no. 2 (1972): 205-16.
Filmer, Cemil. *Hatıralar: Türk sinemasında 65 yıl*. İstanbul: Emek Matbaacılık, 1984.
Fortna, Benjamin C., Stefanos Katsikas, Dimitris Kamouzis, and Paraskevas Konortas. *State-Nationalisms in the Ottoman Empire, Greece and Turkey: Orthodox and Muslims, 1830-1945*. New York: Routledge, 2013.
Gökçe, Ramiz. *Hacı Ağalar Albümü*. Istanbul: Pulhan Matbaası, 1946.
Heper, Metin. Türk kamu bürokrasisinde gelenekçilik ve modernleşme: siyaset sosyoloji açısından bir inceleme. İstanbul: Boğaziçi Üniversitesi Yayınları, 1977.
Keyder, Çağlar. State and Class in Turkey: A Study in Capitalist Development. London: Verso, 1987.
Koçak, Cemil. Türkiye'de millî şef dönemi: 1938-1945. İstanbul: İletişim, 1996.
Ökte, Faik. *The Tragedy of the Capital Tax*. London: Croom Helm, 1987.
———. *Varlık vergisi faciası*. İstanbul: Nebioğlu Yayınevi, 1951.

---

[49] Interview conducted with the late Burhan Ulutan on 2 August 1992.

Parla, Taha. The Social and Political Thought of Ziya Gökalp, 1876-1924. Leiden: Brill, 1985.

Weber, Max. *Economy and Society: An Outline of Interpretative Sociology*. Vol. 2. Berkeley: University of California Press, 1978.

CHAPTER 7

TURKISH ATTITUDES *VIS À VIS* THE ZIONIST PROJECT*

Ayhan Aktar and Soli Özel **

The relations between Turkey and Israel are going through a renaissance. Not only are the two countries enhancing their collaboration on military matters and moving closer to one another politically and strategically, but there is a virtual boom in cultural and trade relations as well. Although the two countries insist that their rapprochement is not directed against any third parties, the Middle East political equation has been greatly effected by these recent developments. Within Turkey, despite the consensus that exists among the elites as to the advantages of strengthening political, economic, strategic and military ties with Israel, there are those who question the wisdom of so open and public a flirtation.[1]

From Turkey's perspective there are expectations of tangible returns to this rapprochement: The ability to buy from Israel the military hardware denied to Turkey by the US; the Israeli assistance in upgrading old military equipment, notably fighter planes; the possibility of joint production in some weapons systems; sharing of intelligence information between the two countries and the increasing volume of trade and tourism come to mind. In addition to these, Turkey expects that her close relation with Israel would bring her the moral and political support of the Jewish lobby in the US when she needs to fight her political battles in the US Congress. Effective lobbying groups in Washington and elsewhere regularly attack Turkey because of its human rights violations, its democratic deficit and the concerns specific to the Armenians or to Greeks and Greek Cypriots.

This new situation marks, almost with a vengeance, the end of the ambivalence that colored Turkey's attitude *vis à vis* the Jewish state since its inception. Indeed one could argue that this ambivalence goes all the way back to the British Mandate period in Palestine. In this paper we will try to examine and illustrate some aspects of this ambivalence and present

** Soli Özel is a Lecturer at the Department of International Relations, Kadir Has University.
[1] M. Hakan Yavuz, "Turkish-Israeli Relations through the Lens of the Turkish Identity Debate," Journal of Palestine Studies : A Quarterly on Palestinian Affairs and the Arab-Israeli Conflict Journal of Palestine Studies 27, no. 1 (1997): 22–37.

a reflective account of Turkey's attitude toward and perception of the Zionist project and, then, the state of Israel.

One of the rare accounts of the early period of Turkish-Israeli relations is the doctoral dissertation by George E. Gruen, which in our view remains unsurpassed in many respects.[2] In this article we do not attempt to give as comprehensive a picture of the origins of Turkish-Israeli relations as Gruen presented. What we try to do is to put the evolution of the relations in their proper context, reflect on the important turning points and evaluate these in terms of Turkey's strategic perspectives and its complicated and sensitive relations with the Arab world. To this end, we went over the collections of daily newspapers like *Ulus, Cumhuriyet, Vatan* and *Ayın Tarihi*, a compilation of news and commentaries published by the Press office of the Prime Ministry.

It is interesting to note that throughout the period from the summer of 1947 through March 1949, the official newspaper of the ruling Republican People's Party (RPP), *Ulus*, gave a decent amount of coverage to the developments in the region and most of the commentaries in the paper, which were rather well-informed, concerned themselves mainly with one political aspect: the involvement of the Soviet Union in the area and the likely presence of Soviet troops as peace-keepers or in any other guise. Israel was seen as a possible Soviet ally and thus politically undesirable. Especially important in this respect are the dispatches and commentaries of Ahmet Şükrü Esmer from Washington, DC. In the period prior to the UN decision on partition through the recognition of the state of Israel (first *de facto*, then *de jure*) *Ayın Tarihi* devoted considerable space to developments in Palestine and to commentaries about the evolving political, diplomatic and military situation in the region.

The most prominent and persistent commentator on the issues of Palestine throughout the late 1930s and 1940s is Ömer Rıza Doğrul, who was writing in *Tan* and *Cumhuriyet*. Whereas *Cumhuriyet* gave precious little space to developments in Palestine when the Soviets did not loom large and its chief columnists and others only wrote once or twice on the matter, Doğrul devoted a considerable portion of his writings to the developments in the region.[3]

---

[2] George Emanuel Gruen, "Turkey, Israel and the Palestine Question, 1948-1960: A Study in the Diplomacy of Ambivalence." (Unpublished Ph.D Dissertation, Columbia University, 1970).

[3] Born and brought up in Cairo from a Turkish descent, Doğrul was bilingual in Turkish and Arabic. Started his journalistic career in Cairo at *eş-Şa'b*, he moved to Istanbul during the First World War. He later became an active member of the Turkish literati. Ömer Rıza Doğrul was connected to modernist/Islamist circles in the early years of the republic. Married to the daughter of Mehmet Akif Ersoy, he later published his articles in several Islamist periodicals mostly informing the Turkish readers on the social and political developments in Islamic world. His translation of the Quran, published under

Other important figures from the press such as Burhan Belge, Nizamettin Nazif, Selim Ragıp, Burhan Felek, Mümtaz Faik Fenik, Hasan Ali Ediz, Sabah Can, Asım Us and retired general Emir Erkilet and political figures like Nihat Erim have from time to time commented on the matter. We shall give samples of their commentaries which we judge to be representative of the intellectual and policy-making elite of Turkey. Our conclusions are based on the way the Turkish elite looked upon the Zionist project. At a time when press freedom, especially on matters of foreign policy was rather limited, we assumed that they would be reflective of official policies as well as indicative of some popular sensitivities that are not elaborated. Needless to say, the opening of the Turkish Foreign Ministry Archives would have helped matters greatly.

Limited Interest, measured cooperation

The 1930s was a period when important developments took place both in Palestine and in Europe, that would have a bearing on the future of relations between two nationalisms under the British mandate. The persistent resistance of the Palestinians to the consolidation of the Zionist gains under the Mandate periodically blew up in violence, the last important example of which took place in 1929. The Passfield White Paper that was prepared by the British government was unfavorable to the Zionists and generated considerable worry among the political leadership of the settlers.[4] The early 1930s saw the Jewish communities, most notably in Germany and Central Europe, beginning to feel the mounting pressure against them. The war loomed large in the horizon and the Zionist leadership did everything in its power to secure the continuation of migration into Palestine.

The eruption of the Arab Rebellion in 1936 was arguably a critical turning point in the history of the Palestine Mandate right before the War. The Rebellion led to the drafting of the Peel Report, and on the part of the Arab states marked the beginning of their diplomatic involvement in the Palestine issue in earnest. With the war almost eminent in Europe, the British government felt the need to consolidate its position among Arab countries and called a conference in London that was to determine its new policy after the failure of the Peel Report.

A survey of *Ayın Tarihi* indicates that the Turkish press watched very

the title of *Tanrı Buyruğu*, made him famous both in Islamic and secular circles. During the inter-war period, he published his articles in *Cumhuriyet* and *Tan* mostly on Middle Eastern affairs using his extensive knowledge of the Arab and Islamic worlds. In his political writings, Doğrul argued that Turkey should use her authority to unite Islamic countries under an "Islamic front" in opposition to Western and Eastern fronts that existed in his period. For best biographic article on Ömer Rıza Doğrul, see, *Türkiye Diyanet Vakfı - İslâm Ansiklopedisi*, vol 9, 489 - 492.
[4] Charles D Smith, *Palestine and the Arab-Israeli Conflict* (Boston: Bedford/St. Martin's, 2001). Ch. 4.

carefully over the developments in Palestine. At a time when Turkey virtually turned its back on the Middle East, this was all more remarkable. Looking at the writings of some senior opinion makers, one can draw the following conclusions on the way these writers evaluated the Zionist endeavor and the nature of the struggle in Palestine. Zionism was treated as an imperialist movement and was associated with the expansionism of Western powers in the region. Both in the writings from this specific period and later, this is a recurring theme. For instance, a senior figure in the press, Burhan Belge who visited the region in 1937 wrote that,

> Zionism can rightly be considered an imperialist movement. (...) History is the biography of all nations, but it does not constitute a title deed for any nation...The Jews felt the need for a homeland of their own because of the persecution and insults they suffered everywhere ... The Jew had become universalistic, tolerant and liberal because of this suffering...Zionism denies all this. It adopts violence and uses money as its means (...) What difference does it make if a man has been uprooted by force, insults and reservation camps or by the cold and material arrogance of gold?[5]

At a later period, another prominent journalist also commented that, "the late 19th century immigration to Palestine is closely linked to the interest that the great powers have entertained for Palestine. In fact ... it was first the Germans and then the British who supported the Zionist movement."[6]

Remaining within the logic of this "imperialist presence" and believing that the Zionists would keep on asking and getting more land for the realization of their project some writers noted that this development was also fostering the rise of nationalist feelings among the Arabs and the Palestinians. For instance, the most informed commentator of the period, Doğrul, who looks favorably upon such a development, remarks that "the Arabs want migration to stop and wish to control their destiny in their homeland."[7]

Most commentators in the press saw the struggle in Palestine between the two communities as the contest of two nationalisms. The periodic eruption of violence and the ineffectual efforts of the British to contain these are seen as the natural consequence of the irreconcilability of the interests of the two nationalisms. According to Doğrul, "the reason why this issue appears so intractable and why it constantly generates confrontation is the attempt to squeeze into this tiny land two peoples

---

[5] Burhan Belge, *Tan*, 22 July 1937.
[6] Hasan Ali Ediz, *Cumhuriyet*, 15 August 1947.
[7] Ömer Rıza Doğrul, *Tan*,19 May 1939

who detest one another, whose interests are incompatible."[8]

Although we know less about the normative evaluations of the Turkish government *vis à vis* the Zionist project in this period, there are number of interesting contradictions one can observe in the actions of the Turkish government. While the Jewish population of Eastern Thrace was being virtually forced to migrate to Istanbul,[9] and at a time when the Turkish government closed down the all associations including the Turkish branches of B'nai-B'rith[10], Ankara was extending its welcome to Jewish professors from Germany who were being persecuted by the Nazi regime in Berlin.[11] The Turkish government did not permit the presence or the activities of indigenous Zionist organizations. Yet, according to Gruen, Ankara had close relations with the Jewish Agency, the paramount Zionist organization in Palestine in those days. Turkey participated in the Zionist sponsored Levant fair in Tel Aviv in 1936. For its part, the Jewish Agency "first participated in the İzmir International Fair, and then the Foreign Trade Institute, founded by the Jewish Agency in cooperation with the Palestine Manufacturers' Association, established a branch in Turkey" in 1938. [12]

During the War, the Turkish government either turned a blind eye or supported the migration of Jews to Palestine allowing them to use its territory. On the other hand, this was also the period when the Ankara government enacted the infamous Capital Levy, which was applied to the detriment of the non-Muslim minorities, as will be discussed later. The Turkish government was under pressure both from the Nazis and the British. The former asked for the return of those Jews who managed to cross the border in order to put them in concentration camps. Britain told the Balkan countries not to allow their Jewish citizens to escape to Turkey and asked the Turkish government not to accept Jewish refugees and not to allow the use of its port facilities for passage to Palestine.[13] The most tragic incident of the period resulting from this pressure was the sinking of *Struma* in the midst of Second World War. This was a steamer with 769 Jewish refugees on board, which was refused the permission to go through the Straits because of British pressure on the Turkish

---

[8] Ömer Rıza Doğrul, *Tan*,5 May 1939

[9] See Ayhan Aktar, "Trakya Yahudi Olaylarını 'Doğru' Yorumlamak," (Correct Interpretation of the Jewish Exodus from Eastern Trace - 1934) *Tarih ve Toplum*, (İstanbul: İletişim Yayınları) No 155, Kasım 1996. pp. 45 - 56

[10] Records of the Department of State Relating to the Internal Affairs of Turkey 1945 - 1949 (M 1224), Dated 3 July 1935, 867. 4016 Jews/17

[11] The memoirs of Professor Fritz Neumark are quite revealing on this intellectual migration. See, Fritz Neumark, *Boğaziçine sığınanlar: Türkiye'ye iltica eden Alman ilim siyaset ve sanat adamları, 1933-1953* translated by and Şefik Alp Bahadır (İstanbul: İstanbul Üniversitesi İktisat Fakültesi Maliye Enstitüsü, 1982).

[12] Gruen, *ibid*, 22.

[13] For an interesting analysis of this period, see Stanford J Shaw, *The Jews of the Ottoman Empire and the Turkish Republic* (New York: New York University Press, 1991), 256-257.

government. *Struma* was torpedoed just outside of the Bosporus and all but one of its passengers perished.[14] As Stanford Shaw observed, "while Nazi and British pressure at times forced Turkey to overtly limit ... Zionist rescue activities by closing the *Aliyah* office and limiting Jewish immigration to those who could show British permission for them to enter Palestine, the Turkish government allowed...the unofficial *Aliyah Bet* organization to continue to bring in Jewish refugees and send them to Palestine on an 'illegal' basis."[15]

The Question of Partition

At the end of the Second World War, Turkey found itself in a rather lonely position. The policy of "active neutrality"[16] that served Ankara well during the course of the war appeared insufficient in the post-War era to resist Soviet expansionist demands. Only six months after Turkey finally declared war on Germany so as to qualify participating in the San Francisco Conference that founded the United Nations, Soviet foreign minister Molotov asked for joint control of the straits and expressed the wish to annex two of Turkey's northeastern provinces.[17] Thus, Turkey found itself faced with the same geostrategic challenge that defined the last two hundred years of the Ottoman Empire: Russian/Soviet expansionism at its expense. As British Secretary of State for Foreign Affairs, Lord Halifax noted carefully during the war, Turkish foreign policy was always conducted with an eye to the intentions and behavior of Russia and then the Soviet Union.[18] It was obvious that the warm relations that served both countries well in the inter-War period were no

---

[14] On the *Struma* affair, see Bülent Gökay, "Belgelerle *Struma* Faciası - 25 Şubat 1942," [A Documented Account of the Struma Tragedy – 25 February 1942] *Tarih ve Toplum*, No. 116, (August 1993), 42 - 45

[15] Shaw, ibid, 257

[16] Active neutrality was defined by PM Saracoğlu in a speech to the Grand National Assembly on August 6 1942: "Turkey does not pursue adventures beyond her frontiers, she has sought means of remaining outside the war and has found them in a conscious and active neutrality...Turkey could not have safeguarded her position by passive neutrality and cannot do so in the future." This was cited in Selim Deringil, *Turkish Foreign Policy during the Second World War: An "Active" Neutrality* (Cambridge: Cambridge University Press, 1989), 136.

[17] On June 7, 1945 Molotov told the Turkish Ambassador Selim Sarper that good relations could be restored only if Soviet demands were accepted. Although there is a controversy among the scholars whether Soviet demands were officially pronounced or not at that time, nevertheless Ankara government practically felt the pressures coming from the north. Especially with the memorandum given to Ankara government on 7th of August 1946, the antagonism between Ankara and Moscow reached to its climax. See inter alia, İsmail Soysal, *Soğuk savaş dönemi ve Türkiye: olaylar kronolojisi (1945-1975)* (İstanbul: İsis, 1997). And also, Bruce R. Kuniholm, *The Origins of the Cold War in the Near East: Great Power Conflict and Diplomacy in Iran, Turkey, and Greece* (Princeton: Princeton University Press, 1994).

[18] A memorandum from Viscount Halifax to HM's representatives at Moscow, Angora, Athens, Belgrade, Bucharest, Sofia, Budapest, dated July 5, 1940 stated that: "In the long run, Turkey's foreign policy is governed by that of Russia - the hereditary enemy, whose age-long ambition is to rest the Straits from Turkey. Whatever country is opposed to Russia is, *ipso facto*, favored by Turkey. Thus, in the last war Turkey sided with Germany, largely because Germany was Russia's enemy and Great Britain was Russia's ally." *Further correspondence respecting Turkey. Part XL - July to December 1940.* Public Records Office, FO 424/285, R6703/G.

more. The fact that in June 1945 the Soviet Union was still an ally of the Western democratic front and the Cold War was not yet on the horizon, meant that Turkey could be alone facing the Soviet threat. As we will see later, for Turkey's policy makers and opinion makers alike, the fear of Soviet expansionism would be an important factor in evaluating the creation of the state of Israel and the policy Turkey should adopt accordingly.

On the Zionist side, the most important development was the favorable disposition of President Truman to resume Jewish migration to Palestine. In fact, his suggestion that 100,000 Jews be admitted to Palestine sent shock waves through the Arab world, and led some Arab countries to warn of dire consequences should such an act take place. Truman went a step further in his "Yom Kippur statement" of October 1946, and in a rather ambiguous way supported the creation of a Jewish state. On the ground in Palestine, both the Jewish terrorist groups and the mainstream Zionist political groups were agitating for immigration to be free and for the promise of a "Jewish national homeland" to be fulfilled. The declaration by Britain that it would no longer assume the responsibility of governing Palestine as the mandatory power and its decision to turn the matter over to the United Nations in February 1947 were a critical juncture on the road to the formation of the Jewish state.[19]

Turkey's analysis of the situation in Palestine was inspired by political and geostrategic considerations. However, Turkey was also in a bind. On the one hand, it feared the expansion of Soviet influence to the south of its borders. On the other hand it wanted to be in good terms with the powerful American Jewish community in order to receive its support "in turning public opinion and policy makers in the United States in favor of Turkey."[20] So, according to the prevalent view at the time, courting Jewish public opinion in the United States to further Turkey's relations with Washington was in the national interest. These relations were already cultivated during the San Francisco Conference. In order to pursue their own agenda and to manage to institutionalize Turkey's relations with the emerging leader of the democratic front, the United States, they understood the need to further deepen their contacts.[21] However, doing so would also necessitate having a favorable view on Jewish migration to

---

[19] William Roger Louis, *The British Empire in the Middle East: 1945-1951 ; Arab Nationalism, the United States and Postwar Imperialism* (Oxford: Oxford Univ. Press, 1998), 394-395.

[20] Gruen, *ibid*, 29.

[21] The chief press officer of the Turkish delegation to the United Nations' 1945 San Francisco Conference later recalled "how greatly influential and well organized American Jewry is and of what tremendous assistance it was to us in awakening public opinion to our cause at a time when the Soviets were demanding the Straits and our eastern provinces" Falih Rıfkı Atay, *Dünya*, 9 November 1955. Quoted in Gruen, *ibid*, 11.

Palestine.

Ordinarily, this would not constitute a problem for the Turkish administrations. However, in this particular issue, as well Turkey was in an *impasse*. Accommodating Jewish wishes would lead the administration to allow migration of Turkish Jews into Palestine. On the other hand, Turkey did not wish to offend the Arab countries. Gruen presents the details of the Turkish record on that matter. Although the Turkish delegate to the United Nations remained silent during the talks over partition, Turkey ultimately voted with the Arab countries in every turn, including on November 29, 1947 when the UN accepted the partition of Palestine between a Jewish and an Arab state. However, true to Turkey's ambivalent stance on this matter, Foreign Minister Necmettin Sadak told an American correspondent the following: "Turkey as a faithful and honorable member of the UN - cannot separate itself from the decisions [the UN] adopted."[22]

On *realpolitik* terms Turkey's decision was inspired by the fear that the inevitable civil war between Arabs and Jews that will ensue from the partition decision of the United Nations would lead to a regional war. This, in turn, might later lead to a more general war. It could also lead to an increase in Soviet influence in the Middle East, a most undesirable outcome for Ankara. As Foreign Minister Sadak noted in an interview with *Ulus*,

> Turkey knew that the partition decision would lead to violence and instability. The correctness of this evaluation has been proven in a most tragic manner ... we hope that by the time partition becomes a reality, a kind of agreement can be reached that would be satisfactory to both parties. Otherwise, we fear that the east would become a battlefield that would draw the entire world to turmoil.[23]

Turkey always prided itself for its ability to make foreign policy decisions on the sole criterion of realistic political assessments. On the face of it, the reasoning Sadak offered about Turkey's vote against partition was consistent with that principle. Against claims by Jewish organizations in the United States that religious solidarity might have played a part in Turkey's stance, policy makers insisted that their support of the Arab position on Palestine had nothing to do with Muslim solidarity. It is true that Turkey's rulers were weary of a Jewish state that they thought would be sympathetic to the Soviet Union and that could easily become a launching ground for Soviet expansionism in the Middle

---

[22] Quoted in Gruen, *ibid*, 38.
[23] *Ulus*, 18 February, 1948.

East.

Our contention here is that, as Gruen also intimates, at least part of the reason why Turkey opposed partition and voted with the Arabs had to do with the sensitivities of its population. In the new multiparty era that Turkey has just entered in 1945, the policy makers in the ruling People's Republican Party were not as insulated from popular sentiments as they were before and wished to remain in the future. This also shows that in foreign policy making there is perhaps an invisible limit to what a government can do that goes against the sensitivities of a large segment of its population. When one looks at the writings of commentators in the period between the partition decision and Turkey's recognition of Israel, one sees that utmost care was given to stress the Muslim and "two millennia long" Arab possession of the land. As much care was given not to raise the sensitive issue of how those lands were lost by the Ottoman Empire at the end of the First World War. This was an issue that was raised only after the recognition of Israel and commented on the Turkish press, especially by Ömer Rıza Doğrul.[24]

Fear of Soviet Influence

The fear of growing Soviet influence increasingly colored the interpretation of the events by Turkish commentators. The future Zionist state, and then Israel at the beginning were treated as potential allies, if not puppets of the USSR. Both the Americans and the British were chastised for their lack of political wisdom in different periods between the partition decision and the actual declaration of independence by Israel and the ensuing war. So when the United States no longer seemed certain of the wisdom of the partition decision and wanted to send a multilateral force to Palestine, the commentators were almost unanimous in condemning the move:

> Since Russia would obviously want to participate in this endeavor by sending its troops, England and the US would have brought in the Russian power into a region of primary strategic importance, of their own free will ... It is only now that the Americans begin to understand the meaning of the Russian vote in favor of the partition of Palestine.[25]

Till the day when partition was to take effect, Turkish commentators paid a great deal of attention to the developments and called upon the international community to take wise steps to prevent the impending war. Major newspapers sent senior reporters or correspondents to the region

[24] Ömer Rıza Doğrul, *Cumhuriyet*, 30 March 1949
[25] Ahmet Şükrü Esmer, *Ulus*, 29 February 1948.

to evaluate the evolving situation. Although their sympathies were for the Arabs, or at the very least they did not favor the creation of a Jewish state of Israel, most of the reporting and commentary from the area did not give the Arabs much of a chance to win their battle against the Jews. For instance Nizamettin Nazif, commenting in *Gece Postası*, made a very realistic assessment of the Arab countries' military capabilities and called upon them to choose the road of negotiation rather than a war they could not win.[26] The concern over the "Russians" went so far as reporting their alleged presence in Palestine. Throughout the period between the UN decision on partition and the declaration of independence on May 15 by the Jewish authorities, the newspapers echoed the government's view that, at all costs a Russian presence in Palestine had to be avoided. Thus, the idea of an international force advanced by the Truman administration, which presumably understood the mistake it made earlier by supporting partition, was relentlessly attacked. The Americans were even condescended for not being astute in matters of international affairs. In a typical, alarmist commentary written the day after partition was to take effect and the state of Israel was proclaimed Sabah Can stated that

> The Russians will come to this country before anyone else and wreak havoc in the Middle East. Under such dangerous conditions to who is the mandate administration turning this country over to? Does England find it suitable for its interest that the Russian influence and power enters the Middle East in such a wide and legitimate manner?[27]

As was expected by everyone, the proclamation of the state of Israel was followed by the immediate attack of the Arab countries against the infant state. What was shocking for the Turkish opinion makers and uncomfortable for the administration was the fact that the Soviet Union recognized the new state shortly after the United States, which extended its recognition almost immediately. The Soviet recognition, in the mind of those who were concerned about a Soviet presence in the Middle East, was a confirmation that the Soviets would make every effort to influence the developments in the region. Since, the Soviet intentions were, by definition, subversive of Turkey's interests, the Soviet move generated almost a hysteric response. In a representative commentary, Professor Ahmet Şükrü Esmer wrote that,

> Russia has suddenly become a friend of the Zionists and the enemy of the Arabs. Russia has taken a favorable attitude towards the Zionist whom it considered a tool of English imperialism until recently ... Russia has taken it upon itself to make sure that the

---

[26] Nizamettin Nazif, *Gece Postası,* October 12, 1947
[27] Sabah Can, *Ulus,* 15 May 1948.

partition succeeds and a Jewish state is established.[28]

As we have suggested earlier, this fear of Soviet intentions and expansionism persuaded the policy makers in Ankara that Turkey had to find its rightful place in the evolving world order. Already with the Truman doctrine Turkey was considered a country of importance for Western interests and where the West drew the line against Soviet expansionism. Turkey was also included, along with Greece, among the recipients of the Marshall Plan. Later on Ankara would work very hard to become part of the emerging Atlantic Alliance since it wished to institutionalize its relations with the West.

For the government in Ankara, relations with Israel would be an important part of that endeavor as we will see later. To that end, relations with the American Jewish community were considered to be critical. Gruen also makes clear that the Jewish community in the United States and the Jewry as a whole considered Turkey's position *vis a vis* the creation of the state of Israel as very important. Turkey's relaxation of migration rules for its Jewish citizens were thought to be important to get the new state much needed manpower both to fight the war and to build the country. We will show that the Turkish government favored the migration of its Jewish citizens to Palestine. In this respect, there was common ground in the political agenda of both parties. Yet, the American Jewish community proved itself to be very sensitive to Turkey's negative wartime record concerning its minorities. Some representatives of the Jewish community held Turkey accountable for the implementation and consequences of Capital Levy and used their influence to put pressure on the American government to persuade Turkey to recognize its wrongdoings. We now turn to the story of the migration of Jews to Palestine and the story of the notorious Capital Levy.

The Capital Levy and the Exodus of Turkish Jews to Palestine

Dispatches sent from US diplomatic missions to Washington and documents in the US National Archives suggest that during the same period Turkey's desire to be a part of the Western side of the Cold War divide could also be linked to the Jews and the formation of the state of Israel. Recognition of the new state was a card which Turkey could use to get closer to the United States and perhaps more importantly to ingratiate itself to the increasingly influential Jewish community, which had taken a very unfavorable note of Turkey's treatment of its minorities especially during the war.

Since the formation of the Turkish Republic in 1923, the relationship

---

[28] Ahmet Şükrü Esmer, *Ulus*, 6 June 1948.

between non-Muslim minorities and the Kemalist regime had been at times uneasy and somewhat precarious. The newly forming Turkish nation-state implemented "Turkification policies". In this context "Turkification policies" meant to be the domination and positive discrimination for the Turkish ethnic identity in nearly every aspect of social and economic life.[29]

During the single party period, the most drastic Turkification policy was Capital Levy (*Varlık Vergisi*), which was implemented in the midst of the Second World War.[30] Promulgated in the Turkish Parliament in November 1942, the declared purpose of this law was to tax extraordinary profits which were accumulated due to war conditions. However, the tax assessments were made by the so-called independent local committees in an arbitrary fashion. The assessments were to be posted within a period of fifteen days, and the tax had to be paid within a month of the date of posting.[31] Failure to pay made the defaulter's property liable to seizure and sale. And the defaulter himself was deported to a labor camp in eastern Anatolia.

The declared purpose of this law was to tax huge profits made through war-time profiteering and to penalize profiteers themselves, as well as to combat inflation through the reduction of bank notes in circulation. But the Capital Levy turned out to be an excellent measure to expropriate the non-Muslim minorities and weaken their hold in the economic life of the country. Careful analysis of the figures provided by Faik Ökte, the Director of Finance in Istanbul, illustrates the fact that out of 62,575 tax payers in Istanbul, 87 per cent came from various minority groups. In other words, not only the rich minority merchants paid the tax but taxi drivers, secretaries, wage-earners, peddlers, self-employed small producers were forced to pay the Capital Levy as well. Anyway there was not a single Turkish/Muslim defaulter among the 1229 persons deported to and made to work in the Aşkale labor camp.

Due to war conditions, the Great Powers did not intervene on behalf of the minorities. Anyway they were busy fighting against the German and Italian Armies on different fronts. At that point Turkey's neutrality was very valuable for both parties. Therefore there was little press coverage of the disaster of the Capital Levy in the English-speaking world. In the summer of 1943, Cyrus Sulzberger from the *New York Times* visited Turkey and this was a turning point on the part of the Ankara government

---

[29] See the article in this collection on "Turkification" policies.

[30] For detailed account of the Capital Levy, see the article in this collection.

[31] On 27 December 1942, the lists were prepared and made known to the public all over the country. There were 114,368 tax payers all over the country and they were to pay TL 465,300,000 which was equal to 50.9 per cent of the total state expenditures in the 1942 national budget. Tax - payers in Istanbul had to pay nearly 75 per cent of the total Capital Levy assessed in Turkey.

vis a vis the defaulters. On his return, Sulzberger published a series of articles in the *New York Times* from September 9 to 13 in 1943. He underlined the anti-minority bias of the Capital Levy. Sulzberger stressed the fact that "many observers concluded, however, that the tax was intended to drive non-Moslems out of business and thus solve once and for all the problem of minority control of much of Turkey's commercial life."[32] This must have created a feeling of unease in Ankara in that only four days later, on 17 September, the Parliament approved a law authorizing the Minister of Finance to cancel unpaid assessments under Capital Levy on small employees receiving daily or monthly wages and on peddlers and persons of similar occupation whose daily gross revenues were small.[33] Soon after, in the first week of December 1943, the defaulters in labor camps were permitted to go back to Istanbul. And the Capital Levy was practically terminated.

In April 1948, only four and a half years later, the formation of the Israeli state created an important pull-factor for the Jewish minority in Turkey. Especially the poor Jews working as laborers or the unemployed were thrilled. At last there was an alternative place for them to migrate. Soon after the formation of the Israeli state, great enthusiasm prevailed among the Jews in Istanbul and they started to apply for visas to travel to Israel. In his study of the Turkish Jews in Israel, Walter Weiker states the fact that "according to official statistics, 4,362 Jews came from Turkey between May and November 1948. Those who came after the founding of the state can be divided into two groups. One was the great wave of 1948-49 (...) Some 33,000 Jews moved to Israel from Turkey between 1948 and the early months of 1950."[34] The exodus of Turkish Jews could also be followed in Turkish population censuses. According to 1945 census there were 76,965 Jews in Turkey. This figure was reduced to 45,995 in 1955.[35]

In his interviews, Weiker also observed that most of the Turkish Jews who migrated in this period came from the poorer sections of the Turkish urban population. In his interviews, Weiker found out that most of the

[32]Cyrus Sulzberger's article in *New York Times*, 11 September 1943.
[33] Turkish Minister of Foreign Affairs Numan Menemencioglu expressed his concerns to Robert F. Kelley, US Charges d'Affaires in Ankara about "a slanderous campaign is being carried on in the American press against Turkey in regard to the Tax on Wealth." Kelley immediately informed his ambassador who was in Washington at that moment about the complaints of the Turkish side. Ambassador Laurence A. Steinhardt discussed the matter with Mr. Arthur Sulzberger of the New York Times and has been assured that the New York Times will publish no more articles on the Turkish Tax on Wealth (Varlık Vergisi)." See, Records of the Department of State Relating to the Internal Affairs of Turkey 1930 - 1944: Dated 6 October 1943, 867.512/245
[34] Walter F Weiker, *The Unseen Israelis: The Jews from Turkey in Israel* (Lanham; London: University Press of America, 1989), 21.
[35] Devlet İstatistik Enstitüsü [State Institute of Statistics], *İstatistik Yıllığı* [Yearbook of Statistics] Ankara, 1959.

Jews migrated in this period because "they had little reason to stay."[36] Turkish Jews' decision to migrate was quite spontaneous as well. Weiker mentions a case that "L. B. in Bat Yam recalled that he was impelled to go when one evening he heard on the radio that a Jewish state had been founded, whereupon he packed and left in a matter of hours."[37] Many of them migrated in the first wave and sold out their remaining property at ridiculously cheap prices in Turkey. In other words, they were burning all bridges.

The documents in the US National Archives contain important testimonies by the American diplomats stationed in Turkey at that period. E. C. Macy, American Consul at Istanbul mentions that at least 2500 Turkish Jews applied for travel visas to Palestine until in November 1948 and it is further estimated that this figure would rise to 5,000 within a few months.

In his dispatch to Washington, Macy argues that "the present departure of Turkish Jews is not the consequence of any propaganda but is partly due to the difficult economic situation of many of the Jews in Turkey, which commenced with the Capital Levy of 1942 ... many local Jews who have been waiting for the past four years for an opportunity to leave Turkey are rushing to take advantage of the present favorable conditions."[38] In this report Macy also argues that the applicants were mostly from the poorer class of Jews and the great majority of emigrants were single youths, 17 to 25 years of age. He also adds that there were few families applying for exit visas and these were divided families where the younger members had already migrated to Palestine in 1944 and they wished to join them when the opportunity has arisen.

When one looks at the timing of this migration and the rather liberal attitude of the Turkish authorities on that issue an interesting point can be made. Turkey allowed the migration of its Jews at a time when it did not favor the partition of Palestine, voted with the Arab countries in the UN and was still concerned with the possible Soviet influence in the politics of the new state and the Soviet presence in the region. In fact, the Arab countries strongly protested this policy. We suggest that Turkey was still pursuing a "dual track strategy", or in Gruen's parlance, its "politics of ambivalence." By allowing and at times encouraging Jewish migration, it was keeping its relations warm with the Jewish communities and organizations, was not taking a totally hostile position against Israel,

---

[36] Weiker, *ibid*, 23.
[37] *Ibid*, 25.
[38] From US Consul General C. E. Macy to the Secretary of State in Washington. Records of the Department of State Relating to the Internal Affairs of Turkey 1945 - 1949: Dated 2 November 1948, 867. 4016/11-248

which after all, was being supported by the United States. At the same time, by its refusal to recognize the new state it was also trying to keep its relations with the Arab countries unharmed.

There was a temporary suspension of permissions and visas granted by the Turkish authorities in the closing months of 1948. Two weeks later, in another report written by P. C. Hutton mentions that Jewish emigration had been halted temporarily by the order of Ankara government. Hutton gives background information that the latest action of Turkish authorities was the "result of the intervention in Ankara of the Egyptian Minister, who had objected to the fact that so many young Jews were leaving Turkey to reinforce the Israeli army."[39] This observation supports our suggestion that the Turkish government wished to sit on the fence until the end of hostilities in Palestine, and did not wish to alienate Arab countries.

In the same period, the appointment of a prominent Turkish journalist, Hüseyin Cahit Yalçın as a member to the "United Nations Conciliation Commission to Palestine" also contributed to the change of policy by the Turkish authorities to limit the number of visas issued to Turkish Jews. In a January 8, 1949 dispatch written by US Consul P. C. Hutton, it is argued that "while the Turks in their hearts are still pleased to have as many Jews as possible leave Turkey for Palestine or wherever they choose, they do not wish to subject themselves to any possible criticism in the eyes of other members of the United Nations by permitting the Jews to leave Turkey."[40]

Four months later, in a report written by the American Consul General John J. Macdonald, mentions that the total number of Jews who had sailed for Palestine reached 10 - 12,000 by the end of April 1949. Turkish Jews' emigration to Israel must have created certain problems for the newly established Jewish state as well since even the Israeli authorities wanted to have a more strict control of Jewish immigrants pouring in from Turkey.

Abraham A. Mayer, unofficial representative of the Jewish Agency in Istanbul, who returned from Israel in those days complained to the American Consul General Macdonald that "the bulk of present day immigrants consists of persons from lowest social and financial classes, who have not exhibited sufficient capacity to earn more than a bare subsistence in their countries of origin, who are pouring into Palestine in the expectation of finding there a ready-made Utopia." Mayer adds that

---

[39] From US Consul P. C. Hutton to the Secretary of State in Washington. Dated 15 November 1948, 867. 4016/11-1548
[40] ibid.

in this case, "the obvious loser is the Israeli Nation."[41]

Turkey's Recognition of Israel: The Capital Levy at the background.

Nearly a year before the formation of the Israeli state and Turkey's recognition of it, a peculiar type of external pressure was exerted on Turkey. In those days, it was quite obvious that Turkey was looking for a place in the Western camp as the Cold War was coming into being. Since she feared the Soviet threat diplomatic moves of Ankara were directed towards the West. Many in Turkey still argue that the well-orchestrated move towards a multi-party regime was also part of the attempts to befriend the United States.[42] In terms of its need for foreign aid and economic development, Turkey had to go to Western capitals and/or to the new economic institutions of the Bretton Woods system. There were also critical notes in the press on the declining feasibility of growth within the "étatist" development model, thus insinuating a more liberal, western-style capitalism and less state interventionism. Turkish currency was devaluated in order to promote exports and a more liberal trade regime was in the making. Turkey wished to be included among the recipients of the Marshall Plan funds in order to partake of American generosity that was to rebuild a devastated Europe.

At this point, in the high circles of American Jewish organizations, the issue of Turkey's treatment of its minorities during the Second World War came to the fore. Especially the wounds of the Capital Levy were still sore. In March 26, 1947, only fifty days before partition was to take effect, the President of The American Jewish Committee, Joseph M. Proskauer sent a letter to Dean Acheson, the US Secretary of the State, in which he wrote that:

> The government of Turkey is now seeking economic and political support of the United States. This would seem a proper occasion for the United States government to make its attitude clear on the treatment of minorities in Turkey. Our people would be much inclined to give support to the Turkish people if we knew that all Turkish citizens including Christians and Jews were treated on a basis of equality and justice ... it should at once redress the outrageous injustices of the Varlık [Tax] Decree which have brought economic ruin to the Christian and Jewish citizens of Turkey. Even a partial restitution would be an indication that the

---

[41] From US Consul General John J. Macdonald to the Secretary of State in Washington. Dated 5 May 1949, 867. 4016/5-549
[42] An excellent treatment of this period could be found in the memoirs of late Professor Berkes. See, Niyazi Berkes, *Unutulan yıllar* ed. by Ruşen Sezer (İstanbul: İletişim, 1997).

Turkish Government is altering its course in the direction of justice to all its citizens without regard to race and creed, in accordance with the principles of democracy which our country is desirous of promoting all over the world.[43]

Judge Proskauer also mentioned the articles written by Sulzberger in order to support his argument. This letter was answered back by Gordon P. Merriam, the Chief of the Division of Near Eastern Affairs, stating that there is an evidence of a "liberal trend" in Turkey. He also stated the fact that recently members of minority communities were elected to the Turkish parliament in 1946 elections, freedom of education and press were secured etc.[44] These exchanges and reports from the archives suggest to us that the recognition of Israel by Turkey was one of the steps that the Turkish Government has taken in order to get closer to the United States. Needless to say, once it became obvious that the new state would endure and was not going to be a Soviet ally, the strategic consideration was also shifted.

Recognition

The progress of the Turkish position towards recognition after war broke out in Palestine is admirably and masterfully analyzed by Gruen.[45] We share one of his contentions that the results of the elections that took place in Israel on January 25, 1949 reassured the Turks that the new state was not going to be a Soviet puppet. In fact, the moderate left won a victory in Israeli elections and the Communists were totally marginalized.[46] Gruen argues that the timing of Turkey's *de facto* recognition of Israel on March 28, 1949 and its earlier participation in the Palestine Conciliation Commission reflected its concerns to be inside the emerging Western security structures.[47] Thus, it needed to prove that its foreign policy was not based on religion or religious solidarity. Furthermore, to repeat a point made earlier, having good relations with

---

[43] From J. M. Proskauer, President of the American Jewish Committee to Dean Acheson, Secretary of the State. Dated 26 March 1947, 867.4016/3-2647.

[44] In his second letter, the President of The American Jewish Committee, Judge Proskauer made his demands more explicit: the losses of the Jews had to be compensated! Quite bluntly Proskauer stated the following: "In all my study of forms of economic persecution I have run across none more devilish in its ingenuity than this *Varlık* business in Turkey. It may be a great interest that there is now a liberal trend in Turkey which will respect minority groups, but it is not going to restore one penny to these Christians and Jews who have been robbed; and if the United States is to help Turkey, it is certainly within the bounds of reason that it may ask Turkey to make reparation to these people who have been despoiled." From J. M. Proskauer, President of the American Jewish Committee to Gordon P. Merriam, Chief, Division of Near Eastern Affairs. Dated 15 April 1947, 867.4016/4-1547.

[45] See Gruen, especially Chapter 3

[46] Peretz Merhav, *The Israeli Left: History, Problems, Documents* (San Diego; London: A.S. Barnes ; The Tantivy Press, 1980), see Ch. 12.

[47] Gruen, *ibid*, 82.

Israel was sen as a way to get a hearing in Washington as well.

Looking at the matter from another perspective, Israel's victory and the disarray of the Arabs relieved Turkey of its constraints and led it to recognize the state of Israel. In the period between the declaration of Israeli independence and the recognition of the new state by Turkey (de jure recognition came on March 9, 1950), the opinion makers in Turkey continued to follow the developments in Palestine carefully. The issue of Jerusalem, of refugees, the plan by Count Bernadotte and his murder by Jewish terrorists were discussed at length. For our purposes we will deal finally with the reflections on the decision to recognize Israel. We chose a lengthy quotation from Doğrul, who was consistently taking an anti-Zionist, anti-Israeli stance and whose views were very sympathetic to the Arab positions.

Angered by the Arab claims that Turkey betrayed them and the Muslim world, and probably not daring to oppose the government's decision on such a delicate matter, Doğrul put his position succinctly in a piece he wrote two days after *de facto* recognition of Israel.

> The military aspect of the war between Israel and the Arab world that has begun in mid-May last year and has de facto reached an end a while ago resulted in the establishment of Israel in a part of eastern Mediterranean and to the recognition of this fact, either implicitly or explicitly, by the Arab states ... therefore our recognition of Israel is just a recognition of a fait accompli. We don't think that such recognition will have an adverse effect on the Arab world and it is impossible to think that it could. Because in this affair we have shown utmost respect for the dignity of our Arab neighbors and friends and have shown that we never intended to undermine the wishes of our Arab friends by postponing this act as long as possible ... So long as the struggle continued between the two parties we did not wish to recognize Israel and have done so only after the Arabs have rested their arms signed the cease-fire agreement. Thereupon since the matter has come to a close we no longer find it improper to extend our recognition.[48]

We have argued throughout this essay that Turkey's relations with Israel had a dimension that went beyond the bilateral relations. As Gruen states it, "the value of relations with Israel lay not only in direct bilateral trade and regional defense cooperation but also in Israel's role as a 'window to the West'."[49] Yet, even at the height of the two countries close

[48] Ömer Rıza Doğrul, *Cumhuriyet*, 30 March 1949
[49] Gruen, *ibid*, 86.

relations in the 1950s Turkey did not wish to display the intimacy between the two very openly. The Israeli Prime Minister, David Ben-Gurion could only come to Turkey, *incognito*, in 1958 to see the late Prime Minister of Turkey, Adnan Menderes. We think that this supports another one of our suggestions that even as insulated a foreign policy establishment as Turkey's cannot disregard the public sentiment. Certainly not in a democratic environment, which Turkey enjoyed in the 1950s.

Turkish policy makers were right in claiming that their policies were always guided by rational calculations. Once the Zionist movement showed its strength and appeared to have the capacity to influence Washington in favor of Turkey, the Turkish attitude to it and the state of Israel changed considerably. In brief, Turkey found in Israel a natural ally, even if this fact was consistently understated until the openings in the 1990s.

Bibliography

Archive documents

US National Archives
Records of the Department of State Relating to Internal Affairs of Turkey, 1945-1949 (Microfilm no: M1292).

Daily Newspapers

Ulus, Cumhuriyet, Vatan, Tan, Gece postası
Ayın Tarihi

Published Works

Aktar, Ayhan "Trakya Yahudi Olaylarını 'Doğru' Yorumlamak," [Correct Interpretation of the Jewish Exodus from Eastern Trace – 1934] *Tarih ve Toplum*, 155, [Kasım 1996): 45 – 56.
Berkes, Niyazi, *Unutulan yıllar.* Ed. by Ruşen Sezer. Cağaloğlu, İstanbul: İletişim, 1997.
Deringil, Selim. Turkish Foreign Policy during the Second World War: An "Active" Neutrality. Cambridge: Cambridge University Press, 1989.
Gökay, Bülent "Belgelerle *Struma* Faciası - 25 Şubat 1942," [A Documented Account of the Struma Tragedy – 25 February 1942] *Tarih ve Toplum*, 116, (August 1993): 42 – 45.
Gruen, George Emanuel. "Turkey, Israel and the Palestine Question, 1948-1960: A Study in the Diplomacy of Ambivalence." (Unpublished Ph. D Dissertation, Columbia University, 1970).
Kuniholm, Bruce Robellet. The Origins of the Cold War in the Near East: Great Power Conflict and Diplomacy in Iran, Turkey, and Greece. Princeton: Princeton University Press, 1994.
Louis, William Roger. The British Empire in the Middle East: 1945-1951 ; Arab Nationalism, the United States and Postwar Imperialism. Oxford: Oxford Univ. Press, 1998.

Merhav, Peretz. *The Israeli Left: History, Problems, Documents.* London: A.S. Barnes ; The Tantivy Press, 1980.

Neumark, Fritz, *Boğaziçine sığınanlar: Türkiye'ye iltica eden Alman ilim siyaset ve sanat adamları, 1933-1953.* Translated by Şefik Alp Bahadır. İstanbul: İstanbul Üniversitesi İktisat Fakültesi Maliye Enstitüsü, 1982.

Shaw, Stanford J. *The Jews of the Ottoman Empire and the Turkish Republic.* New York: New York University Press, 1991.

Smith, Charles D. *Palestine and the Arab-Israeli Conflict.* Boston: Bedford/St. Martin's, 2001.

Soysal, İsmail. Soğuk savaş dönemi ve Türkiye: olaylar kronolojisi (1945-1975). İstanbul: İsis, 1997.

Weiker, Walter F. *The Unseen Israelis: The Jews from Turkey in Israel.* Lanham; London: University Press of America, 1989.

Yavuz, M. Hakan. "Turkish-Israeli Relations through the Lens of the Turkish Identity Debate." Journal of Palestine Studies : A Quarterly on Palestinian Affairs and the Arab-Israeli Conflict Journal of Palestine Studies 27, no. 1 (1997): 22–37.

CHAPTER 8

ECONOMIC NATIONALISM IN TURKEY:
The Formative Years, 1912 – 1925 *

History, despite its wrenching pain,
Cannot be unlived, but if faced
With courage, need not to be lived again.

Maya Angelou

Turkish nationalism was first clearly articulated and presented itself as a well-defined political ideology after the 1908 Young Turk revolution. The major aim of this article is to focus on only one dimension of Turkish nationalism, namely, economic nationalism. In this article, economic nationalism will be treated as a special characteristic of Turkish nationalism in its formative years, 1912-1925. Its place and articulation within Turkish national consciousness will be analyzed at different levels of abstraction.

The Problem

Economic nationalism, in general, can be defined as a set of protective or neo-mercantilist economic policies implemented in a particular country in order to safeguard the domestic market from the destructive effects foreign capital and goods. This definition naturally introduces the modern nation-state as an agency which formulates a set of rules to protect the domestic market via tariff systems, foreign exchange regulations, and the abolition or restriction of privileges granted to foreign companies. Simultaneously, in a backward capitalist country, an autarkic - or a rather self-reliant model of industrialization could be adopted in order to promote economic development. In short, economic nationalism inevitably brings the state into focus. The active function of the state as a mediator between the private and public spheres of society, or its interventionist role over and above the society, can be seen as a continuum. The intensity of state intervention may change in time. The crisis of accumulation or distribution may redefine the actual nature of state intervention. In this context, I shall argue that state intervention

* I am grateful to Professor Feroz Ahmad and Professor Liah Greenfeld for their valuable contributions on the earlier version of this article. I would also like to thank Irvin Cemil Shick and Arus Yumul for their helpful comments and editorial advice.

cannot be analyzed by itself: it is always related to the level of economic development, the actual nature of capital accumulation, the formation of social classes, and finally the type of nationalism(s) existing within the society in question.

Before going into the details of Turkish nationalism, the second dimension of economic nationalism must be stressed in order to comprehend the Turkish case: the question of "economic nationalism as a domestic policy." This may sound like a redundancy since all economic policies that come under the umbrella of economic nationalism are indeed "domestic" policies. I shall argue that economic nationalism was implemented as a domestic policy, in the form of economic or extra-economic measures in multi-ethnic and basically agrarian empires during the process of disintegration into various nation-states. From a sociological point of view, these disintegrating empires presuppose a social structural context in which an ethnic or religious division of labor in the economic domain is predominant. Furthermore, in these disintegrating empires, there may be some clear-cut structural incongruities between the "political/administrative" and "business" élites. In other words, an ethnic or religious minority may control commercial and business activities via its elite. In contrast to the preponderance of minorities in commercial activities, if a political élite holds a firm position within the state apparatus and furthermore considers itself as the sole representative of the nation then a clash may be expected to occur between the two groups. In this context, "economic nationalism as a domestic policy" would serve as a means to shape the market by undermining the prominent position enjoyed by the commercial bourgeoisie.

However, as the Turkish case will illustrate, economic nationalism is only the first step in the nationalization of nearly every aspect of a once multi-ethnic and multi-religious country. As we shall see later, the clash between competing nationalism(s) may also take more severe forms: population exchanges, the expulsion of minorities, and other policies may also be utilized in order to achieve a more homogenous society. The nation-states that come into existence after the disintegration of an empire may also become arenas of struggle, although on a smaller scale. For example, after gaining independence most of the Arab states implemented several anti-minority measures which could be classified as economic nationalism in a specific sense. They started with the boycotts against minority and foreign firms in the 1940s in Egypt and Iraq and later deported Jews and other non-Muslim minorities in the 1950s. In analyzing the process of economic nationalism, we should keep in mind that the implementation of economic nationalism may require the use of legitimate or illegitimate coercion. In order to have a more concrete definition of the problem, one may scrutinize the position of Indian minorities throughout Black Africa, where several offensives were made by African post-colonial governments to eradicate their privileged position in the economic domain.[1]

Economic nationalism as described above defines the nature and content of capital accumulation in these newly formed nation-states. The actual behavior of central authority on economic matters, i.e. taxation, nationalization or state-subsidies can only be comprehended by analyzing the inherent fundamental principles of such nation-states. Here the specific formulation of nationalism as a social and political consciousness serves as the fundamental principle. Indeed, the study of the genealogy of a newly rising business élite can only be understood vis-à-vis the previously prevalent ethnic or religious minority which formerly held a strong position in the economic domain. As my research indicates, some latent tendencies towards the expulsion of minorities from economic fields may come to the surface in an international crisis. In order to make my argument clear, first I would like to illustrate the political context within which economic nationalism will be studied.

The Broader Context

The Ottoman Empire was always a poly-ethnic and multi-religious social entity. There was always a clear-cut social division of labor based upon ethnic and religious cleavages. In the Classical Age (1300-1600), this mosaic-like social fabric was perfectly compatible with the needs of an agrarian empire, in which the ruling Turkish/Islamic element in the center was content with the extraction of economic surplus in the form of taxes. In other words, the Ottomans created a society which granted a large degree of autonomy to its minorities while creating a fiscally sound and militarily strong center.

This type of economic rationale was based upon the provision of goods and services within the Empire and forced the Ottoman center to grant certain economic privileges and capitulations to foreigners. When the Empire weakened, some members of the non-Muslim minorities preferred to seek foreign protection in order to benefit from commercial privileges given to foreigners. Through this process, by the end of the nineteenth century, the non-Muslim minorities came to dominate commercial activities within the Empire. However, as the Ottoman Empire was integrated into the world economy, the strategic position of

---

[1] On the deportation of Ugandan Asians by President Idi Amin in 1972, see Ram R. Ramchandani, *Uganda Asians: The End of an Enterprise : A Study of the Role of the People of Indian Origin in the Economic Development of Uganda and Their Expulsion, 1894-1972* (United Asia Publications, 1976).

non-Muslims, with ever increasing demands for national independence, and hence secessionist tendencies within the Empire, shaped the overall political agenda of the nineteenth and early twentieth centuries. On the one hand, the Ottoman minorities were influenced by the idea of nationalism which flourished in the West; on the other, the Ottoman center was not in a position to resist the centrifugal tendencies within the Empire. As in the case of Egyptian autonomy in 1833, the Ottoman bureaucracy was forced to sacrifice its periphery in order to consolidate its political power at the center. The existence of the so-called 'administrative genius' of Ottoman bureaucracy in the nineteenth century can be explained by efforts to give necessary concessions to the Great Powers of Europe in the form of promises for social reforms within its domain in order to delay the political resolution of the "Eastern Question." Throughout the nineteenth century, non-Muslim minorities in the Ottoman Empire acquired a much-privileged position where their civil rights and social status were also guaranteed by international agreements.

Parallel to the growing pressure exerted upon the Ottoman center by the foreign powers which claimed to be the protectors of non-Muslim subjects, Ottoman reformers formulated "Ottomanism" as an ideological umbrella to stop the disintegration of the Empire. However, this policy did not succeed, because Ottomanism attempted to eradicate all national and ethnic differences and unite all Ottoman subjects, regardless of religion and ethnic affiliation, under one political program. As has been pointed out, "Reform and Ottomanism were the proposed remedy... But the effort failed. One could not be a citizen of a sovereign nation, the protégé of a foreign power, and the subject of a would be egalitarian Empire at one and the same time. Neither physics nor politics allows such things to occur, at least not for long."[2]

Just a few years before the outbreak of the First World War, Ottoman Turks discovered the importance of economic nationalism. Economic privileges and capitulations were discussed widely in the libertarian atmosphere created by the 1908 Young Turk Revolution. However, it was in the critical days of the Balkan Wars that economic nationalism was first implemented as a domestic policy.

The Birth of Economic Nationalism

The following quotations are taken from a series of pamphlets distributed in Istanbul during the Balkan Wars in 1912-13. Written and formulated by the Committee of Union and Progress (CUP), the general

[2] Benjamín Braude and Bernard Lewis, *Christians and Jews in the Ottoman Empire: The Functioning of a Plural Society* (Holmes & Meier Publishers, 1982), 33.

theme of these pamphlets was a call for a boycott against the Greek shop owners in Istanbul:

> Oh my God, how we are going to celebrate the day when Turks and Muslims buy things only from each other and consume the goods produced in Turkey as much as possible. [Gentlemen,] we are not asking for a great sacrifice from you in order to reach that day... In the beginning, this might seem difficult. However, we shall eventually get used to it. The main task is to learn the addresses of those Muslim stores and Turkish shops that carry products necessary for your household. And we should not be too lazy to visit those shops even for the purchase of a tiny box of matches worth 10 pennies... The most important task is to consume Turkish products as much as possible. In fact, compared to imported European goods, some of our products seem a bit expensive and of inferior quality. This ruggedness should be regarded as [a part of] our honor and pride. That high price paid should be perceived as something cheap indeed and more beneficial to us. If the empty-headed [ladies] who are proud of their nice dresses and the elegant ribbons crowning their hair could realize the satisfaction they would feel in their souls by wearing a domestically produced but rugged and certainly less colorful dress. If they could appreciate the national pride by saying 'those goods are made here and they are the products of our looms" (*A way of Liberation for Muslims*, 1913)

To the Muslim Shop owners:

In most of your shops, the names of the owners are not written anywhere on the premises. This situation creates a further complication for the customers looking for a Muslim proprietor. Immediately, have your names written over your shops in a visible manner. Furthermore, please be aware of the fact that some of the non-Muslim shop-owners recently had [Muslim] names written over their premises, like Yakub, Necib, Selim etc. Do not show any negligence at all in having your real Muslim names like Ahmed, Mehmed written and adding your fathers' names as well. We also find it unnecessary to remind you to assign this job to a Muslim calligrapher [!][3]

The messages in these popular pamphlets are among the first examples of economic nationalism as a domestic policy, hitherto unknown to the men in the street. The boycott was quite successful and functioned as a

---

[3] For the Turkish text of pamphlets and a detailed analysis, see Zafer Toprak, 'İslâm ve İktisat: 1913-1914 Müslüman Boykotajı', *Toplum ve Bilim* 29/30 (1985),179 - 99.

"consciousness-raising" program for the Turkish/Muslim community in general. Printed lists of Muslim shop owners in the city were distributed free to the public, and soon nearly 500 Muslim/Turks established their own companies and entered the market as the newcomers in trade, and were later favored by the Unionist government.[4] In order to understand the immediate and popular success of this boycott, we must examine it within the socio-economic context of the period.

First, we must understand the overall hegemony of Greeks and Armenians in the trade sector of Istanbul that laid the groundwork for a boycott. This hegemony functioned as the 'necessary condition' for the formulation of economic nationalism as a domestic policy. Commenting on the ethnic division of labor in 1917, Sussnitzki underlines the following characteristics:

> We first note the fact that in nearly every form of trade, Armenians and Greeks dominate the field... these two groups have succeeded, in the course of time, in securing an extraordinarily strong position in commerce. They hardly allow other national groups the possibility of developing their own economic powers... A final cause of the standing of the Greeks and Armenians should be considered: the protection they enjoyed from foreign powers, whose subjects they sometimes were, thus becoming, thanks to the former Capitulations, exempt from taxation ... these factors explain the fact that, in petty trade and petty credit activities, but also in wholesale internal trade, import and external trade, and in the high finance of Turkey, the Greeks and Armenians... have played the decisive role... two of these peoples are preponderant almost everywhere. Neither the Arabs and Persians, who are able traders nor by and large Jews can compete with them.[5]

Secondly, a sufficient condition for the boycott was the donations made by the Istanbul Greek community to help with the war expenses of the Greek Kingdom, fighting against the Ottomans during the Balkan Wars. News of the purchase of a battleship by a Greek citizen Georgios Averoff and its donation to the Greek Navy created an upsurge of emotion within the Turkish/Muslim community of Istanbul. Moreover, this powerful battleship blocked the Dardanelles during the war preventing the Ottoman Navy from sailing to the Aegean Sea.

In the first round of the Balkan Wars, the Ottoman Army was brutally

---

[4] *Ibid*, 181.
[5] A. J. Sussnitzki, "Ethnic Division of Labor," in *The Economic History of the Middle East, 1800 - 1914*, ed. Charles Issawi (Chicago University Press, 1966), 120-121.

defeated in Thrace, and the advancing Bulgarian army was halted merely forty miles outside Istanbul.[6] While cannons could be heard in Istanbul, nearly 250,000 Turkish/Muslim refugees from Balkan countries fled into the city.[7]. All the mosques, including Hagia Sophia, were converted into shelters for the homeless refugees. Soon, hunger and grief were merged with a destructive disease. Of those who took shelter in Hagia Sophia alone, it is estimated that around seven hundred refugees died of cholera.[8] These adverse political circumstances, no doubt greatly contributed to the immediate success of the boycott.

The Balkan Wars were among the first tragedies to be encountered by the Muslims and non-Muslims of the Empire alike in the next ten years. No doubt, it was a bitter experience and created important repercussions in the collective consciousness of both communities. Furthermore, I believe that the Balkan Wars may be regarded as a turning point in state-minority relations in the late Ottoman Empire. Indeed by the end of this conflict, the Ottomans had not only lost most of their territories in Europe, but they had also abandoned all hopes of protecting the unity and integrity of a multi-ethnic and multi-religious empire. Between 1912 and 1922, Ottoman lands became an arena where the different nationalisms contested, conflicting projects for newly emerging nation-states competed, and consequently several bloody wars were fought.

The general tone of the pamphlets discussed above was that of a steady stream of confessions and self-accusations for the Muslim/Turks. In the pamphlets, it was first argued that the Turkish/Muslim community itself was guilty of greatly contributing to the situation by purchasing goods from Greek merchants. They blamed themselves for enriching the Greeks and other foreign merchants. As one can expect, the political consequences of this popular movement were detrimental for non-Muslim minorities.

Throughout this boycott, and for the first time at the popular level, the Turkish/Muslim majority discussed its economic position in comparison with minorities in Ottoman society. The first practical recommendation for the boycott was quite defensive: Muslims had to buy from Muslim merchants only. However, in terms of inter-communal relations, this meant a further development of hatred and mistrust between the two communities. A Muslim/Turk had to be suspicious of the Greek grocer in his neighborhood, who would probably be a typical

[6] Feroz Ahmad, Feroz Ahmad, *Young Turks: Committee of Union and Progress in Turkish Politics, 1908-14.* (Oxford University Press, 1969).
[7] Arnold J. Toynbee, *The Western Question in Greece and Turkey* (Boston: Houghton Mifflin Company, 1922), 138.
[8] Mary A. M. D. Poynter, *When Turkey Was Turkey: In and around Constantinople* (London: G. Routledge, 1921), 121.

Karamanlı, a Greek from Central Anatolia. In those days, *Karamanlı* Greeks did not even speak Greek; they read a special version of the Bible in Turkish but written in the Greek alphabet. As Arnold Toynbee rightly observed, "the arrival of the Rumelian refugees from the end of 1912 onwards produced an unexampled tension of feeling in Anatolia and a desire for revenge; and so the Balkan War had two harvests of victims: first, the Rumeli Turks on the one side, and then the Anatolian Greeks on the other."[9]

At the same time, these pamphlets pronounced the first anti-colonial and anti-minority sentiments of economic nationalism in the Ottoman Empire. Presented in a religious cover or recommended as a Muslim praxis in general, the main objectives of this boycott could be summarized as follows:[10]

1. An emphasis on the creation of a new group of entrepreneurs entirely from the Turkish/Muslim community.

2. Reducing in volume and in number the prominent positions enjoyed by non-Muslims in the trade sector in Istanbul.

3. Inviting the Turkish/Muslim element to be more active in the economic domain, either as tradesmen or manufacturers.

4. Favoring of Turkish workers and craftsmen in terms of employment opportunities.

5. Urging consumers to purchase goods produced in Turkey. In economic terms, this meant moving towards self-reliance and import substitution. However, consuming Turkish products also entailed a special satisfaction and served as the culmination of national pride and honor.

6. Recommending the already existing Turkish shopkeepers to utilize more modern sales techniques and advertising as ways to compete with minority firms.

Finally, the boycott underlined the one-to-one correspondence between the national wealth as a source of pride and powerful nation-state as a symbol of strength. Moreover, the boycott clearly identified the commercial bourgeoisie of Istanbul as a "comprador bourgeoisie" in the

---

[9] Toynbee, *The Western Question..*, 139.
[10] Moise Cohen a. k. a. Tekinalp, the ideologue of the CUP on economic matters, discloses the tactics of boycotters as follows: '[Boycotters] sought after a judicious mingling of the religious and national impulses. They realized only too clearly that the still abstract ideals of Nationalism could not be expected to attract the masses, the lower classes, composed of uneducated and illiterate people. It was found more expedient to reach these classes under the flag of religion. Religion has a universal appeal, whereas Nationalism is a finer instrument which requires good training if it is to be properly handled.' See, Jacob M. Landau, *Tekinalp, Turkish Patriot, 1883-1961* (Istanbul, 1984): 121.

Latin American sense. Emphasizing the common interest between the non-Muslim merchants and European capital which determined the agenda of economic nationalism in general: non-Muslim minorities were regarded as agents of imperialism, and the blueprint for "total independence" inevitably included the expulsion of minorities and foreigners from the economic domain. Thus, the commercial bourgeoisie of the Empire had to be Turkified. Capital had to be transformed into something socially beneficial to the Muslim Turks only. We now turn to the examination of the formation of national mentality corresponding to this economic/political agenda.

Turkish Nationalism within a Corporatist System of Thought

In the second half of the nineteenth century, the Ottoman intelligentsia developed the intellectual basis for the formation of modern Turkish nationalism. However, this substructure mostly consisted of works on Turkish history, the literature on the uniqueness of Turks, and fierce debates on language and literature.[11] Naturally, this intellectual movement remained primarily within the confines of the Ottoman urban elite and did not influence either the masses or decision-makers within the Empire.

Turkish nationalism was first formulated and codified as a clear-cut worldview during the years of the Balkan Wars. The most sophisticated ideologue of Turkish nationalism was Ziya Gökalp (1876-1924). Having deconstructed Gökalp's system of thought in his pioneering work, *The Social and Political Thought of Ziya Gökalp*, Taha Parla argues that Gökalp not only codified the founding principles of Turkish nationalism but furthermore 'Gökalp's corporatist thinking has provided the paradigmatic worldview for the several dominant political ideologies and public philosophies in Turkey'.[12] In other words, Gökalp not only influenced the intellectual and political atmosphere of the Second Constitutional Period (1908-1918) in the last years of the Ottoman Empire, but his ideas also provided the intellectual and political matrix of modern Turkey. In Parla's words:

> Gökalp's system may be taken as a codification of the dominant ideas of his time, blending European corporatism and elements of national political mentality... In other words, his system fixed the parameters within which mainstream political discourse and action has been conducted in Turkey. To put it differently, the major ideological positions in Turkey have been derived from his pervasive corporatist model, occasionally explicitly acknowledged

---

[11] See, David Kushner, *The Rise of Turkish Nationalism, 1876-1908* (London: Frank Cass, 1977).
[12] Taha Parla, *The Social and Political Thought of Ziya Gökalp, 1876-1924* (Leiden: E.J. Brill, 1985), 7.

and often only implied.'[13]

Combining the solidaristic corporatism of Emile Durkheim, the heterodox Sufi traditions of Islam and developmentalist/modernist currents of European thought into a well-defined sociological model, Ziya Gökalp not only laid the foundations of Turkish nationalism, but his model served as a foundation of Kemalist Republicanism in modern Turkey. As a follower of Durkheim, Gökalp tried to create, in his own words, "an ideal which existed in the realm of imagination, not in the realm of reality."[14] Criticizing the Westernization programs of nineteenth-century Ottoman reformers Gökalp argued that they had uncritically accepted Western cultural values at the expense of traditional values. For Gökalp, the Ottoman reform movement's "fatal mistake sprang from its failure to take into consideration the fact that the ideal of nationalism had become the driving force of the age"[15] Defining the term "civilization" as the international product of modernization, and Turkish/Islamic "culture" as the basis of Turkish national solidarity, Gökalp combined both of these concepts in his corporatist model. Taha Parla outlines the characteristics of Gökalp's synthesis as follows:

> In Gökalp's view, Turkish nationalism represented a cultural ideal, a philosophy of life which laid the basis of social solidarity. He believed that that applied to every nationalism. His was non-racist, non-expansionist, pluralistic nationalism. Similarly, his unorthodox, Sufi brand of Islam with its emphasis on ethics rather than politics, reinforced solidarity. Thus, Turkism became the cultural norm and Islam the moral norm in his societal model. Westernism or modernism, which Gökalp used interchangeably, meant the scientific, technological, industrial achievements of European capitalism, which were to form part of his program of national revival ... Moreover, corporatism as the solidaristic perception of society as an analytic discipline, also served as a philosophical model of the society. The system as a whole took the shape of idealistic positivism: the method was scientific in the positivistic sense, and the ideology was solidarism, a variant of corporatist capitalism, as opposed to Marxist socialism or liberal capitalism. Gökalp labeled it social idealism (*içtimai mefkûrecilik*)'[16]

In Gökalp's model, membership in the national collectivity was defined at the cultural/linguistic level, and not at the ethnic/particularistic level. As Parla states "his nationalism... is a matter of subjective

---

[13] *Ibid.*
[14] Ziya Gökalp, *Türkçülüğün Esasları [Principles of Turkism]* (Istanbul: Kadro Yayınları, 1976), 11.
[15] Ziya Gökalp, *Türkleşmek, İslamlaşmak, Muasırlaşmak* (Istanbul: Türk Kültür Yayınları, 1976), 15.
[16] Parla, *The Social and Political,* 26.

identification, language, and acculturation, and has nothing to do with elements of race and ethnicity."[17] Gökalp in answering his political opponents who claimed that he was of Kurdish descent, he contended that his grandfathers were indeed Turks. He also added, "however, I would not hesitate to believe that I am a Turk even if I had discovered that my grandfathers came from the Kurdish or Arab areas, because I learned through my sociological studies that nationality was based solely on upbringing."[18]

Thinking about the ethnically and religiously heterogeneous character of the Ottoman Empire, Gökalp's criterion was quite convenient. In the beginning of twentieth century, it was practically impossible to preach particularistic nationalism in the Ottoman Empire. In formulating Turkish nationalism, Gökalp inevitably recognized the long tradition of the "*millet* system" even though it had legally abolished and practically disintegrated. In this context, Gökalp's emphasis on Islam should be perceived as a moral force to achieve social solidarity, and not as a "necessary condition" for Turkish nationalism. This instrumental definition of Islam could be one of the reasons why Jewish intellectuals like Moise Cohen (a. k. a. Tekinalp) and Abraham Galante (1873-1961) took active part in the ideological kitchen of Turkish nationalism. Tekinalp (1883-1961), a follower of Friedrich List, was the most important ideologue of the Young Turks on economic nationalism and on Turcification of the national market.[19] Similarly in its earlier phases, when Arab nationalism defined Islam at cultural and linguistic levels, the earlier generation of Christian Arabs made substantial contributions to its formation. As Arab nationalism transformed more along the Islamic lines, Christian Arab ideologues were either disillusioned or eliminated by Islamic fundamentalists in their respective countries.[20]

Gökalp's emphasis on the sociological foundations of nationalism and national consciousness was a novel contribution in comparison with the European nationalist ideologues of his age. His utilization of the Durkheimian concept of "collective conscience" served as a framework for constructing the source of morality and the basis of social solidarity in his own work. In analyzing the scientific and industrial superiority of contemporary Western societies, Gökalp made a clear-cut distinction

---

[17] Ziya Gökalp, *Türkleşmek*, 10.
[18] Ziya Gökalp, *Turkish Nationalism and Western Civilization. Selected Essays*. Translated by Niyazi Berkes (New York: Columbia University Press, 1959), 44.
[19] See, Jacob Landau, *Tekinalp, Turkish Patriot, 1883-1961*.
[20] For the earlier generation of the Arab nationalists' definition of Arabism, see E. Chalala, 'Arab Nationalism: A Bibliographic Essay,' in Tawfic Farah, *Pan-Arabism and Arab Nationalism: The Continuing Debate* (Boulder: Westview Press, 1987), 20-22. On the relationship between Islamic modernism and Arab nationalism, see Ernest Dawn, 'The Origins of Arab Nationalism,' in Rashid Khalidi (Ed.), *The Origins of Arab Nationalism* (New York: Columbia University Press, 1991), 7.

between culture and civilization. For him the technological and scientific developments of the Western world had to be perceived within the domain of civilization, whereas liberalism as a value system for the individual, parliamentary democracy as a form of political participation, and the unrestricted functioning of the market mechanism as the regulator of economic life as part of the cultural domain. It was quite clear that Gökalp was influenced by the European critics of industrial society of his age, who were unhappy with the overall behavior of "homo economicus" or possessive individualism and tried to bring the individual back to his natural environment, i.e. the community. This line of reasoning, which was similar to J. J. Rousseau and F. Toennies in some respects, enabled Ziya Gökalp to perceive the idealized Turkish individual stripped of his egoism and merging with the community. In this respect, Gökalp's social solidarism functioned as a magic key for bringing the individual back to his natural community. On the basis of his distinction between "culture" and "civilization", Gökalp criticized the Westernizing Ottoman elite as follows:

> There is in our country a class, the so-called Levantines or Cosmopolitans, who try to adopt the aesthetic, moral, philosophical tastes, and entire customs, ceremonies and behavior of the West rather than its scientific methods and industrial techniques. That is, they try erroneously to imitate the cultures of other nations under the name of civilization.[21]

The concept of "national revival" in Gökalp's system inevitably brought the economic sphere into discussion. In other words, the role of the individual as an agent of economic activity, of the state as the regulator of economic life, and of the property and production relations as the basis economic domain were redefined in Gökalp's system. At this point, Gökalp's solidaristic nationalism deserves further scrutiny.

What Type of Nationalism?

I would like to emphasize certain characteristics of Gökalp's nationalism by utilizing the conceptual framework developed by Liah Greenfeld in her study of nationalism, which could set the agenda for further research in this field. Greenfeld defines nationalism as an idea, a particular perspective or style of thought which bases itself on the idea of "nation."[22] Following up the semantic changes in the meaning and definition of nation throughout the centuries, Greenfeld argues that "in early sixteenth-century England the word 'nation' in its conciliar meaning

---

[21] Ziya Gökalp, *Hars ve Medeniyet* (Ankara: İş Matbaacılık, 1972), 9.
[22] Liah Greenfeld, *Nationalism: Five Roads to Modernity* (Cambridge, MA: Harvard University Press, 1992), 4.

of 'an elite' was applied to the population of the country and made synonymous with the word 'people'[23] This novel elevation of people to the level of the elite and at the same time defining the people as 'the bearer of sovereignty, the basis of political solidarity and supreme object of loyalty' marked the beginning of the era of nationalism. This was also the beginning of a new type of identity "which derives from membership in a 'people,' the fundamental characteristic of which is that it is defined as a 'nation." Indeed, the new definition of the nation did not entail any form of particularism such as common territory, history, language, race or the shared traditions. In its birth, the original nationalism was only a new political ideology which did not necessarily have to be identified with any specific community. Emphasizing the liberating and democratic consequences of this development in England, Greenfeld expands her analysis to other parts of the world where an already crystallized nationalism met others: other countries and communities are now defined and conceptualized as "a unique sovereign people."[24] Here the original non-particularistic conception of nation is transformed into its opposite in foreign lands because the others might lack the social structural conditions for the adaptation of nationalism in its original definition. Greenfeld develops her Weberian model as follows:

> The emergence of the original (in principle, non-particularistic) idea of the nation as a sovereign people was, evidently, predicated on a transformation in the character of relevant population, which suggested the symbolic elevation of the 'people' and its definition as a political elite, in other words, on a profound change in structural conditions. The emergence of the ensuing, particularistic, concept resulted from the application of the original idea to conditions which did not necessarily undergo such transformation.[25]

The theoretical and practical implications of this approach are quite revealing. First, Greenfeld underlines the peculiarity of the English case. As in the development of capitalism in England, the original version does not repeat itself identically in other parts of the world. Second, the birth and rise of nationalism in England creates many mirrors and images of itself on the world scale - although these transmissions were quite uneven in time and space - where the original "idea" mutated considerably. In other words, the social and structural conditions that preceded the formation of original nationalism in England also inspired its original formulation and shaped the creation of democratic institutions where

---

[23] *Ibid*, 6.
[24] *Ibid*, 8.
[25] *Ibid*, 10.

English people truly exercised popular sovereignty. However, the original image that traveled to the rest of the world created totally different representations of the same phenomenon. Emphasizing the differences between these cases, Liah Greenfeld argues that "the importation of the idea of popular sovereignty - as part and parcel of the idea nation - initiated the transformation in the social and political structure."[26]

Here it is necessary to underline that Greenfeld's treatment of the dissemination of nationalism on a world scale is quite unconventional. Contrary to the popular orthodoxy where nationalism is treated as the by-product of modernization process, Greenfeld rightly puts the cart before the horse and argues just the opposite: the transformation in the social and political structure (i.e., modernization itself) was created by nationalism. However, before going into the details of the transformation of the social and political structure, we must follow up the analysis of Greenfeld on how some countries reinterpreted popular sovereignty without actually exercising it.

Greenfeld makes a distinction between the "observable" and "theoretical" sovereignty of people. In the first case, the English case, of course, the sovereignty of people was "observable," experienced by the people, acknowledged and rationalized by the political system through political institutions, i.e., parliament etc. The national principle which was based upon this experience was "individualistic" and the individual actors actually lived with it. The second case that is quite meaningful for analyzing the Turkish case constructed as follows:

> The theoretical sovereignty of people in the latter case, by contrast, was an implication of the people's uniqueness, its very being a distinct people, because this was the meaning of the nation, and the nation was, by definition sovereign. The national principle was collectivistic; it reflected the collective being. Collectivistic ideologies are inherently authoritarian, for, when the collectivity is seen in unitary terms, it tends to assume the collective individual possessed in a single will, and someone bound to be its interpreter. The reification of a community introduces (or preserves) fundamental inequality between those of its few members who are qualified to interpret the collective will and the many who have no such qualifications; the select few dictate to the masses who must obey.[27]

From those two different interpretations of popular sovereignty, Greenfeld constructs two major types of nationalism, **individualistic-**

---

[26] Ibid.
[27] Ibid, 11.

libertarian and **collectivistic-authoritarian**. This typology is further refined by the criteria of membership in the national collectivity, "which may be either '**civic**,' that is, identical with citizenship or '**ethnic**.' In the former case, nationality is at least in principle open and voluntaristic; it can and sometimes must be acquired. In the latter, it is believed to be inherent - one can neither acquire it if one does not have it, nor change it if one does; it has nothing to do with individual will, but constitutes a genetic characteristic. Individualistic nationalism cannot be but civic, but civic nationalism can also be collectivistic. More often, though, collectivistic nationalism takes on the form of ethnic particularism, while ethnic nationalism is necessarily collectivistic."[28] According to Greenfeld, this typology should serve as a model to analyze specific nationalisms where the above constructs are treated as ideal types in Weberian sense. However, in the real world of specific nationalisms, Greenfeld argues that the most common type is a mixed one. The following chart makes it easy to understand the different types of nationalism(s) developed by Greenfeld:

Figure 1. Greenfeld's Ideal Types of nationalism.

	Civic	Ethnic
Individualistic-libertarian	Type I *(England, USA)*	*Void*
Collecitivistic-authoritarian	Type II *(France)*	Type III *(Germany, Russia)*

Greenfeld's model and ideal types are extremely useful for analyzing the inner structure of Gökalp's version of Turkish nationalism. Using Greenfeld's model, we can classify Gökalp's version of Turkish nationalism as a collectivistic and authoritarian type. Gökalp's criticisms of individualism and his glorification of social solidarity are sufficient to classify his model of nationalism as collectivistic and authoritarian. However, Gökalp's criteria of membership in the Turkish national community are not based on race or ethnicity but on culture and education. Repeating Gökalp's definition, the

> Nation is not a racial, ethnic, geographical, political, or voluntary group or association. Nation is a group composed of men and women who have gone through the same education, who have received the same acquisitions in language, religion, morality, and aesthetics... Men want to live together, not with those who carry the same blood in their veins, but with those who share the same language and same faith.[29]

---

[28] Ibid.
[29] Ziya Gökalp, Turkish Nationalism and Western Civilization, 137.

This very broad anthropological definition of culture naturally covers a belief system, i.e., the *Sufi* version of Islam as the basis of social solidarity. For Gökalp, "education" (*tahsil/eğitim*) is certainly different from "training/socialization" (*terbiye* in Turkish). According to Gökalp, education is a system of learning where human beings get acquainted with the products of civilization such as techniques that are universal. On the other hand, training is a process of socialization, during which the cultural values are transmitted from one generation to another. In Greenfeld's terminology then, Gökalp's perception of the individual's ties to the national community is more close to "civic" than to "ethnic" criteria. Finally, we can conclude that **Gökalp's version of Turkish nationalism is authoritarian and collectivistic and the individuals' membership criteria to a national community are civic.** Now we should try to see how this nationalism is situated in a more general conception of state and society where the social structural relationship between the individual and state was formed.

Corporatist Capitalism as a Model for Nation-State and Society

Deconstructing first and later rebuilding Gökalp's nationalist system, Taha Parla argues that Gökalp's model was a variant of corporatist capitalism. Parla defines corporatism as a "system of thought and a set of institutions that presuppose a predominantly capitalist mode of production with its central elements of the primacy of private property and enterprise. Corporatism is, by definition, anti-socialist and anti-Marxist. It is also anti-Liberal (in philosophy, politics, and economics), but not anti-capitalist."[30] In this definition, it is very important to underline the anti-liberal but not anti-capitalist essence of the corporatist system of thought and praxis, because later in the single-party period in Turkey (1925-1945), this dimension constituted the backbone of Kemalist étatism. Kemalists described their étatist nationalism as a unique social system and maintained that Kemalism constituted a clear-cut alternative to socialism and liberalism. This was the main argument of Kemalists who asserted that their system was a "third way," in opposition to both socialism and liberalism.

In Parla's work, corporatism is constructed as a broader umbrella to cover both the solidaristic corporatism of Ziya Gökalp and the fascistic corporatism of Europe in the interwar years. At this moment, it is necessary to point out that the type of corporatism under discussion is not at all related to the concept of "neo-corporatism," developed by Philippe C. Schmitter and others, who explicitly define corporatism as a form of articulation of political representation and state intervention.

---

[30] Parla, The Social and Political, 45.

Although Schmitter develops a typology of several corporatism(s) in the Western industrialized societies, his main criteria are nevertheless at the level of political representation and the state's role in combining conflicting class interests within the decision making body in the public sphere.[31] The role of multi-national corporations in affecting the decisions of the central authority could be analyzed within this perspective. However, this rather simple definition of corporatism is too limited in scope to explain the power and dominance of corporatist political ideology in the interwar years. In this respect, Parla's model is more coherent, and stems from the earlier and more realistic formulations of the European corporatist thinkers during the interwar years.[32] Parla constructs his broader model as follows:

> Corporatism... has two main species: solidaristic corporatism or solidarism and fascistic corporatism or fascism - the former still bearing certain residual tenets of political and cultural liberalism as particular ideals, but rejecting liberalism as a holistic model of economic, social, and political organization.... Corporatism, with its solidaristic and fascistic variants, is but a derivative of the 'first way' i.e., capitalism, and it is a category at the same abstraction level as liberalism, or liberal capitalism, and socialism, or Marxist socialism - replacing the former as the supersedent rationale of modern capitalism.[33]

According to Parla, the emergence and dominance of corporatist models are the consequences of the "crisis of capitalism." There are two types of crises which capitalism faces in the process of development: accumulation and distribution crises. The first one can be observed in the backward capitalist countries where capitalist development was retarded where "the corporatist formula serves economic development of a particular kind by providing a disciplined labor force for accelerated private accumulation under the protection of neo-mercantilist policies of a state capitalism."[34] However the second type of corporatism, i.e., its fascistic variant, is a response to distribution crisis experienced in an industrial society where class polarization and class struggle between organized labor and capital reaches destructive levels. Here "the corporatist formula serves the containment of class polarization between numerically and organizationally advanced labor and a monopolistic

[31] Philippe C. Schmitter, 'Still the Century of Corporatisim,' in Philippe C. Schmitter and Gerhard Lehmbruch, *Trends toward Corporatist Intermediation. Edited by Philippe C. Schmitter and Gerhard Lehmbruch.* (London-Beverly Hills: Sage, 1979), 7 - 52.
[32] For instance, see Mihail Manoilescu, *Le Parti Unique: Institution Politique Des Regime Nouveaux* (Paris: Les Oeuvres Françaises, 1936). And also Mihail Manoilescu, *Le siècle du corporatisme: Doctrine du corporatisme intégral et pur.* Paris: Felix Alcan, 1934.
[33] Parla, The Social and Political, 45.
[34] Ibid.

capital."[35] Constructing solidaristic and fascistic corporatism(s) as ideal types situated at the opposite ends of a continuum, Parla further comments on their structural characteristics and on transitions between the two:

> In either context, the corporatist variant may take either solidaristic or fascistic dimensions depending on the specific nature and intensity of crisis, and on secondary, intervening variables such as the social organization, class balance, political culture and institutional traditions of a particular country. Thus, I do not assume a one-to-one correspondence between fascism and monopoly capital, as do some of the Marxist analyses; neither do I imply a linear transition from solidarism to fascism.[36]

The ideal types constructed by Parla provide a valuable research tool for operationalizing corporatism in general. Parla sees "corporatism first as a philosophy-ideology about a model of society and economy, second a set of economic and class policies and actual procedures for conducting representation of interests, third a particular form of political institutionalization and authoritative decision-making."[37] Furthermore, he argues that corporatism cannot be observed at all three levels in every case. Here, the social structural context that precedes the formation of corporatism plays a decisive role. Nevertheless these three levels of analysis could be used as a starting point. Parla further expands on this notion, stating that,

> It is not always the case that corporatism is simultaneously manifest at three levels, hence fully crystallized and readily recognizable. It may be that we have indications of the second and only partial materialization of the third levels, but no subjective expression and formulation, yet, of the first. Furthermore, both partially and fully unfolded forms of corporatism can have the more pluralistic and libertarian solidaristic and the more totalitarian and autocratic fascist variants. Corporatism as a model and philosophy of society, then, may be expressed in the form of a well-formulated, programmatic political ideology, or it may remain as a loose worldview. At another level, or dimension, corporatism is a system of actual practices and policies that are the result of, or in conformity with, such a world-view or ideology. At a third level or dimension, corporatism, beyond the *de facto* manifestations of the second level, unfolds in *de jure* manner as

---

[35] Ibid.
[36] Ibid.
[37] Ibid.

tangible political institutions and legal structures.[38]

Not only does Parla thus construct his model in a persuasive manner to observe corporatism in different societies in different periods, furthermore these three levels of analysis provide a valuable agenda for actual research. Clearly the quotation above serves, to a certain extent, as a guideline for examining transitions between different forms of corporatism without losing touch with their common characteristics. The third level of analysis, which invites the researcher to examine the political/legal aspects of corporatist systems, is especially very effective.

Corporatism and Economic Activity: The Social Base of Economic Nationalism

Within the corporatist system, the overall economic activity of the individual is perceived as being within the limits of compatibility with the "public interest" (*kamu yararı* or *amme menfaati* in Turkish) Keeping private property and private initiative as basic individual rights, corporatist ideology puts forward public interest so as to restrict the destructive and egoistic tendencies of "homo economicus." Furthermore, the anti-liberal criticism inherent in corporatism was conceptualized as a "new type of individual" who could function within a "new order" without undermining social solidarity. Here public interest as an entity, by definition, greater than the sum of individual concerns, was perceived as an arena where the social solidarity was served and fulfilled perpetually.

The transcendence of competitive capitalism and the critique of liberalism bring us to a new understanding of the state. In this context, the state was defined as an active element in constituting a harmonious society where no conflict of interests or class struggle between the classes is anticipated. In the corporatist system, state intervention was welcomed in nearly all aspects of economic and social life. The state's interventionist role over society was preached in such a manner that in some cases the individual social actor is stripped of most its autonomy and simply functions as a tiny organ or the extension of the state. Depending upon the type of corporatism, the expansion of the public sphere developed and was shaped by the crises of accumulation or distribution. In this organic conception of society, social harmony and work peace is supposedly created by occupational groups that are functionally interdependent and mutually complementary organs of the same social state mechanism.[39] As Parla aptly argues, corporatism tries to transcend the short-term interests of the individual capitalist for the sake of a so-

---

[38] *Ibid*, 46.
[39] *Ibid*, 56.

called higher rationale:

> Corporatism, by defending the long term survival of general, total capital(ism), furnishes the capitalist society with a higher rationale, definitely superseding the previous liberal rationale, which could only justify the narrow short term interests of individual private capital(ism)s. The profit maximization logic of capitalism in its competitive phase has been subordinated to, but not displaced by, another higher logic of capitalism, the logic of system-maintenance, in its post-competitive, monopolistic phase - be it in advanced industrial or neo-mercantilist, statist contexts.[40]

Returning to our starting point, it is necessary to summarize Gökalp's conception of the economic revival and productive activity in general. However, we must first underline the "elective affinity" between Ziya Gökalp and the founding father of economic nationalism, Friedrich List (1789-1846). It is no coincidence that both List and Gökalp worked in the Chambers of Commerce in their respective countries. List was elected Secretary General and functioned as the editor of the journal of the 'Union of German Merchants and Manufacturers' in Frankfurt from 1819 to 1821.[41] Gökalp became Secretary General of the Chamber of Commerce in Diyarbakır in 1902, a position he kept until the Young Turk revolution of 1908. As a Young Turk, Gökalp established cordial relations with local notables in Diyarbakır, and published his first articles on the economic issues during this period. In other words, both men lived in close touch with the economic activities surrounding them.

Gökalp's views on national economy were quite close to Friedrich List's in many respects. Both wished that their respective countries to develop national economies. Gökalp stressed that Turkey should achieve an industrial revolution and establish a "national economy." He believes that the national economy would substitute the municipal (local) economies and the large-scale industry for handicrafts. Gökalp defined national economy, first as a modern developed market economy with advanced division of labor and organic/occupational solidarity and functional interdependence as opposed to the self-sufficient agricultural communities. Second, his understanding of national economy did not recognize class tensions or economic self-interest detrimental to the public interest. In other words, the economic domain was perceived as an instrument for securing social solidarity. Third, like List, Gökalp always preached the neo-mercantilist policies of nationalistic state capitalism. In Gökalp's nationalist system, state intervention was indispensable. The

---

[40] Ibid.
[41] Roman Szporluk, *Communism and Nationalism: Karl Marx versus Friedrich List* (New York; Oxford: Oxford Univ. Press, 1991), 98.

accumulation crisis of a backward capitalist economy could be solved only with active state intervention. In his last and fundamental work, *Türkçülüğün Esasları* (Principles of Turkism), Gökalp put forward his position on different economic systems as follows:

> Turks love freedom and independence; therefore, they cannot be socialists. But since they love equality, they cannot be liberals either. The system best suited to Turkish culture is solidarism. Private property is legitimate in so far as it serves social solidarity ... The social ideal of Turks, therefore is to prevent usurpation of social wealth by individuals without abolishing private property, and to preserve and increase social wealth in order to spend it for the benefit of the public.[42]

The solidaristic version of corporatism is dominant in here. Anti-liberal criticism of market economy and an emphasis on public welfare and public interest were the underlying characteristics of Turkish nationalism. Another dimension of Gökalp's solidaristic nationalism was the critique of the individual's economic advantages realized through market mechanisms such as speculation, hoarding, etc. Especially, on these matters, the solidaristic corporatism of Gökalp invited complete and unrestricted state intervention. State intervention and public ownership were justified on the grounds that society itself contributed to capital formation in the economy, therefore public ownership was considered to be a remedy for the sacrifices endured by the society. Gökalp reiterates his point quite clearly when he argues that, "along with private property, there must be public property. Surplus profits that are the result not of the labor of individuals but of the sacrifices and hardships undertaken by the society should belong to society. It is not legitimate for individuals to appropriate such profits for themselves."[43]

In a manner reminiscent of the traditional Ottoman logic of taxation and confiscation, Gökalp here puts forward the idea of surplus appropriation, probably via extra-economic measures. Gökalp also argues that the state's assumption of an active role in the economy is also a moral service to the nation. Without state intervention this moral service cannot be realized. Here, economic nationalism in general, and as a specific domestic policy comes to the fore. The question of legitimacy in the appropriation of profits is especially crucial in understanding the later developments in the Kemalist single-party period (1925-1945). In this respect, Gökalp's criticism of liberal capitalism and imperialism was harsh. In an article written during the Lausanne Peace Conference (1923) - which shaped the modern Turkish Republic and secured its international

---

[42] Ziya Gökalp, *Türkçülüğün Esasları*, 168.
[43] *Ibid*, 104.

recognition - Gökalp justified his choice of state capitalism as follows:

> This would prevent the formation in our fatherland of a new class of profiteers composed of speculators. This class, called 'capitalist' in Europe, a mere criminal group, was entirely exposed when their ambitions were unveiled during the [Lausanne] peace conference... Today, European imperialism is based on liberal capitalism. If we adopted the system of state capitalism, we would prevent the emergence in our country of an avaricious and rapacious gang, the so-called capitalists.[44]

It is quite obvious that Ziya Gökalp as the codifier of Turkish nationalism aims to solve the accumulation crisis of the backward capitalism by utilizing the state apparatus. Discrediting the capitalists as a "rapacious gang," Gökalp inevitably seeks a new type of capitalist, a "national merchant" (*milli tüccar*) which had to be created and nurtured by the state. The members of this new class are supposed to act in harmony with the solidaristic essence of Turkish nationalism.

Keeping in mind Gökalp's earlier criticism of the Levantine and cosmopolitan way of life prevailing among the westernized Ottoman elite, we can guess at possible candidates for this mission. It was quite clear for the Young Turks that the "comprador bourgeoisie" - mostly consisting of Greeks and Armenians - could not be trusted at all. The new national bourgeoisie had to be created among the Turkish/Muslim element within the empire. The creation of an indigenous bourgeoisie was on the agenda not only in the last years of the Ottoman Empire but it remained as a major mission to be completed after the formation of the Turkish republic.

Creating a "National Bourgeoisie"

The grand scenario of creating a "national bourgeoisie" was one of the main themes in the politics of Young Turks between 1913-1918. The bitter experience of Balkan Wars and the rising anti-minority sentiment among the masses helped the Young Turks to implement nationalist economic policies effectively at popular level. Radical officers in the government had done everything possible to invite the Turkish/Muslim element to be supported as the entrepreneurs in a new economic environment.[45] The so-called "national companies" instigated by the state

---

[44] Ziya Gökalp, 'İktisadi inkilap için nasıl çalışmalıyız,' *Küçük Mecmua*, (5 March 1923) cited in Parla, *ibid*, 109. This extremely critical approach of Gökalp towards 'profiteers and speculators' has been repeated by the Kemalists during the World War II in the implementation process of notorious anti-minority Capital Tax of 1942-43.

[45] See, Zafer Toprak, *Türkiye'de Ekonomi ve Toplum, 1908-1950: İttihat-Terakki ve Devletçilik*, (Istanbul: Tarih Vakfı Yurt Yayınları, 1995). And also, Zafer Toprak, *Milli İktisat, Milli Burjuvazi*, (Istanbul : Tarih Vakfı

and protectionist duties were introduced by the abolition of all privileges granted to foreigners in the late Ottoman period. The outbreak of First World War in Europe enabled the Ottoman government to abrogate the capitulations. A whole set of new laws and regulations was prepared and implemented hastily. For example, in May 1915, a language reform was put into effect prohibiting usage of French or English in commercial correspondence. As Keyder rightly argues, this was one of the first attempts to increase the employment of the educated Turkish elite in private companies, and was aimed at the non-Muslims and particularly Levantines who did not speak or write Turkish.[46]

During the war, shortages created favorable conditions for the capital accumulation and development of a Muslim commercial bourgeoisie through nepotism/corruption and by the allocation of certain public facilities to this nascent bourgeoisie. Due to price differences for basic foodstuff between big cities and the countryside, anyone who obtained a special permission to transport goods to Istanbul via public railways became rich overnight. The term "war profiteers" (*harp zenginleri*) entered the daily language of urban masses. Furthermore, the Young Turks organized urban artisans and tradesmen into associations. It was assumed that these associations would control the market and regulate prices. However, just the opposite happened. Soon, most basic goods disappeared from the market, and the prices skyrocketed in the black market.[47] In the meantime, the so-called "work peace" had been secured, because all strikes had been banned. In addition, the Young Turks did everything possible to reorganize and reform the state apparatus of a collapsing empire: the transition from tax-farming to direct tax collection, the promotion of indigenous manufacturing industry by special legislation, and the printing of paper money as the basis of a sound monetary policy were the main aspects of these reforms.

In the provinces, the "national companies" were formed along the same lines. The Ottoman public bureaucracy, mostly supporting the nationalist policies of Young Turks, favored the formation of such national companies. As Keyder coherently stresses, "there was usually one-to-one correspondence between the roster of Committee of Union and Progress local organization and the shareholders of new companies."[48] In the beginning, these national companies did not create

---

Yurt Yayınları, 1995).

[46] Çağlar Keyder, *State and Class in Turkey: A Study in Capitalist Development.* (London: Verso, 1987), 62.

[47] Feroz Ahmad, 'Vanguard of Nascent Bourgeoisie: The Social and Economic Policy of the Young Turks,' in Osman Okyar, and Halil İnalcık, eds. *Türkiye'nin Sosyal ve Ekonomik Tarihi (1071-1920) - Papers Presented to the Conference on Social and Economic History of Turkey (1071-1920)* (Ankara: Hacettepe Üniversitesi, 1980), 339.

[48] Keyder, *State and Class*, 63.

a major economic transformation in the countryside. However the organizational networks formed during the First World War served as the basis for the creation of the national resistance movement against Greek occupation of Anatolia a few years later (1919 -1922). In short, the long-term political gains of economic nationalism were far more important than the actual economic changes.

In order to understand the complete picture of this movement, it is necessary to mention the sociological characteristics of the architects of Turkish nationalism. Most of the prominent nationalists in the CUP were born and raised under the oppressive but modernizing regime of Sultan Abdülhamid II (1876-1909). To a certain extent they were the products of the educational reforms implemented by the Sultan they had overthrown in 1908. Within the CUP, the ideologies of Ottomanism, Pan-Islamism and, Pan-Turkism functioned together, though in changing proportions over the years. Naturally Gökalp and other prominent ideologues preached Turkish nationalism. However none of the ideologues of Turkish nationalism was given active government duties. In those years Ziya Gökalp worked as the professor of sociology at Istanbul University. The essential core cadres of the CUP consisted of army officers and some civilian members of the Young Turks who had organized the domestic or external opposition to the regime of Sultan Abdülhamid II before 1908. Moreover they were different from the typical urban cosmopolitan Westernizing Ottoman elite. Some members of the CUP Central Committee were officers and state employees with provincial background. In this respect, the Unionists never constituted a homogenous group in terms of social background and well-defined set of implemented politics, and political ideology. As Feroz Ahmad clearly points out,

> The Unionists saw themselves as the representatives of the evolving Ottoman nation and the agents of change. Their movement was essentially urban though it had filtered into countryside through the administrative machinery and by means of their alliance with the landowning 'aristocracy'... The Committee was the first political organization in the Empire to have a mass following and this gave the politics of the day a populist basis... The Committee had too broad a social base and too heterogeneous a class structure to be elitist.[49]

However this novel radical social group had two important social characteristics that formed all their actions: First, they had no organic relationship with any of the productive classes of the empire such as the

---

[49] Feroz Ahmad, *Young Turks: Committee of Union and Progress in Turkish Politics, 1908-14* (Oxford: OUP, 1969), 162.

peasantry, workers or the urban commercial bourgeoisie (which was predominantly non-Muslim anyway). Second, they possessed no social sphere independent of the state apparatus they were mostly coming from the bureaucratic elite. In other words, the Turkish nationalists linked their status and future to the existence of the state. As the members of the Turkish bureaucracy and intelligentsia, they sublimated the Turkish nation in such a manner that the nation itself lost its actual referents. In Greenfeld's terms, they had reified the nation. This hypothetical conception of the nation was then equated to the party, and the CUP established its identity with it. This authoritarian self-image shaped the nature of their action and the texture of their radicalism. They became the only interpreters of the collective will of the Turkish nation. All of their efforts to modernize and centralize the state apparatus must be seen as attempts to secure the status and existence of Turkish bureaucracy. It is not exaggeration to say that for the Turkish nationalists, the act of saving the state from destruction was a gamble where the stakes were their own lives.

Ideologues of the Turkish nationalist movement were quite aware of the fact that they could not survive as a group unless they created a social base whose loyalty could be secured by political means. In other words, the implementation of nationalist economic policies and the creation of a national bourgeoisie had to benefit the state in the long run. Naturally this omnipotent state under Unionist direction set out to create its social bases by étatist means. For instance, Yusuf Akçura, the editor of *Türk Yurdu* - the first theoretical journal of Turkish nationalism - argued the following in 1914:

> The foundation of modern state is the bourgeois class. Contemporary prosperous states came into existence on the shoulders of bourgeoisie, of the businessmen and bankers. The Turkish national awakening in Turkey is the beginning of the genesis of the Turkish bourgeoisie. And if the natural growth of the Turkish bourgeoisie continues without damage or interruption, we can say that the sound establishment of the Turkish state has been guaranteed.[50]

Yusuf Akçura's flourishing Turkish bourgeoisie would, in the long run, create a strong state and the appropriate climate for the existence of Turkish nationalist intelligentsia. All nationalistic economic policies implemented by the CUP served to secure this end. As Keyder argues, their "ideology was mostly incidental and it resulted from the desire to save the state (and to safeguard the position of the bureaucracy in the

[50] Quoted from *Türk Yurdu* (first series), no. 63, April 3, 1914. p. 2102-3. Cited by Niyazi Berkes, *The Development of Secularism in Turkey* (Montreal: McGill University Press, 1964).

social structure) and the material conditions of the Empire in the international capitalist context."[51]

Non-Muslim Minorities and the Commercial Bourgeoisie

Although the military facet of Turkish War of Independence (1919-1922) had been concluded with the liberation of Izmir in September 1922, the international political recognition of the victorious generals of the Ankara government came only a year later. Today, after nearly seventy-three years, the Lausanne Treaty remains the only effective international treaty signed after the First World War. Many important issues were discussed and settled in Lausanne, including the question of the non-Muslim minorities in Turkey. One of the first demands of the Ankara government was the abolition of capitulations, which had been resented by nationalist elite as a symbol of inferiority and subservience. Thus another important step towards "total independence" was accomplished. In fact, European financial control over Turkey was related to the existence of non-Muslim minorities. As Pentzopoulos observes "to the minds of the Turkish leaders, the existence of national minorities and the practice of foreign intervention in their domestic affairs were inter-related in a manner of cause and effect. Consequently, they viewed the elimination of the heterogeneous groups as a necessary prerequisite to achieving absolute sovereign independence."[52]

As a logical conclusion, it was agreed that the local Greek population in Anatolia would be exchanged for the Muslim/Turks living in Greece. As a result of the population exchange agreement, nearly 1,200,000 Anatolian Greeks were exchanged for 354,000 Muslims between 1923 - 26.[53] This exchange thus completed the "Turcification" of Asia Minor. This was one of the largest forced population transfers realized in this century. The massive population exchange between India and Pakistan seems to be most destructive of all population exchanges where about 200,000 people had been killed from both sides in disturbances and massacres. Penderel Moon sums up the total number of refugees as follows: "Between August 1947 and March 1948 about four and half a million Hindus and Sighs migrated from West Pakistan to India and about six million Muslims moved in the reverse direction."[54]

The population exchange created another shock for the Turkish economy, and later molded the nature of the political systems in both

---

[51] Çağlar Keyder, *ibid*, 59.
[52] Dimitri Pentzopoulos, *The Balkan Exchange of Minorities and Its Impact upon Greece*, Kentron Koinōnikōn Epistēmōn Athēnōn. Publications ; 1 (Paris: Mouton, 1962).
[53] *Ibid*, 69.
[54] Penderel Moon, *Divide and Quit* (London: Chatto & Windus, 1961).

Greece and Turkey: in the long run, Greece became more and more dependent on foreign aid to solve the refugee question.[55] Turkey, on the other hand, invested less than five per cent of the total amount spent by Greece on the settlement of refugees, and not borrowing credit from the international bankers became more immune to European financial control. However, Turkey also lost the most progressive elements of its population - non-Muslim merchants, skilled workers, Levantines specialized in international trade - in terms of economic development, and resorted to a more "autarkic and étatist models" of development. In this manner, so-called the question non-Muslim minorities in Anatolia resolved forever. The Greek community of Istanbul and the Turkish community of Western Thrace were exempted from population exchanges.

The texture and distribution of the population in Turkey changed considerably between 1913 and 1926. The Balkan Wars of 1912-13 and the First World War created great social and political turmoil. Finally the Turkish War of Independence not only exhausted the last economic and social resources of Asia Minor, but it also shaped the political nature of the newly formed Turkish nation-state. Çağlar Keyder sums up the transformation of the population as follows:

> According to the census of 1906, the Ottoman population within the border of present day Turkey was around 15 million. Approximately 10 % of this population were Greeks, 7% Armenian and 1% Jewish. Moslems counted over 80%. Between 1914 and 1924 the composition of this population changed dramatically; according to the 1927 census the total population was 13.6 millions of which the non-Moslems accounted for 2.6 per cent. There were 120,000 Greek speakers and 65,000 Armenian speakers. Part of the change in the figures were due to the ravages of war. For instance it has been estimated 18 per cent of the Moslem population were killed between 1914 and 1922. Of the Armenian population, a proportion perished as a result of expulsion or death in 1915, and another part migrated or was forced to migrate, to Syria, Russian Armenia and other countries. The Greek population suffered less in terms of actual deaths: according to 1928 census in Greece, there were close to 1.2 million refugees from Turkey, and Greeks had also migrated to the other parts of the world. Thus slightly over one-quarter of the 1913 population were no longer there in 1925: compared with the 18 per cent of the Moslem Turks who perished, only one-sixth of the non-Moslem population remained. To express it differently,

---

[55] Pentzopoulos, *The Balkan Exchange of Minorities and Its Impact upon Greece.*

before the war, one out of every five persons [20 %] living in present-day Turkey was non-Muslim, after the war, only one out of forty persons [2.5 %] was non-Moslem.[56]

As a result of this process, only the non-Muslim minorities in big cities like Istanbul, İzmir and Bursa retained their power in the economic sphere. For the victorious generals, the ten-years of wars and the ratification of Lausanne Treaty not only signified breaking all ties with the Ottoman heritage, but also marked the beginning of a new epoch. The architects of this period, who were born and raised under the rule of Sultan Abdulhamid II (1876-1909) experienced several setbacks. Not only had the human topography and methods of commercial interaction been transformed, furthermore the actual designs and targets of the new regime had changed. The establishment of the republic, the abolition of the caliphate and the deportation of the Ottoman royal family formed the cornerstones of Kemalist regime. The complete removal of non-Muslim elements in Anatolia and the decreasing number and political influence of non-Muslim commercial bourgeoisie in Istanbul left the Turkish bureaucracy unchallenged in coming years.

Concluding Remarks

The political upheavals, wars and population exchanges transformed the social fabric of Anatolia between 1912 and 1924. Non-Muslim commercial bourgeoisie of relatively developed Anatolian cities like Samsun, Trabzon, Erzurum, Adana, and Gaziantep either subjected to ethnic cleansing and genocide (Armenians) or exchanged (Greeks) in masses. Apart from the commercial bourgeoisie, artisans and craftsmen of non-Muslim origin found their way either to Europe and/or other neighboring countries like Greece, Syria etc. Thus, the entrepreneurs and the most skilled section of late Ottoman working population perished within ten years. Recently developing Turkish bourgeoisie and urban artisans was far from replacing the minorities in all sectors of economic and social life. Moreover Turkish commercial bourgeoisie only wanted to have an upper hand or a more feasible bargaining position in their transactions with foreign capital.[57] As a newly developing social class their aspirations and actual capacity were awfully limited and inadequate for a better vocation. Thus the development and dissemination of a more skilled industrial working population had to wait for some more decades. Naturally, human inventory of a country cannot be altered overnight.

Losing the most strategic elements of its urban population, the Republican ruling elite resorted to a more autarkic model called étatism

---

[56] Çağlar Keyder, *ibid*, 79.
[57] *Ibid*, 250 – 252.

(*devletçilik*). Under these adverse conditions Ankara government was forced to adopt more nationalist economic policies in order to solve accumulation crisis, hence to foster economic development. During the single party period (1925-1945), all attempts were made to build a self-sufficient economy. State economic enterprises were established and industrialization programs were implemented in order to restore pre-war production levels. Although the étatist measures helped the administrative elite to achieve some kind of development in the economy, the traditional characteristics of the Turkish urban elite remained intact. Very few Muslims, however, chose to take part in entrepreneurial activities. In the big cities like İstanbul, Bursa and İzmir remaining non-Muslim minorities nevertheless held a firm position among the members of the commercial bourgeoisie and small producers.

Given the foundations laid by Gökalp in the formative years of Turkish nationalism, the Republican ruling elite went a step further in taking a more collectivist and authoritarian position on defining the actual properties of Turkish nation-state. In the formative years, certain characteristics of Turkish nationalism had remained at the level of political ideology only. However during the single party regime, *de facto* and *de jure* manifestations of solidaristic corporatist political ideology became more observable. Young Turkish Republic and its ruling elite were quite successful in transforming the image into reality. Thus the process of political institutionalization, conduct of decision making and finally the formulation of certain legal principles had all evolved on the same line and made their minor contributions towards a more well-defined and coherent solidaristic corporatist regime.

In this reconstruction process, even Gökalp's original formulation of Turkish nationalism was modified. In the last decade of the Ottoman Empire, while Gökalp defined individual's ties to national community more on cultural therefore close to "civic" lines, the Republican elite resorted to more "ethnic" definition of the individuals' membership to national community. Ankara government, that was divorced of its imperial traditions and limited its sovereignty to Anatolia only, could not have responded otherwise. Already transformed human geography of Anatolia made it vain to provide an umbrella to cover Jewish tinker, Armenian tailor and Turkish soldier at once. A well-defined Gökalpian "culture" which functioned as a "collective conscience" and believed to have united the Turkish people even though they were divided by the lines of status, class, locality, religion, and in some cases ethnicity was not meaningful anymore. Gökalpian cultural unity, which is believed to have molded different individuals into one nation, had been overdue by then. Political formulations that had belonged to the age of ethnically and

233

religiously heterogeneous empire became somewhat outdated within ten years.

Bibliography

Ahmad, Feroz Young Turks: Committee of Union and Progress in Turkish Politics, 1908-14. Oxford University Press, 1969.

———. 'Vanguard of Nascent Bourgeoisie: The Social and Economic Policy of the Young Turks,' in Osman Okyar, and Halil İnalcık, eds. Türkiye'nin Sosyal ve Ekonomik Tarihi (1071-1920). Social and Economic History of Turkey (1071-1920). Ankara: Hacettepe Üniversitesi, 1980.

Berkes, Niyazi. The Development of Secularism in Turkey. Montreal: McGill University Press, 1964.

Braude, Benjamín, and Bernard Lewis. Christians and Jews in the Ottoman Empire: The Functioning of a Plural Society. Vol. I. Holmes & Meier Publishers, 1982.

Farah, Tawfic. Pan-Arabism and Arab Nationalism: The Continuing Debate. Boulder: Westview Press, 1987.

Greenfeld, Liah. Nationalism: Five Roads to Modernity. Cambridge, Massachusetts; London: Harvard University, 2003.

Keyder, Çağlar. State and Class in Turkey: A Study in Capitalist Development. London u.a.: Verso, 1987.

Khalidi, Rashid. The Origins of Arab Nationalism. New York: Columbia University Press, 1991.

Kushner, David. The Rise of Turkish Nationalism, 1876-1908. London: Frank Cass, 1977.

Landau, Jacob M. Tekinalp, Turkish Patriot, 1883-1961. Istanbul, 1984.

Manoilescu, Mihail Le siècle du Corporatisme: Doctrine du corporatisme intégral et pur. Paris: Felix Alcan, 1934.

———. Le Parti Unique: Institution Politique des Regime Nouveaux. Paris: Les Oeuvres Françaises, 1936.

Moon, Penderel. Divide and Quit. London: Chatto & Windus, 1961.

Parla, Taha. The Social and Political Thought of Ziya Gökalp, 1876-1924. Leiden: E.J. Brill, 1985.

Pentzopoulos, Dimitri. The Balkan Exchange of Minorities and Its Impact upon Greece. Paris: Mouton, 1962.

Poynter, Mary A. M. D. When Turkey Was Turkey: In and around Constantinople. London: Routledge, 1921.

Ramchandani, Ram R. Uganda Asians: The End of an Enterprise : A Study of the Role of the People of Indian Origin in the Economic Development of Uganda and Their Expulsion, 1894-1972. United Asia Publications, 1976.

Schmitter, Philippe C, and Gerhard Lehmbruch. Trends toward Corporatist Intermediation. Edited by Philippe C. Schmitter and Gerhard Lehmbruch. London-Beverly Hills: Sage, 1979.

Sussnitzki, A. J. "Ethnic Division of Labour." In The Economic History of the Middle East, 1800 - 1914. Ed. by Charles Issawi. Chicago University Press, 1966.

Szporluk, Roman. Communism and Nationalism: Karl Marx versus Friedrich List. New York; Oxford: Oxford Univ. Press, 1991.

Toprak, Zafer. "İslâm ve İktisat: 1913-1914 Müslüman Boykotajı." Toplum ve Bilim 29–30 (1985): 179–99.

———. Milli Iktisat, Milli Burjuvazi. İstanbul : Tarih Vakfı Yurt Yayınları, 1995.

———. İttihat-Terakki ve Devletçilik. İstanbul : Tarih Vakfı Yurt Yayınları 1995

Toynbee, Arnold J. The Western Question in Greece and Turkey. Boston: Houghton

Mifflin Company, 1922.

Ziya Gökalp. Hars ve Medeniyet. Ankara: İş Matbaacılık, 1972.

———. Türkçülüğün Esasları [Principles of Turkism]. İstanbul: Kadro Yayınları, 1976.

———. Türkleşmek, İslamlaşmak, Muasırlaşmak. İstanbul: Türk Kültür Yayınları, 1976.

Ziya Gökalp, Turkish Nationalism and Western Civilization Selected Essays. Translated and edited by Niyazi Berkes. Westport (Conn.): Greenwood Press, 1981.

www.ingramcontent.com/pod-product-compliance
Lightning Source LLC
Chambersburg PA
CBHW050350270326
41926CB00016B/3681